Veronica's Bird

Dear wishes
Richard Newman
&
Veronica Bird OBE

Veronica Bird and Richard Newman

Clink
Street

London | New York

Published by Clink Street Publishing 2018

Copyright © 2018

First edition.

ISBN: 978-1-912262-61-8 paperback
978-1-912262-62-5 ebook

Other books by the author

Novels: Crown of martyrdom
The Potato Eaters
The horse that screamed
Non-fiction: The Green hill
Brief encounters
A Nun's story

Having twice been down a deep coalmine and switched my lamp off to stand in absolute darkness, it feels right that I acknowledge the generations of miners who have worked and died bringing our coal to the surface particularly around Barnsley

*

Robert, 'Bob' Duncan is a highly respected, now retired, Prison Governor who has always bucked the rule to strike out on a pathway of his own making. The prisons he has worked in list like a Who's Who of the penal service. They include Wormwood Scrubs, Gartree and Wakefield (all top security), Liverpool and Pentonville. On retirement Bob worked as a volunteer with the Butler Trust, the Retired Governors Association and the Shannon Trust where he was Chair of Trustees for nine years. He was also invited to be a special advisor to the House of Commons Home Affairs Select Committee. He is currently Chair of the Independent Monitoring Board at Elmley Prison. He has produced two books: one on Wakefield Prison, the other on Pentonville.

He is also, a very nice man.

Deputy Governor Gary Poole, Pentonville Prison went out of his way to show us anything and everything we wanted to see in his prison. He is a very busy man but he stopped for us. Thank you.

Lynne Carter HR Directorate – HM Prison and Probation Service was extremely helpful to us in ensuring the manuscript was accurate and reflected current policy.

CONTENTS

FOREWORD   by Bob Duncan   ix

PREFACE   1

PART ONE   I might be better off in
               a children's home   7

Chapter One   Doncaster Road   9
Chapter Two   A world away   29
Chapter Three The Cheap option   50
Chapter Four   Some light ahead   71

PART TWO   Climbing   85

Chapter Five   Chamber pots and chaos   87
Chapter Six   'Everything alright Veronica?'   119
Chapter Seven   Styal, first time round   141
Chapter Eight   Grisley Risley   154
Chapter Nine   Back to Styal as Governor   168
Chapter Ten   Thorn Cross-Males only   183
Chapter Eleven   Armley – The hard one   191
Chapter Twelve   Buckley Hall – 'In control'   211
Chapter Thirteen Brockhill – 'A basket case'   219
Chapter Fourteen Ivanovo   236

PART THREE   Why do we lock people up?   259

Chapter Fifteen 'It's an irony'   261
Postscript   277

A FOREWORD BY ROBERT DUNCAN

This is the deeply moving story of how a down-trodden child, by sheer determination, courage and self-belief, overcame repeated obstacles that would have defeated and crushed most children. It is a salutary lesson to all, of what can be achieved with fortitude. Every life is special and has potential; Veronica had this in spades.

I have known Veronica for some forty years, both as a colleague and a friend. We have also both undertaken voluntary work for two prison charities, the Butler Trust and the Shannon Trust (a literacy scheme where trained prisoners teach others to read and write.) It is my privilege to have Veronica as a friend and it gives me much pleasure as an ex-Governor, that her remarkable achievements were accomplished at the time, in a male dominated and 'Cinderella Service.' This though, is not a fable; it is a real-life story, of a young woman and of her achievements to the highest levels in the prison service, where she rose, like a phoenix (also a symbol of the Prison Governors Association) out of an an overcrowded, poverty-stricken and dysfunctional family to become a unique and remarkable individual.

The Government's mantra is that '...every child should reach their full potential through free education'. This ethos failed miserably to reach the Bird family. If it had not been for Kitty, her loving mother, shrewdly recognising the determination and single-mindedness of her daughter, who had seen there could be a better life, it would almost certainly have been a very different ending.

Against all the odds and the fact, she could barely read herself, her mother ensured an application for a scholarship to Ackworth school was completed and signed off, ending in a frantic run to the Town Hall to ensure the letter was received in time. Then, when, miraculously, Veronica gained a place, her mother had to find the funds to fit her out in the uniform and kit required of a Boarding school, for Veronica had only known threadbare, hand-me-down clothes from her elder sisters.

This book is also about how the Service operates from someone who knows every facet of the real issues of 'life behind bars'. It portrays humour, sadness and despair, but most of all, it conveys compassion and hope. It reveals the knowledge that prisons can be managed and that staff will respond to empathetic leadership. It is probably the most moving, accurate, balanced and honest account of prison life I have read.

From a one pound a week skivvy, to an audience with the Queen, her life's journey is almost too much to comprehend – but that is Veronica.

Robert 'Bob' Duncan   Winter 2017

PREFACE

She moved a hand towards the arm of her chair, the better to steady herself in her need to tell me something of importance and personal. Her countenance changed as she caught my eye.

'They've no idea, you know, Richard, they haven't a clue.'

At the time, this was during my first interview in September, I had no impression of her early life, nor for that matter, what made up her later success.

Towards Christmas, with the first dozen interviews in the bag, the reasons for her earlier stress had become crystal clear. Passed on from friends, overheard at Ladies Luncheon Clubs, unkind comments gleaned from neighbours, the word was: 'Veronica must have been born with a silver spoon in her mouth.' It was the only time I heard her speak with such exasperation, despite the misery of her young life which, to listen to, was almost unbearable at times, that such 'things' (I search for another word in frustration) could happen in the mid-Twentieth Century.

Veronica is a small lady, petite and only five feet five and a half inches high with blue eyes and a voice, tremulous at times, as she begins to recall her early life. I had expected, and experienced with other subjects, one memory recalling another then, yet another, until, at last, there comes a nod of understanding, as sense begins to form out of earlier uncertainties. 'Possibly', 'maybe' and 'perhaps' are turned, one by one into signs of relief, a liberation from previous confusion.

Whatever the time of year or the weather, it makes no difference, for she always talks with confidence, reflecting her need to express herself clearly as she has done throughout her life, knowing her facts are backed up with access to prison officer's diaries written by colleagues, together with her own large file containing mementoes of her thirty-six years of service.

What is it that drove a young girl into such a tough, male-orientated world as was the Prison Service, particularly at a time when women were shunning any idea of being shut up for long hours of each day alongside murderers, rapists, grand thieves and child molesters? Surely, there were better things to do when Britain was just beginning to break out of its Second World War strait-jacket of war-time regulation and conformity?

It is an irony, is it not, that completely innocent people with no criminal record whatsoever allow themselves to be held behind bars in grim prisons each day, where they can smell, and feel the experience of the inmates doing their stretch. It is a strange coincidence also, is it not, that the day Myra Hindley was imprisoned for life on 6th May 1966, Veronica Bird entered the Police Service and the month Hindley died, November 2002, Veronica retired? All those years as we grew up, and aged, one of Britain's worst mass murderers had been shut away to keep our children safe, a diminutive young woman was forging an outstanding career, ensuring, amongst other things, this evil woman would never see the outside wall of her prison.

One must wonder why Veronica never married. There have to be many possibilities, none of which is difficult to speculate upon. Maybe, having had first-hand and close-up experience of her cruel father, with her mother always in fear of an explosion of rage from her husband, it put Veronica off pursuing a happy relationship? She could see how sad, marriage could be. What, therefore, was the point, she might well have questioned herself?

Veronica confirmed to me early on, that the Prison Service

was '…. her home and her family,' For the first time in her life, at the age of 21, she was away from the cruelty, the drinking bouts and her meddlesome brother-in-law, ever intruding deeply into her life, which kept her from taking on a similar nightmare. Perchance it was the constant need to aspire, to achieve well above her eight brothers and sisters, to show them that one could climb, if painfully, out of their shared deep pit and stand in the sunshine, that there had been no time to find a husband. Of these and many other options, there is one, the truth, which I am aware of, but have agreed never to mention; it could upset others in the narrative and Veronica has no intention of doing this.

Instead, she was driven always to have a new goal in life, the next level up, to replace the boss above her, her mantra, '….is there promotion in the job…?' and once this was in the bag, to look around to assess yet another giant step upwards, a hardening glance at the staircase which became steeper as time consumed her.

Veronica claims she was never driven, but the evidence to the contrary is there. For her, she was always seeking a new post and taking it up with evident pleasure – a higher position and a more difficult challenge. It was always in her nature to try, if it took her in an upward move.

It was certainly a combination of several factors that Veronica is still on her own today, respected, listened to: even the Queen saw fit to award her the Order of the British Empire; but she is still alone. The damage is too deep and too hurtful.

All of this, paints a dismal picture, one maybe you are familiar with; the usual story of the deprivation of coal miners' lives, the general lack of colour with only tints of grey and black in those early post-war years. But, Veronica's later life is filled, stuffed full in fact, of humour and colour. When one is facing a ten year stretch there are two ways to go, one being to fill it with as many laughs as possible to soften the daily chore of prison life. To deal with this you will find that Part One is monochrome, fascinating yet cruel, her life without the tints which came later to her as she blossomed into her profession, which she speaks about in Part Two.

When I first heard Veronica speaking at a U3A meeting, reminiscing on her life in Russia, her stories were peppered with humour and I could see it was important to her. With a jest or an absurdity, her own days would have been quickened, a smile to and from a prisoner who only wants, perhaps, to get through the day without trouble? And the staff? How could they carry on year after year without allowing a chuckle at a joke or a twitch of a mouth at a particularly outrageous suggestion from a prisoner?

It has been a long way from the dark years of Doncaster Road in Barnsley to filling one's days with enjoyment and the admiration of her peers. There could hardly have been a single hour in her youth when Veronica would not have found herself looking over her shoulder at an approaching shadow or straining in exhaustion as she lifted the heavy bags of potatoes into the market at three in the morning when dressed in threadbare clothes. There could not have been much to smile at in life when her thoughts would have been on stocking up the carrots and cabbages on the stall so she could move on to the washing and ironing or calming the fretting younger children. It is an almost daily occurrence to read as a headline, a red top paper demanding heavy penalties on the exploiters of children in Britain, but only fifty years ago, it appears it was quite permissible to allow these abuses to continue as 'accepted' norms. When we complain today of the country unable to sort itself out and '…. wasn't it better in the Sixties?' perhaps it might be a good thing to remember that we have advanced enormously since that era in terms of Welfare and Social Care. Of course, the coal industry with all its terrors and blackness, is a mere shadow of itself, the people better educated, better housed and better paid. They are safer. The emancipation of women allows them to match, or better their men in so many ways, has brought a new relationship to partnerships. Men washup and help make the beds these days; it is with such small changes of attitude as these, taking place everywhere which, eventually, bring new, positive and strong connections into being. Veronica's life might have been very different if she had had access then to twenty-first century attitudes.

Seventy-four years ago, Veronica Bird was born into a world so utterly different to ours today that George Bird, her father, might have taken himself off to the Dove Inn to sort it all out in his mind. But it was his sixth child and his third daughter, the one on the far fringe of his life who finally showed his family that there was hope; there was a way to climb out of that pit into the sunshine. Veronica took that decision to lock herself away so she could be freed of persecution. It was, paradoxically, the making of her.

When I asked Veronica, what her family, all those still alive, might think of her story she replied quickly: 'It is the truth. It is all true, we can't change history. All we can do is to learn and try to be better citizens as a result.'

PART ONE

I MIGHT BE BETTER OFF IN A CHILDREN'S HOME

CHAPTER ONE
DONCASTER ROAD

A letter to our house was so rare that to see the slim white envelope in my mother's hand was a surprise, to say the least. The fact it was addressed to me was mind-numbing, particularly as understanding was immediate, connecting quickly to a deep anxiety as I grasped the fact of what, almost certainly, was inside.

The room, always noisy, always argumentative, had fallen silent. Mother had placed her rough hands on her pinny as she gazed at her third daughter. Father had turned away, dismissing the slightly theatrical atmosphere. Besides, neither my mother nor my father could read or write, save for their signatures, so it would have been left up to me anyway to inform them of the contents.

You can have no idea of the stress I was under. For eleven years, I had been existing, no more than that, always hungry, dressed in threadbare passed-on clothes, the frequent chance to feel my father's belt across my backside. There was the ever-present stench of coal dust drifting in from the Pits, the grime and the filth of the kitchen floor while Jack, my eldest brother's epileptic fits increased in their severity every month; there were no signs it might ever get better.

For as long as I could remember, I had dreamed of leaving this house, running as fast as my short legs would take me as far as they could, never mind where, so long as it was away. There had often been the threat from my father in one of his drunken rages to send me to the local Children's Home, though hardly a red danger line to me, for I know I would have been happier there than to remain in the harsh atmosphere of our house in coal-mining Barnsley in post-war Britain.

I received a nod and a smile from my mother but I cannot recall if my hands were shaking in the best tradition of the tense thriller, but I am fairly certain I stopped breathing.

She held out the single sheet of paper, nothing else, too slim to say much, but then, how many words does it take to say '…. sorry…. but.'

Fail or Pass: it would be one of those two words. I began to read to myself, not to the family.

Like one of those ludicrous Bake-Off programmes I said nothing for such a long time even my father turned around to look at me. He sniffed loudly to draw attention to himself as if to say, 'Well?'

'I've got it! I've got in. I've won a scholarship … Ackworth School,' I added as if they did not know the origin of the letter.

There was a silence, just the hiss of the coke in the grate until, with a rush and a roar, Gordon my brother of eight years my senior, grabbed me and threw me into the air.

'Well done, well done,' he said with a grin.

I answered with my own big smile as I struggled to regain my feet. I was very pleased, no, wrong word, perhaps over-the-moon might be better, try blown away for the modern vernacular equivalent, for it was rare any of the family would ladle out praise upon another, let alone me. Father turned away without a comment to light a cigarette and to ease his damaged leg. Mam, though, came over to me and squeezed me tight.

'I knew you could do it,' she said with a look of pride. She gave me a hug, defiant of what my father might have thought. This was one time when she could stand up to him without receiving too many glares. It had been her idea for me to apply.

'The uniform…. the trunk, the-'

She cut me off. 'We'll find the money; don't you worry your head.'

I turned away from my brothers and sisters who were already wondering what might happen now. They knew very well I would almost certainly change beyond all recognition to them; I was just about to become posh.

In Barnsley, it was difficult, no, bloody difficult, to be posh. I knew that only too well.

I turned my head back to the fire, remembering the awfulness of almost every day of my brief life. There had been nothing to laugh about, barely a smile, for the shadow of my father shivered at every corner as I sought to hide.

*

The first light of day disturbed my newly formed eyelids on a cold morning in February. It was 1943 and the war was already well into completing its fourth year. Although I was unaware of the cataclysmic events going on around the world, the gloom of the war and the lack of real progress shaped a grubby pessimism which laid itself upon the town. For better or for worse I had arrived; I had yet to learn it was for the worse.

Barnsley was coal, plain and simple, with many of the familiar pit names such as Grimethorpe, Houghton Main and Cortonwood in the surrounding area. Because the town was ringed by pits, the coal dust hung in the air and settled during the rain. It turned anything with a hint of colour to a shade of grey. Never mind Fifty Shades of Grey, Barnsley had a thousand shades of black.

There was so much coal below the town that it had grown rapidly, attracting glass blowers and linen weavers along the way into a complete anthology of heavyweight industries. When Dad was born, trams would have rattled down Cheapside towards the seventy collieries which lay within fifteen miles of Barnsley's town centre. There was an urgency about the town and it was known as a good place to be if you wanted work. As the town expanded, villages such as Monk

Bretton and Carlton were absorbed into its boundaries as the tide overtakes the sand, before disappearing altogether in the endless rows of tiny back-to-back houses.

It was as if coal stocks would last forever, as if Britain itself was composed of coal, and with coal came steel. How could such a source of wealth end?

In nineteen-eighty-four, Arthur Scargill launched his National Coal strike. It split families and communities right down the centre leaving deep wounds still open today. In the end, logic triumphed, for coal was too expensive to mine, with cheap imports already arriving in the country. Besides, the country was urgently demanding, newer, cleaner sources of energy. Green was the new mantra, green was the colour of choice.

As I write, there are no coal mines remaining open in Barnsley, just sad reminders, like a winding tower, abandoned here and there, of the glory days to show what Barnsley had stood for. The streets are clean now, so is the air, and businesses have graduated towards a service economy. It does mean the community spirit of the mining families never travelled to the new Estates when everyone moved out of the centre.

Seventy-four years earlier I arrived on the Third of February but, as no-one was particularly interested in me, being the sixth child in a poverty-stricken home, there had been a misunderstanding over the actual date and the fact was, the family believed I had been born a day earlier than the actuality, only revealed by my long lost, then rediscovered, Birth Certificate.

This was the year of Barnes Wallace's Bouncing Bomb and the first Bevin Boys were conscripted to work in the coal mines. The first jet aircraft, the Gloucester Meteor flew its maiden test flight at Cranwell, as Churchill began to realise we could lose the war not by the lack of guns but from the real possibility of mass starvation due to the serious increase in U-boat operations.

In Barnsley, the hunger was real. It was a time of trying to find enough to eat each day, for the family was too large and had become a constant worry for my mother. She had delivered me at our rented house close to my grandmother's home. Gran ran a Fish and Chip shop, an essential element in the life of Yorkshire at the time, the forerunner of the Take-Away, a cheap meal for the many on subsistence levels. A bag of fish and chips, wrapped in a copy of the Mirror would have cost 6d, that is 6d not 6p.

I suppose one of the first dramas in my life, certainly one that sticks close in my memory was when I practically collided with a bus soon after I had learned to walk at eleven months. It reads quite dramatically and by the very fact you are reading this book, you know I survived, but at the time I almost died before I had reached the age of one. For some reason, I had made up my mind to cross Doncaster Road holding my mother's hand urgent as a dog on a lead. Off I stepped, no idea of the dangers of course, seeing only the other side of the road and nothing in between. Mam screamed out as the bus clipped me but I was already flying up in the air in a parabola, removed to safety by the strength of her arms, though covered in cuts and scratches and more tearful at the alarm in my mother's voice than in the danger I had placed myself, as I completed more of a cartwheel than a full somersault. There was a doctor's surgery just up the road past the school where I was taken and a declaration made I was very lucky. Not soon after this alarm, there came a second incident, far more painful, when a glowing lump of coke spat out of the fire and embedded itself under my cheek. It left a scar, a reminder of those days of coal fires and the ever-present danger of young children in front of the grate.

As I grew, not as fast as many, as I never had enough to fill my stomach, I became aware of my mother, in part warm towards me, in other ways distant. I was yet to understand that with five other children at that time, (there would be nine) to look after, and Alwyn, already next in line to appear, with Jack a very sick, oldest son constantly needing her attention, there was a need to distribute love and comforts evenly.

There was a second key presence in my life. This one was frightening, a dark, brooding menace with blackened face who, having almost no time for me, would always lash out, making me jump. It was my dad, George Bird, thirty-seven years old when he saw me for the first time, and angry with it because he could not afford, or would not use contraception. There would be two more sons and another daughter, nine in total, a seemingly never-ending expansion of the Bird dynasty, only stopping when my mother died far too early. Meanwhile, for Alwyn as well as me, for whatever reason, we would remain the butt of Dad's frequent anger.

Father was a coal miner in Carlton Main Colliery along with his three brothers. There had been a fourth brother but he had died in the First World War. Dad was born before the First World War in 1906, a man who grew to five feet ten inches in height but unlike so many coal miners he was relatively slim, with no sign of a beer belly which might well have resulted from the enormous quantities of beer he downed each night. He shaved each day but this didn't mean he ever wore a suit or even a jacket. His brown hair remained with him all his life.

In a football-obsessed town like Barnsley, some, who like to think on such things, might have noted it was also in 1906 that Manchester United was promoted to the First Division. To all the miners that year came real hope as the Labour Representation Committee in Parliament became the Parliamentary Labour Party.

George Bird was in a reserved occupation as a miner in the Second World War. This might never have happened for he had been involved in a terrifying and massive fall of coal and rock in 1933. He was hauled out of the pit on the assumption he was already dead, as he was smashed up so badly. His brain was open, with a huge hole, and miners just shook their heads when they saw his body on the stretcher. But, he was to defy all the pundits. Clever surgeons placed a metal plate over the hole to protect his brain and sent him home. Extraordinarily it worked. He lived, just, only to find, like miners in those days, that he was laid off and he was left with a pittance to live on.

At the age of twenty-seven with two children, one of them seriously ill with epilepsy, in a tiny cramped house, he had only his skills as a miner to fall back on. The world collapsed in on him. One day he found Kitty, his wife, in tears and asked what the matter was.

Mother said through her sobs: 'How are we going to live? What are we going to eat?'

Even George's heart, hardened to life, must have softened that day as reality set in. Abruptly, he made the decision to ask his brothers for a loan. They obliged, and although I have no idea how much they raised for him, he managed to buy a cart and a horse with the proceeds. It was indeed, a strange purchase for a proud miner.

'What are you going to do with those?' The comment was rightly tinged with suspicion seeing their hard-earned cash begin to melt away in hay and harness.

'I've got my allotment. I'm going to expand it, up the production, then I'm going to go around the streets selling veg. Carrots, lovely potatoes, onions. Folks round here will think it bloody lovely.'

'Bloody rubbish more likely. You'll never stick to that. You're a miner, not a bloody farmer!'

But my father was a determined man. Besides, what else could he do? 'There's a Depression on. You wait and see.' Dad would have shrugged his shoulders as if to throw off the world. He knew better.

Surprising his brothers, he prospered, as the shortage of everything in those unhappy days made his hawking cries popular. There was a ready demand for his fresh vegetables and, no doubt, they were a reasonable price. He began to make a little money and we survived.

By the time my eyes could focus, he had gone back into the mine. The hole in his head had somehow repaired itself sufficiently to be passed fit for work. The camaraderie of the miners was fused deep within him and formed an unshakeable bond. His improving health had made him turn his back on his allotment and he said goodbye to his horse. It was wartime, there was a massive demand for coal, and he sought solace in the company of his trusted friends. I remember it as a time when I would try and read his blackened face, an ogre from hell, with red, staring eyes, judging whether he would over-turn the kitchen table again when the potatoes were not quite ready for him to eat. When he was in such a state he never cared who came within his firing line.

One of the first real hurts in my life, apart from the burning coke, not his fault, and boiling water thrown over me, which was his fault, enough to need hospitalisation, was the realisa-tion my father had a favourite in the family, his eldest child, Joan, fourteen years older than me. She, to my youthful mind was an adult in every way and enjoyed a much better, stress-free life than the rest of the family. Joan could not understand why everyone complained (quietly) so much. This gap formed an early chasm between the rest of us. It focussed me on the inequalities of life as I grew up, for we lived on the hand-me-down principle. By the time I received something to wear it had already been passed from Joan, then Pat before reaching me, threadbare. And something warm for the winter could pass through five siblings before I could pull it over my face.

For George Bird, fate stepped in again, unexpectedly as always. Maybe it was the hole in his head, maybe the beer which was more than likely. One day he stumbled on the pave-ment edge in the bus station. His leg was badly crushed in collision with a bus and the ensuing damage was bad enough to oblige him to wear a calliper for the rest of his life. Again, he survived, but his bitterness with life caused him, when in one of his tempers, to snatch the brace off his leg and throw it at Alwyn, the youngest in the family, who was quite unable to understand the anger pouring out of his Dad.

There was a single exception to this never-ending round of unhappiness. It was an isolated event which stood out like a beacon of warmth in a cold sea. Perhaps God made the decision Himself, who knows? Maybe He smiled that day when an aunt, or was it just a good friend, I cannot remember who now, felt sorry for me. Whoever it was, they gave me a bright red, new cardigan. I could not believe my luck; it was wonderful, magical and it was mine. It was new, that was my point. It was thick, it had no holes, it wasn't darned repeatedly and it smelt of something I could recognise now: newness. It never happened again until I left home for good. Re-reading this, it seems quite ridiculous to say I was so happy over one single red cardigan but when you have had nothing, this was like being taken to the circus and the pantomime in the same day.

We had moved from our rented house in Carlton to the Corner Shop No.89 Doncaster Road. The stone-built house, as they all were, was coated in black grime as if the whole street was part of a coal mine itself. We were separated from St. Peter's church next door by a steep slip road. The church was a large red-brick building completed three years before the start of the First World War. It was funded with pennies donated by miners, though whether they realised it was going towards somewhere to worship in the Anglo-Catholic tradition, that is, an Anglican church which recognises Catholic roots history, is not recorded anywhere. I would play around its stark brick plinth, not realising then how it would play such a large part in my early life. For those interested in such fragments of history, St. Peter's was described by Sir John Betjeman as '…. a hidden gem,' although, hidden was probably the wrong word, being of red brick which thrust out into Doncaster Road robustly, as if it was one of the sea cliffs at Sidmouth.

Moving to a new house did not improve my father's temper which manifested itself in sudden swings of anger. There were no warnings. The new house was not an improvement, not a step up as most house moves should be. His black scowl had been packed along with our few sticks of furniture only to be re-opened as soon as we arrived. So much for Mam hoping the change might help.

17

Across the road, we could see a Fish and Chip shop and a sweet shop next to it. Lack of pocket-money of any description prevented me from buying any of these goodies, but at least I could dream, dream of a future when I would be able to call into such a shop whenever I wished and order two ounces of... (such a choice) of.... liquorice twirls...or how about jelly babies? Alongside these was a cobbler who maintained an immaculate house, always a talking point with the local wives. It formed a stark contrast with our own house showing just what care and attention could do for a similar property.

Hungry, belted too frequently, though Dad was careful to be out of sight of my Mam when he brought a strap to me, and cold in the winter, I had grown used to being smudged in soot and coal dust, as the black stuff was as much inside the house as in the street. A combination of Dad's anger and the grime formed in me a desperate urge, when I reached the age of six, to get away, anywhere from the house. My wish was granted in the form of a refuge provided on the doorstep, so to speak: it was Betjeman's hidden gem, St. Peter's.

Mam never took us to church, nor did she attend herself. She would always help with the cooking for the fêtes and outdoor parties in the summer. But the church became a foil to my loneliness and a shield against my brutal home life. What our Priest thought of his newly moved in parishioners, owning a ragamuffin who sought sanctuary, is not documented in the church crypt. Although in 1949, rationing of clothes was removed, it made no difference to me. Same dress, same cardigan each week. It was the church which allowed me to escape from the noise, the anxiety, the fear and the lack of privacy. Surprisingly, although surrounded by people I did not know, where the roof almost disappeared into clouds, it was so lofty, I could easily lose myself at the back, behind the other regular worshippers who packed the pews for every service. They, from time to time, might have registered my presence with a slight condescending smile and a gracious nod of a head whose hat had been carefully adjusted in front of a mirror, before entering onto the street. How sweet, quaint even, one would indicate with her eyes to another parishioner, at the waif, a Dickensian character perhaps, before passing on down the aisle to a seat which had not yet been possibly contaminated with grime.

I enjoyed singing, so much so, that later I took to Evensong as well. It had a curious knock-on effect later for being well versed in hymns, I carried this enjoyment and knowledge with me when I eventually left Barnsley.

I remember the day the Priest announced that deaths in the mining workforce were reported to have fallen to a record low since nationalisation two years earlier. Safety had come too late for my father, though I am sure wives and mothers slept better, cheered at the news. Such an announcement in a strong mining community as Barnsley, would have had a considerable impact on the close-knit families. Do you remember those black and white, grainy television images of women gathering at the pit head as yet another mining disaster was announced? Faces would be drawn in desperation, reddened hands thrust into their aprons or tucked into tightly folded arms as they sought any news of their men trapped underground? Such scenes always triggered a nation-wide sympathy for the entombed men and we were reminded, yet again, of how dangerous the job was to get the coal into your grate.

Poor Jack, my eldest brother was trapped too. He was an epileptic with few medicines to treat him in 1950. It was only, in that year, epilepsy was brought into the public domain in an attempt to change public attitudes towards this condition affecting the brain. Jack was imprisoned, literally speaking, for as his condition deteriorated he had to be locked in the boys' bedroom. It was feared he would harm himself if left on his own. He was my father's eldest son and I am sure Dad would have been planning for Jack to follow him into the pit when he came of age. To his exhausted mother, Ethel, or Kitty as she was known to everyone on the street, it was an added worry to keep to herself every day. Dad, as with everything else, blamed Mam for his son's disease saying she had worn corsets which had been too tight when she was pregnant. I think there might have been more truth in the suggestion that as Jack was kicked in the head by the horse, Dad owned, this had led to the onset of the disease. Doctors today are pretty clear on this – a severe injury can cause epilepsy.

We moved twice again, the second time to Park Road, a ludicrously small property with just two bedrooms and a box room. In this tiny space eleven of us had to find our way in life. Even my eldest sister, Joan, was still in the house though she was to leave, sensibly, in 1952 to be married. It became obvious to my father he had made two mistakes in buying houses, and he did not want to repeat his errors, not that they were ever admitted. Having managed to put aside some money when he gave up his market garden venture to return to mining, it gave him a new chance to buy a Fish and Chip shop, the same one we had looked across the street to the corner by the church, where I had almost been killed by the bus.

It was a good buy, a first good move for the family, for the business lived off the proximity of the Football Ground, Barnsley F.C, 'The Tykes,' just a road or so back behind us. We could hear the roar of the crowd on a Saturday afternoon as one side or the other scored. Without acknowledging the fact, Dad knew the shop would be professionally managed with Mam in charge. He need have nothing to do with its day to day operation. To him, it was vital to have the Dove Inn just a hundred yards up the road as his centre of life, not the drudge of peeling potatoes.

He did, however, work to improve his income, by spending a lot of time separating out his coal allowance he received each month, hiving off the good, large pieces into sacks which he then sold on. He was not allowed to do it, but it was the way in which miners could increase their small pay. Inevitably, the result was that the family had just the slack for their own fire which burnt miserably in the grate before settling into fine dust.

From this new house and workplace combined, I could look

across the street gazing at my Sunday place of refuge while on the town side was the sweet shop, but as near as it might be, it was as far away as if on the other side of the Channel.

The smartly dressed cobbler and his sons were now our immediate neighbours, always a bell-weather to us, demonstrating how one could live with a little care. I deliberate often on those days and wonder what they thought as the bellowing roars of rage from next door transferred through flimsy party walls, followed by the crashing of pots and pans. It was never a contest between us; they lived a life of cleanliness and tidiness, we wallowed in a black pit of grubbiness.

A little further east along this road, more of a hop and a skip in the direction of Goldthorpe, was Doncaster Road Primary School. I attended this from the age of three, a war-time habit where I remained after VE day. Our class was by no means out of the ordinary to begin learning to read and write at such an age. It meant, we children, were kept out of the feet of busy mothers who had been employed to lend a hand towards the production of war materials. I assumed it had to be a Government plan, needing an up and coming stock of relatively intelligent children to fill the empty places created by the ruthless protraction of the war.

I remained there until nineteen fifty-four when I was eleven. With so many other children with parents from poor backgrounds, I merged effortlessly into the rows of wooden desks, taught for two years by a severely reduced number of teachers. Most had gone off to war, many had been killed, some had taken up the opportunity offered to go on to University; it left us with much older men and women to take their places often with the last vestiges of Empire and its old-fashioned ideas to pass on to us. When it came time to revise for Boarding School, I found myself struggling to swot up on some high-powered test papers which did not relate, in the slightest, to our teaching in Doncaster Road.

Down the street would come the babble of excited football supporters on Saturday afternoons. Flat-capped men flooded the street with a boozy, belching bonhomie on the way in, and, depending upon the result of the game, crept grumpily off to the pubs or cheered as they balanced precariously on the edge of the pavement, to everyone they met, as they queued for fish and chips if the Tykes had won. Today, our prim, spotless houses, each with two television sets and strong locks on the houses show how far removed that world has moved from a time when our doors had been left open. There had been a familiarity, almost tactile in its warmth, lost for ever with the disappearance of the mining communities.

There was one exception to the drudge of our lives in those days, a one-off event each year meant to be an exciting day out for us all. It was simply the biggest occasion in our skimpy calendar. The Miners Welfare Club in Carlton would arrange for about sixteen coaches of families to go to Southport for the day. That year, we were separated in the convoy, with Mam and Alwyn together in one and me and the others in another. As luck turns on a spin of the top, her coach was in collision with a lorry before she had reached the half-way mark. Mam and Alwyn were sitting up front where they had found a good seat with a front view. They were hit by flying glass. Her dream day out was stopped before it started and they ended up in hospital having their facial cuts seen to. The cash compensation from the Coach Company was hardly what was wanted. It was so hard; it was the only day of the year Mother could enjoy herself, fully away from the house, the job and the anger, enjoying her children's excitement. It had begun in happiness, with our sandwiches clutched tightly in our hands, a smile on everyone's face. It ended in a short terror, a swirl of antiseptic, and a ration of pain.

We had moved, not because we needed more room, not because it was better, but because of the shop attached to the front; like my grandmother in Carlton we were to be a fish and chip shop business. The shop window faced out onto a stone-flag courtyard where the beginning of the Saturday queues would form. Today it is a women's hair-dressing salon with greater aspirations than our fish shop could ever be. Otherwise, we were just as cramped as before, with father and mother in one bedroom, all the boys in another and the girls in the third room. At the back of the shop was a staircase down to the kitchen with a blackened range sitting on a stone flagged floor. Potato peeling went on in a work- shed out in the dirty yard and further, but not that far away, stood a shared privy. It is still there although it now rebuilt as a much smarter brick built store. (think health and safety). There were no floor coverings in the bedrooms, so we remained permanently chilled in the winter. The only heat came from the fire with its miserable slack and even that struggled to combat the ice-cold damp which came up from the cellar into our feet.

The fish and chip shop was entirely my mother's domain. Dressed in her headscarf knotted up on her head she became well-known in the local community. Father never lifted a hand to help though it was contributing successfully to the family income. She was seen each day in her white jacket, and a blue butcher's apron, always easy-going to her customers. The only time Mam allowed herself to take a break was on a Thursday afternoon, for two hours, when she crossed over to the other side of the road to the church to play Whist.

With this house came more single-minded meanness. There was a tin bath in the kitchen to remove the daily grime of coal dust from my father's body. Thinking he was doing himself a good deal, he got hold of a proper bath and had it installed in the tiny kitchen forgetting how big the bath was. He was forced to build a wooden shelf to fit on top of the rim which enabled us to sit when we ate. To say, *ate*, belies the idea of a normal meal with the family grouped around a table. Father owned the only mug and eating utensils which he kept to himself and washed them up before putting them away. So, although we found enough room to sit, we had to pick our food with our fingers and wipe any grease on our clothes. I should add, that although Dad had a new bath, the water still had to be heated in buckets – there was no other source of hot water.

The introduction of the Fish and Chip shop, a useful and valuable facility in an area such as Doncaster Road, brought additional work upon us all. In the yard, we had a *rumbler,* a potato peeler, which was kept in the shed. As soon as the potatoes had been reasonably stripped of their skins we had to finish them off by removing the eyes before placing them in very heavy pans. If the rumbler broke down we had to do all the peeling ourselves often in freezing conditions. Peeled, we lifted them up the flight of back stairs and entered the shop where they were chipped. Producing raw chips ready to be fried, in winter was generally loathed for in those pre-global warming days, it led to chilblains and reddened hands. There was no heating in the shed and the pressure was always there on a Saturday, especially when football was being played behind the house. The queue before and after the match for Fish and Chips would snake into the distance, causing a constant cry of '…. more spuds.'

We approached the back yard through a lived-over arch, separating the Sweet shop and our house, reached by a steep ramp which led into Snowdrop Terrace where we would play around the lamp posts in front of a row of terrace houses until late at night in the summer months. In fact, it made little difference in the winter as we could kick a ball under the street lights. There was a sort of grass square laid out many years ago by an enlightened town planner who had never, and would never live himself in such a poor area of the town, and I cannot remember it ever being cut. Lank grass mixed with dandelions and pieces of greasy chip paper, usually a page from *The Mirror* as it was known then. One house on the green, singled itself out for us as a family, for a young girl had committed suicide there, with an overdose of pills. With other suicides, this time within the family, I became aware at an early age, of the stresses which can cause someone to take their life; that knowledge would never serve me better than when I began to work in the Prison Service.

Snowdrop Terrace has gone, swept away by the urgent need

for more car-parking. The lank grass has been replaced by tarmac – it leaves just memories of an age long past. When I visited it the other day, the ghosts of my childhood sat at the side, and gazed on willing me, perhaps, to shed a tear but there were no happy memories to cry about and I was glad to leave and move on in my life.

You would have thought we could at least, have enjoyed a plate of fried cod and chips well-dusted with salt and liberally doused in vinegar, after the long hard work, but all we got were the left-over batter pieces lying abandoned and congealing in the draining tray. It would be rare for us to have been given fish and chips ourselves. I suppose I should be grateful to have grown until I achieved five feet five inches tall – any shorter and I might not have made the Prison Service height requirements.

My father's pub, so to speak, the Dove Inn, closed the loop which made up this part of Doncaster Road, marked out by the sweet shop, the cobbler and the church and was our world within the town. The stone built pub is still there, a convenient rendezvous in his day for Father and his brothers after work. We would hear his heavy nailed boots clattering down to the back yard to visit the privy next door to the fish shop, covered in coal dust and sweat, needing a beer but having to wash first. We would wait for his entry into the kitchen, judging the mood of whether he had had a hard day or not. Heads down, we would eat our supper of bread sometimes with dripping or, if very lucky, jam on bread, though never with margarine and not a hope of butter. We would eat in silence. When father returned from the Dove we studied him again through hooded eyes to see if he had had too much to drink. If so, he was known to summon me along with Alwyn and forced to have a bath in Izal disinfectant or drink Epson Salts as a variant. When asked the first and only time why he did this, the reply came '….to clean your insides out.'

Here, amongst the Barnsley community, violence was not uncommon, but Welfare was never called in, and if any one of us had made that decision, the repercussions falling on our heads if we had said something would have been too awful to contemplate. Besides, in those days, the authorities would never have believed a child.

His cruelty continued. I had been given, along with Alwyn, a most precious and longed for, bar of Fry's Peppermint cream, the one in the characteristic green wrapper. This was a one-off, a present from a relative, to be enjoyed slowly, perhaps kept for three days as we devoured every morsel with delight, retaining the last piece as if it was the key to Pandora's box.

My father, enraged that I could enjoy myself in such a way, snatched it from my hand and quickly scooped out the peppermint cream centre with clumsy hands. Then, he filled the hole with mustard and made Alwyn and I eat the mess until we were sick. My mother was helpless to object in such circumstances. She was exhausted, suffering from pernicious anaemia which was beginning to wear her down. The result was, she did not have the strength to protect us anymore.

The threats to send me away to a Children's home did not go away. To keep out of my father's mind and especially the length of his arm, I maintained my Sunday attendances over the road. Other families, I knew, would go on picnics in the summer and walks in the autumn along the river banks, or as a treat, go to the 'flicks.' Not once did our family spend the day together, and I do not remember seeing the whole family as a group at one time. The words 'dysfunctional' and 'totally' were real in our family, and often come to mind these days as I pull out memories for this book; then, I could only look across the street at other families coming home from a day-out and wonder why we did not do the same from time to time.

Those *cruel* times (I use the word advisedly), allowed me to brood on the idea that my father was, as he was, because of the accident he had had in the mine. He had sustained the massive blow to his head from rocks caught up in the fall. What might have happened as the surgeon poked around in my father's brain? He must have pulled out fragments of rock and coal as he sought to clean up the damage to his head but maybe he pulled out something vital at the same time? Perhaps it was that event which brought on his mood swings, his drunkenness and the sheer bloody-minded cruelty? But, when I asked one of my older sisters, did she remember such violence when she was young, her reply was that Dad had always been the same: antagonistic, difficult, a self-serving man. She said the focus was on me and Alwyn at the time simply because we were the youngest.

Whatever the cause, it frayed at my mother's reason and health, leading to need regular injections to counter the debilitating effects of her anaemia. I began to listen to the neighbours who seemed to know something about the disease which was difficult to spell, and to pronounce, yet showed its effects in such a frightening way. I had heard from an aunt it was called the 'Sighs,' a mystery word until I heard my Mam, one day sighing as she attempted to draw breath, which characterised the illness. Others, equally strangely, referred to it as 'The Fogs'. Mam would agree with that, describing it as if she was in a thick fog which caused a mental fatigue and general apathy to spread through her. It was this last development which alarmed me the most for it was at such times I could feel her slipping away from me. In addition to this problem I learned she had contracted Lyme's disease possibly caught from a tick. This often led to depression and fatigue both of which now exacerbated the anaemia. She began to age before my eyes. She became a leaf curling and fading in autumn. I was in a panic that she might leave me altogether, removing the last shield against my father's anger.

To alleviate my worries, I would go and see her in Barnsley hospital where, at one time, she was being treated for the anaemia. After I had said goodbye, I stood looking up at what I though was her window, and she must have been looking out for me. She suddenly pulled aside the curtain and looked down. She waved, a small but defiant wave towards the gate as if to say, '…. I'm alright, go home'.

As she began to detach herself from her strength, I reached the age of ten. It was the last year of Primary School and my last Sports Day, a fairly major event in my calendar for, despite not having a good diet, there was a strength in my legs which allowed me to run that much faster than my friends. I began to appreciate I could move quite swiftly when pressed and gave me an ability, at last, to be better than others in my year if only, out of class. This year was to be different; or rather, the Sports Day was proceeding as the school intended and would start on time. It was only I who had a problem. I had no shoes or knickers, both of which I needed to participate. In anguish, I pleaded with my mother to pin together a pair of her adult size knickers around my waist but I still had no shoes. There were none under the bed nor lying on the stairs, so, in the end I had to miss the big event where I could have shown what Veronica Bird was made of.

It was the one place I could have shone for my family, where, maybe, Dad might have smiled at me if not offering his congratulations. A nod of his head, ever so slight maybe, to recognise my prowess. But, no shoes meant, no running. Owning clothes in our house was shambolic, utter chaos reigning everywhere, with no-one knowing whose clothes belonged to whom and, like musical chairs you had to be very ready when the music stopped. This was just such a day. My brothers and sisters had all slipped out of the house for one reason or another, each with a pair of shoes, not to return until later in the day. By then, it was too late. The cheering parents had gone home, the finishing tape rolled up in the sports teacher's drawer ready for the next year, the Headmaster pleased with attendance…overall.

This disappointment came in 1953, the year of the Coronation with all the exciting and memorable moments it conjured up for most people in this country. For me it would be more of the same; I was in a pit, not of coal but of hopelessness, a bleak and impossible future ahead of me as I waited for the next fearful event, and I could see no way I could dig my way out.

CHAPTER TWO
A WORLD AWAY

A few years earlier I had been lucky to visit a doctor's house in Mexborough. I expect it was because I delivered a box of fruit at some time for there was no other reason I could have been in the house. Vast rooms with tall ceilings, led on to others, hung with beautiful curtains, carpets to sink into and a pervading warmth. I walked around, spinning as if I was a top, arms spread wide to take it all in. The incident had almost been forgotten when I noticed a girl one day, well dressed, in a school uniform. She was even walking nicely. As she passed me I heard her talking to her mother. It was what we would call a 'posh' accent, but that did not make it an unpleasant sound. It was certainly different, strange, alien even, to my own simple selection of Barnsley-accented words. In many ways, she was a world away from my own life yet I could have touched her as she overtook us.

'That's the Ackworth School uniform,' replied my mother in response to my questioning. 'If you wanted to, you could go there but you would have to take an exam, and then there would have to be an interview.'

How she knew all this I don't know. Such far removed comforts were not of normal interest in our family, nor, to be fair, in many families in Doncaster Road. We just didn't associate with people who sent their children to such a nice school. Mam explained what an interview was. I was nine years old and unsophisticated. ''Do you have to speak like that girl....at the interview I mean?'

Mother hesitated for just a moment. 'I don't think they would turn you away because you didn't have a posh accent. You see, these sorts of schools are looking for the brightest children in the country; ones who could go on to University.... even girls, so your accent is not what is important, it is what you can achieve.'

Mam saw the deepening interest in my eyes. She made a small grimace putting a dampener on my newly-forming ideas.

'To go there, you would have to win a scholarship, that is, passing your exams so well you would not have to pay. It is very expensive there.'

'Oh,' I said, deflated. 'So, how do I get a scholarship?'

My mother's tired face smiled down on me. 'You would have to work for it as you have never worked in your life. If you did get one, it would mean you would be a boarder during term-time, staying at the school for the full term, sleep there and eat there.'

Something burst out in my brain. I imagine it was like the alarm going off in a fire-station. The very idea of being away from the anger and my father's belt with, perhaps the possibility of having a bit more food each day....and dressed nicely, was not something I could dismiss out of hand. That was silly. I could not let this idea pass me by at all. Such a vision of the future would be a hundred times better than any Children's' home.

'Mother, I want to get a scholarship. To this school. I want to go to Ackworth. I want-'

She placed a hand over my mouth. She hadn't seen me so urgent in an appeal to her until now. 'Tell you what. I will get the forms for you. You will have to fill them in and I will sign it. But,' she stressed the next few words repeating what she had said. The second time it excited me for I was suddenly filled with hope and confidence. 'But, it will be work as you have never done in your life. You simply won't get through unless you work, work, work. No more hopscotch or playing ball in the street.'

I watched the girl from Ackworth School disappear around the corner and nodded. 'I'll work, Mam, I really will.'

*

The application form, when it arrived, caused some soul-searching and frustration over the time it took to fill in the boxes. It was quite complicated. I was well aware also we would have to get the submission in quickly as we had applied very late. What the school required was personal, intrusive to my way of thinking though, I suppose, to anyone else they were just questions to be answered. There were some I did not understand at all, and there was a need to read out much of what was required of me to my mother who, though being unable to read, could at least, explain what was wanted. It was the first form I had ever seen in my life and it seemed so queer to have to answer questions which had no reason, at least to my youthful and near dormant brain.

There were boxes and areas where there were just no answers at all. We brushed across these as best as we could, though each time we did, I felt it was another black mark against Veronica Bird's submission. Would they even bother to read it? Eventually my mother signed her spidery name at the bottom and, panicking that I could still miss the deadline typed in heavy print on the front, ran all the way to the Town Hall Education Department late that Friday night to slip it into the large brass letterbox on the main door. The deadline was 9.a.m. Saturday. That night I prayed quite hard, well, really hard in fact, squeezing my eyelids tight as I asked God to speed the letter to the school.

He must have been out walking in Barnsley that night, perhaps having decided Bird should have a go at taking the exam. Why not? She might do well.

I *was* asked to sit the exam. It was January nineteen fifty-three.

Everything else should have been placed on hold so I could

read and revise for the exam, but Dad insisted I do my share of looking after the family and staying in while he went out on the town on a Saturday night. Meanwhile my mother's health did not improve, making that New Year a sad and grey place to be.

It was sadder still, for the country was gearing up, aiming at the biggest party of the century as the State shaped the forthcoming Coronation in June. Street parties were being deliberated, bunting sewn and plans drawn up in dozens of Committee rooms. This excitement floated around the town as if everyone had won the football pools at the same time creating a mood to match the town's wish for a bright new era as we all headed for the start of Queen Elizabeth's reign.

I had been told to expect to attend an interview the same day as the exam. I could bring a parent with me, in fact, the school insisted they should meet and talk with my mother as well. The questions in the form confirmed everything I had believed might be the case, an intrusion into my very private life. To make it worse, I was to be laid bare for the examiners, possibly I supposed, so they could smirk at my clothes and my accent. I knew I did not have a hope, recalling the girl in the street and her nice voice and the way she managed herself in her walk, even the way she glanced about the street. She wasn't me and never could be.

Beginning to creep up on me, a brush of an eyelid to begin, then an itch down my spine, the shake of my head as if surrounded by midges, was the realisation of the stupidity in which I had acted. There was no-one to blame except myself. My Mother had only followed my pleading. Everything came back down on me in having this pointless idea which was so far removed from reality I might as well have been cutting coal instead of my father. I wished I had never filled in that damn application form. As I struggled over one fence, the next reared up in front of me. Beecher's Brook for eternity. It began to dawn on me, one option might well be to pass the written exam but fail the interview – badly. There would be the galling experience of failing, not because of my ability but because I did not talk like other boys and girls, nor did I have their manners. The remote possibility of attending the largest co-educational boarding school in the country was so far divorced from my own life it was ridiculous that I had ever pressed my mother. And all because I had seen one girl in a nice uniform talk to her mother in a way that had attracted me to do something myself.

Buggar! Buggar! Buggar! I had learnt those three words very early in my life. I did not say them aloud but I felt their force underlining my stupidity.

So, why had Mam gone out of her way to bring back the forms to the house so I could fill them in? Surely, she would have understood that at the final fence I would fall, and fall hard, but, this time, fully aware of what I had lost? I felt uncomfortable because of her continuing belief in me. She had in fact, opted to place me in a state of enormous disappointment. It was also going to colour my belief in myself for ever. Working class and always to be as such.

This extraordinary, this very special day, stored forever in my mind struggled into a dawn light; it brightened and Mam and I took the bus to Ackworth School. It was a journey of almost eleven miles, past Grimethorpe Colliery and not far from Wakefield. We drove through countryside which had a significance about it as I had never thought of before. As the miles rolled away I knew that in a few hours I would be coming back down this same road, perhaps even on the same bus, having spoken and written words which, when judged, could decide my whole life. It was as pivotal as that. If I impressed, there was a life out there where I could choose a road to step along, not one which was dictated to me.

*

To say the change from Doncaster Road to Ackworth village was enormous is to understate my words completely. Within

two hours of leaving the grime, the rubbish, the rusting corrugated iron and the stinging nettles growing through it all,
I had arrived at the sweeping grandeur of the curving wings
of the main buildings of the school with their soft honey-co-
loured stone. The white clock tower with its gold numbers and
hands, the tennis courts saying come and play with me; the
two-hundred-year-old gleam on the York stone pavings inside
along the corridors, the polished brass bands strapped hori-
zontally across every door. I could go on of course, possibly
for ever. I had simply never seen anything like it in my life. It
was clean, and ordered, and just plain nice. Standing with my
mouth open, gazing up at the main door hearing the chatter
of children like myself going about their lessons I vowed to
myself I would try my hardest to be the best possible pupil and
make my family proud of me.

The exam was short; I thought it would have been longer
so perhaps they were checking to see if I really could read and
write, do a few sums, that sort of thing. I was to be judged
alongside two other children, well-dressed, parents oozing
wealth, who smiled at me in that kindly way rich people smile
to those not as fortunate as they

After the test, we sat outside the study on a long bench
which had seemingly been there for as long as the school had
existed, not saying much, trying to hold in the tremors of our
hands and the worry of what questions would be thrown at us.

'Ah. Mrs Bird, and this must be Veronica. Do come in.'

Both with considerable trepidation, but smiling at almost
anything that moved in case he, she or it might be involved
in the decision-making, we walked into a friendly office. One
which put us at our ease in a trice. A man and a woman shook
hands with us introducing themselves as the Headmaster for
the whole school and a Headmistress who looked after the
girls. This was amazing, that one school could have two Heads
to look after their pupils. I wasn't at all clear at the time if the
Head Master bossed (sorry, administered to) everyone, boys
and girls alike or if he was divorced from running the girls

side completely. The Headmistress gave the impression she was not to be messed with at any time. Red lines and do not cross, came to my nervy mind but, at the same time I felt in control of myself. I could see she had a softness about her if one of her girls got into trouble.

I smiled as brightly as I could, seeing book upon book on the shelves. Sunlight glinted on a silver cigarette box and a bowl of flowers on a stand. A school motto on a plaque read: *Not for oneself, but for all.* It was.... nice. What was more unsettling was the sideways glance given by the Headmistress to my shoes? I had no socks on because I did not have any. My dress was very plain though I suppose I had a cardigan over the top.

The questions were as much directed towards my Mother as me.

She was asked what the conditions were like at home and why did she want Veronica to go to this school? I was asked at what level I had reached and what were my good subjects. They both picked up their ears when I said I was good at all sports. We came to the end of the question and answer session. We all shook hands again and withdrew from the study which reeked of tobacco smoke and ease. On the way back on the bus neither of us said much. I was too shell-shocked now, aware for the first time of what I was going to lose and all for my stupidity in wanting what was clearly not mine to seek. Mam had no idea how I had done. We were simply in the dark as to how my appearance had gone down, or whether Mam's own comments would best push me up the ladder I needed to climb.

The die, was, as they say, bloody well cast. I learned later the other two, a boy and a girl came from a Headmaster's home and the other from an Optician, so no doubt they both spoke politely. I had already noticed their nice clothes.

When we left, I took in as much as I could, memorising the rooms we were shown in case I never came back. My eyes gleamed at the dining halls, the food in the kitchens, the sports equipment, the place where I might sleep.

It was thus in this low state I arrived home from school on

that critical day. My mother was standing in the kitchen, the slim letter in her hand; Gordon was standing in the room, anxiety for me showing clearly on his face. At last, I read the contents. Then I read them again.

Then…I smiled.

Unable to retain himself any longer Gordon grabbed hold of me and literally threw me into the air.

'You're in! You're in!' he cried out in pure delight. 'You are going to Ackworth.' His words, after he had put me down, caused my mouth to go dry with the shock. I *was* going to Ackworth. I *was* going to be given a real chance in life. No-one in my family had ever been given such an opportunity. There had been, in one split second of time, a quantum leap, not just for me but for the whole family. If my father had felt he was not involved beforehand, he was now, whether he liked it or not. From this day forward, I was to be placed in a different and unique box to any of my siblings. There was me going places; and there were all the others in my school. Most of all I felt so pleased for my mother. She, it was, who had pushed me very hard in my books and she it was who had stuck by me from the very beginning and had chided me when I showed nerves before the exam.

A few days later, a brown envelope arrived at the door bringing a sheaf of other information, pictures showing children of my age doing things I had never dreamed of; an equipment list which just fitted on a quarto sheet of paper detailing the need to buy all, not just some, of the items on the schedule, my own personal effects as the school put it. I would have to have possessions so exciting I found I wanted to cry. But, how on God's earth would my mother find the way to pay for all of this? My father would never risk his beer money to buy me a tuck box. Three of everything, like skirts, shirts, all with my name tag sewn inside the collar; shoes outdoor and indoor, gym shoes, a trunk to take it all, sports equipment, pants to vests, socks to handkerchiefs, it would all have a place in my life.

In those days, many women and girls as well, made their

own clothes because we were taught to do so. Another problem arose as we realised we could only buy the uniform from one shop, Mattias Robinsons of Leeds. They were the sole school stockist and could thus charge what they wanted. With careful planning, my mother found the money and time to travel into the city by bus, and work out a budget with the shop before she could even think of raising the money. With good preparation, Mam and I designed my blouses for when I needed to change out of my school uniform, so they could be let out at the seams easily, as we did similarly for that all-important cloak which brought identity to the school. We turned up the hems three times to give me plenty of room for the future, if I ever grew. Because I became very active on the sports fields I did not put on weight; it all helped keep the clothing budget secure. The knowledge that everything I wore at the moment was to be replaced down to nightwear, slippers for the first time and the idea I would push my feet down into a clean bed with sheets and a pillow smelling of soap and lavender, kept me awake at night; just my eyes peeked over the blanket wide and sleepless staring at the ceiling as I attempted to conjure up images of that dormitory I had seen, filled with girls who might become my friends.

I had prayed long and hard and over many years that a school, any school, would accept me on the basis it would be away from home. Now it was to become a reality. Attending a real school where I had only read one book before, which was not a school text book, was going to be an eye-opener. I wasn't in to reading for I needed my sleep before getting up early to go to help in the house.

My whole life had been one of hiding; soon I wouldn't have to hide anymore. School friends at Doncaster Road who learned of the news, first disbelieved me, then they gazed almost in awe as if I had won the Football Pools or a rich uncle had died leaving me his entire fortune. They did not connect my success with the long evenings of study and learning my Times-tables by heart. The assumption was my place at

Ackworth had been secured with money, not talent. It could not have been further from the truth.

There came a flurry of buying, so many things neither Mam nor I had ever experienced such a shopping spree before. It was as if we were suddenly rich and could go out and buy whatever we wanted. I had to assume the scholarship paid for some of it, for there was no way my family could have afforded, or wished to provide for all my clothes and equipment.

Before I had time to blink at my diary, came the day when I was to travel to Ackworth to start school. By some means, my trunk had been packed, paid for I suspect also in part by my grandmother in Carlton, for I had to go over one day dressed in my new uniform to show her. There was no-one with a camera to take a photograph of me, so proud, so happy and even today I implore parents sending their child off to their first school, to record the event which impacts small lives to such an extent. There was no photograph, but smiles all round as I climbed into my brother-in-law, Fred's shooting brake with my trunk and tuck box looking very new in the boot but it wasn't even Fred who drove me. It was one of his lorry drivers detailed to get me to the school. I suppose I had to think I was lucky that I had not been delivered to the school in one of Fred's fruit lorries.

I closed my eyes, batting the image of our poor house out of my mind and out of sight as we set off, saying goodbye to the family and the pale wisp of my mother waving a scarf. I watched the countryside until we reached the, quite magnificent gates, where I was dropped off early with my belongings stacked together. This was so I would not be embarrassed I presume? Mam was not there to see me at the proudest moment of my life, and she was never to see the school again. It was my mother alone who had given me the chance to snatch a life away from the bleakness of a future in Barnsley, without a moment's hesitation for herself.

It was curious, to say the least, that at the time I started at the school, Fred described it as a 'bloody waste of money' yet, years later he sent all of his four grandchildren to private schools which he paid for out of his own pocket.

The tailgate of the car disappeared on its way back home, leaving me standing in my new uniform among other arriving boys and girls scattered around the forecourt. Smart cars, trunks and tearful mothers cluttered the access. At least my new uniform would not show up my poor background from where I had come. We were all the same.

But, of course, we weren't all the same. It soon dawned on me that my position in this world was a long way down the pecking order, in fact there were few girls or boys if any with such obvious working-class backgrounds as the Bird Family. The very steep learning curve on which I now entered showed me up as 'one of the roughest,' at the school. I had little experience in using a knife and a fork. I had no idea what *etiquette* meant though, to give me one saving grace, my manners, beaten into me at home, were as good as anyone in my year. On that first, glorious day, as children cried with home sickness and hugged their loving fathers, I glowed with a supreme happiness.

Rough I might be but I knew I could hone and polish those edges, speak politely if not posh, and show my family that there was at least one member who was going to go places in the world. I was going to be alright, okay, and…. fear-free.

Upstairs, through a bewildering set of corridors and rooms, I was shown my dormitory which held twenty-two girls, eleven beds either side facing in to a central corridor. Each of us had a bedside cupboard in which we kept our pyjamas and slippers, both new for me. Clothes were stored in a near-by locker room. The others had all brought teddy bears and hot water bottles, neither of which had been on the official list for me. I had no photos of my parents to put up beside me whereas some of the new arrivals had a framed photo of their pet dog as well as their parents, taken in a sunny garden, but it didn't seem to matter. What did matter was, I was here and I was going to have the time of my life.

That night, my first night away, my first time with a bed to myself, a first for sheets and a pillow, warmed by hope, my pillow as my Teddy. I said goodnight.to the teacher who was close-by in case of emergencies such as a fire. I almost reached up my arms to kiss her.

I slept.

*

A bell went off in my head causing me to ascend rapidly through multi-layers of sleep.

I stared at the strange patterns on the ceiling before recognition returned.

Muffled grunts crept over me from either side. Sniffs and tears told their own story. We were told to wash in a communal washroom (which is still there) before going down to breakfast where, unbelievably, I had cereal and scrambled egg on toast. My stomach was full for the first time I could remember. I was told the school had its own orchard from which we would be getting apple pie for lunch…. with custard!

While scraping my plate for the last remaining morsel of egg I saw another girl smile at me. It was a sort of a sign saying: 'I think I like you.' I smiled back determined to say something to her at lunch as we could speak during mealtimes. Her name, I learned that day was Sue and our friendship remains cemented together for life.

There has never been a time in my life when food could have been a subject for discussion with friends, just as we did for timetables and choosing team leaders. Food was now exciting; I would plan for the next meal, savouring the simple but delicious dishes in my mind.

It was extraordinary to my way of thinking. We could fantasize on what we might be having for the meal and my mouth learned to salivate as we talked. Lunch, for example, always included a pudding, following a different choice each day of a main course. There was always a change of menu to liven up the day. I would raise my nose like a mole to the air as I reached the corridor leading to the dining room, making me out to be a lioness downwind of a gazelle, already drooling as I recognised that today was going to be Lancashire hotpot followed, with a bit of luck, by sultana sponge pudding…and custard. Nothing was ever left on my plate, not by school edict but by sheer enjoyment the meals brought to me.

At tea-time, I learnt something else which would have been quite incomprehensible at home. Tea might consist of a banana, jam and cheese with fresh bread. What was astonishing was that some pupils would place their cheese and jam on the same piece of bread as if it was quite natural to mix the two together. The banana would then be eaten at the same time, some shortbread perhaps to complete the day, allowing me to go to bed every night with a full stomach.

With a bewildering array of rules, instructions, procedures and guidelines to pick up on – we were expected to know them all in a very short while – there was one area where I was not such a dummy. Ackworth was a Quaker school founded in 1779 on behalf of the Religious Society of Friends. Because of my weekly visits to St. Peter's back in Barnsley I was more than familiar with church services. This allowed me to come to terms quicker than many with the tenets of Quakerism, accepting the *Silences* and the *Expectant Waiting* which were a part of all Quaker Meetings.

On Sundays, after the Meeting, we had about an hour and a half to ourselves before lunch. Then there came another silence imposed on us known as the *Siesta* for the afternoon. The stark contrast with my previous life, now a million miles away, made me realise how lucky I had been. I could have failed, only to find myself crossing the road, avoiding traffic as I set out for church evensong.

There were three exeats, when parents could take their children out for the week-end in each year, leaving the rest of us, as we ate our own tea, wondering what they might be doing. I knew neither of my parents would come and collect me and to be truthful, I had no desire to go home. I could hear the joyful shouts of 'Hullo, Mummy!' and 'Hullo, Daddy!' across the car-park. That was not going to happen, so, to counter any mood of pessimism, I began to fill my Saturdays with sport. I had known for some time I could run, I had an eye for the game in hand and I wasn't afraid of going into a scrum to extract the ball. It brought noise and action to what otherwise might have been neap tides which formed the week-ends. There was no sport I did not try and no sport I did not excel. (Sorry to be so full of myself on this but I needed to achieve, to shine). I simply revelled in the competitive spirit of the games, where I was not only equal with my fellow team mates but often above them. I led in Hockey, Netball, Tennis and Rounders. With our own swimming pool, I found new freedoms, a new independence. There was to be no copy of the repeated home-sickness of my friends. Homesickness implies there is a desire to re-engage with the comforts and love of home. Of course, it would have been nice if one member of my family had come to cheer me on, especially when I scored the winning goal in netball just as the whistle blew – a Johnny Wilkinson moment – to find a very pleased sports teacher demanding to know '…. how on earth did you manage that?' I could have burst with joy.

Flashes of long-term memory include a vision of games stopping, annoyingly, when the River Went broke its banks and flooded the fields much to my exasperation. A fire at the school managed to slip into the local newspaper with the expected parental alarms, but no-one was hurt and work went on as normal. Those days were when there were many fewer helicopter parents to vent their spleen on a school when their children might have got their feet wet for half an hour. These, and many others were the colours in my rainbow and I wanted it to go on forever.

The tuck shop, a mecca in our world, was located on the opposite side of the road to the school entrance; in bounds if we just went to the shop, out of bounds if we departed from the line which connected the two. There, for a few pennies you could buy iced buns and home-made cakes and I would imagine the tiny shop lived off the school. Today, it is gone, just a house now, and no doubt there is a sophisticated shop inside the school, catering to the needs of its diverse population.

Real freedom was found in another form. I would often play in Away matches at other schools which were not always with boarding pupils. Having this urge, perhaps necessity is a better word, to win every time, it became interred within my bones to the extent it has remained with me all my working life.

Like exeats, we had annual events such as an Open Day which was combined with Sports Day. Parents were as competitive as their children, propelling them on as they craned their necks over the white-washed touchlines, their voices hoarse with excitement, yet wondering why such a diminutive girl was so capable of passing their own blonde-haired daughters. It had only been a year earlier, that dark day, when I had wanted to forget, when I did not have a pair of shoes to run in, and stayed at home while my friends ran ahead unchallenged by me, to pass the finishing line. That day I had screamed in my head, '…it isn't fair.' And of course, it wasn't fair, but it *was* life, and I was fast learning. If you wanted to get on you had to grab it by the scruff of the neck and hold on to it.

I wanted to prove that despite my accent, which was already beginning to soften, as words were becoming more rounded, and my etiquette somewhat improving, I could be as good as anyone else. The school had an annual 'posture badge', quite literally an award for being able to sit upright at mealtimes, better than all others. Such an ability, or otherwise, as a slacker, was monitored by the mealtime teachers who sat up on their dais enabling them to look down on the chattering masses, most of whom were attempting to stuff their mouths as full as it was possible, while discussing the latest events in *Girl's Own* paper at the same time. The teachers, meanwhile, would take note of those girls whose back was the least round-shouldered.

The badge for some reason was only awarded to girls (we were split 220 boys and 220 girls) and that year I won, to my absolute delight. It may seem ridiculous that such a small event gave me so much pleasure but it was an accolade awarded to someone who had never received a hint of praise before in her life.

Friends were beginning to look up to me and show me respect, despite my reputation for coming from an area of Barnsley as rough as ferrets bedding. I wanted to write to my mother to tell her, but knew she would be embarrassed to ask a friend to read the letter out, so I left it, filing it away to tell her at the end of the term. There was a determination always to do better, so much so that Spanish became a top subject. At the same time, lessons like dress-making proved to be very useful later on in life when on a very tight budget in the police force.

Sports meant 'colours.' A *colour* was awarded to those who excelled in a particularly sport. The *colour* was added to your tunic so in the end, along with my posture badge I looked like a Girl Scout. A friend lent me her tennis racket and clothes as she hated the sport. I took them gratefully and achieved another *colour* that summer.

In amongst all this whirlwind of sport and leisure we had, of course, lessons. These were concentrated in the morning and afternoon as usual but homework was a monitored affair each evening, with a teacher supervising our efforts. Work also went on into Saturday morning before the welcome release onto the sports field. With Spanish came Biology, Domestic Science as it was then though Maths did not fare as well with me possibly due to the teacher. I had to work harder than most, for I wasn't as bright as many in my year. My reports often…. well usually, spoke of 'Veronica has difficulty in grasping the facts,' truisms which have remained with me all my working life. Veronica's own belief was to have to work ten times harder than others just to keep alongside her friends.

There were disciplines I had never heard of let alone grasp and digest. I found myself interested and devoted to learning, so much so I must have appeared as a trifle sanctimonious, even a bit holier-than-thou to many in the class. I don't recall any exacting disciplines being applied while being taught at Ackworth although they must have been there.

You may have kept in mind my first friend, Sue whom I mentioned earlier? Sue had become a good buddy and told me, a lot later in life, she had got up to stunts at Ackworth. She had given no indication of the shenanigans she was involved with which were going on under my nose and I found it difficult to believe even when I was told years later. It was not being a 'goody-goody', it was the dormant fear of being disciplined at home, a root stock buried very deep. It was so ingrained I steadfastly refused to involve myself in 'japes'. She told me, when she was in the Sixth form, which meant her dormitory block was the furthest away from the main school, she would regularly walk around the village at night in her slippers and go to Wakefield at the weekend. Janet, a girl who won a scholarship at the same time as me, was so naughty her parents were summoned to the Head Mistress and told she would be expelled if there was another transgression. She knew she was in a strong position for she was a very bright A-stream girl. I remained in the C-stream.

With my head down, working hard, winning at sports, I was promoted to Form Captain at the end of my first year. Despite my background, the Head Mistress saw fit to appoint me, possibly, or more likely probably, to boost my self-esteem. Whatever the reason, she selected me. Miss Sadler was one of those enlightened teachers who could see further than an academic mind in a pupil. Not that she was not God. Do you remember those school days when you knew there was a red line, as clear as if it had been drawn on the floor in red chalk which you never crossed? Sure, you pressed up against it from time to time as attempts were made to explore the boundaries of your world which held you in. It all boiled down to respect. She, and the overall Headmaster, Mr Lindley, were respected at every minute of every day for they were always judged to be fair in their edicts. If we transgressed it was because of our own stupid fault. Thus, they were the major deities in my daily world; with glimmerings of my past home-life still sitting like an incubus on my shoulders, it was not difficult to do as I was told.

*

It came as a shock, or perhaps surprise is a better word, when I returned home at the end of the first term for the Christmas holiday to be told by my sisters and brothers I was too posh to be talking to them anymore. Perhaps they were saying it in fun as they made frequent jokes about my burgeoning new accent. Maybe they too would like to have won a scholarship to a nice school, but there was, undoubtedly, a widening channel of water between us which I had to recognise even as we sailed into Boxing Day. I had been a loner before I left home and I remained alone for the rest of the holiday.

Christmas in our family was not a time of exchanging presents. There was no more money in the house than in the summer. The only present I can remember receiving from my father was a chocolate wafer bar he held out in exchange for the bottle of whisky I gave to him, and that was fifty years into the future and nothing in between. What little money there was went into the Dove Inn's takings as likely as not, so I ached for my return to the freedoms of the school. When I did, it was as if Christmas had never ended, for Sue talked incessantly about the number of presents she had received. She was not attempting to impress me, to show how well she had done, for in her world she assumed all the girls in her class received as many gifts. Elizabeth, another friend received letters and parcels daily, for her father who had been an Architect, had died very young. Her mother lived in the south and was unable to get up to see her. I expect the mother/daughter bond had been made the stronger and I could understand why she always had something in the post tray for her to read. Nothing is retained in my mind of anything being sent to me at school. There could not have been a wider gulf between us, but we remained good friends.

But, I lie. I had quite forgotten I did receive one present each Christmas. It naturally, was very special to me. It reminded me there were good people out there to counter my father's meanness. It was not just the present from my brother-in-law's parents, it was the act of giving I treasured. They never forgot to include me, knowing, otherwise, I would receive nothing at all.

To cover my essential costs, I was given a pound note at the beginning of the term to last thirteen weeks. This was for tuck and new shoelaces and ink. It was a reasonable amount for those days (about £24 in today's money) but I had no experience of spending money and I would end up at the end of term with ten shillings and sixpence or thereabouts. A Kit-Kat then was about 5d (2 ½p) that's the large four-bar, the smaller two-bar was half of that, what we called tuppence ha'penny. You could eat quite a lot of them if you so wanted but I have always hated going into debt and I never have. I remember I was also given a ten-shilling note from Fred's parents, a further kind act, knowing how their son would have reacted if he had known. But, I was told to keep quiet about it, which I did and converted the note into four half crowns. One day Joan saw the money and, having messed up with the Sunday banking, had lost some money and accused me of stealing. I had to be very firm and insist she was wrong which, eventually she accepted, but the taste of the accusation remained in my mouth for a long time.

*

By the time the Third year had slid past in a welter of hockey sticks and swimming matches I had collected the title of Bedroom Captain, another strange term, like a youthful Privy Councillor or Master of the Rolls, maybe but considerable responsibility came with the handle and it was my job to ensure the dormitory was kept immaculate right down to the hospital tucks to the beds. (A long way from the duvets of today's bedrooms, which hold just two girls). Again, you may think this a trifle, something we all did. So what? But, it was the second time in my life someone up the ladder had seen fit to make me in charge and I found I liked it. Responsibility is an amazing compliment to be given. How many times have dissolute, drifting teenagers lifted themselves out of the mire when given a responsibility over others? The Armed Forces have always recognised the success of promotion, and such an idea filtered down the ranks until it reached into my dorm.

My new accountability rested surprisingly lightly on my shoulders; it permitted me to see the future. It was important for I only had one more year in the main school dormitory before, as all fifth-year pupils (the term 'students' had not yet arrived on the scene), I would move out to accommodation further from the main buildings. It was a case of, the older you became, the more responsibility you were given, or perhaps trust would be a better word. And I wanted to be trusted.

As the year ended, we clubbed together, amassing an enormous sum based on sixpence each, so we could hold our annual Midnight Feast which we all assumed, in our cabal, to be a deadly secret – cross your heart and hope to die – stuff. But, everyone, including the school cat were fully in the picture and knew when we were meeting, being no other than the bewitching hour, well, twelve that is. Then as the chimes subsided into the blackness of the school grounds we shook and shivered with excitement. We would cosy up to each other, munching biscuits and eating cold baked beans, while whispering, rather too loudly about what we had planned for when we eventually left school. For me, as the clock struck the hour I gazed closely at my knees, tucked up to my chin as I tried to fathom out what I could do to break the bonds of family when I finally left the sixth form. But, at the time, I was very happy with life.

The end of year dance was the same. I had learned to dance

with the boys in the school which meant looking your best and trying not to stand on their shoes which had been polished like a guardsman's boots. Do you remember patent leather dance shoes?

It was school which brought me the first happiness in my life. It tended to obscure other thoughts, so, like an ostrich in a sand pit I never saw the gathering storm.

CHAPTER THREE
THE CHEAP OPTION

Cheap option – synonyms
Got it for a bargain; bought for a song; dime a dozen; marked down; bargain basement; cheapo.

During the holidays, I had gone to live with my sister Joan and her husband Fred Ward. My mother was constantly ill, tired out and unable to cope the demands of my father and the family. Joan had taken charge and brought me and my youngest sister Susan to their house in Doncaster Road, No.85. Leaving my mother sick and stressed, was a wrench, but holidays were only short periods which meant I was soon back in school. It was in nineteen fifty-four I began to feel a nagging prickle in my neck, something I could not, at first, put my finger on. Life, surely, had to be better, separated from my father. I was in a nice house, with my youngest sister and nieces to share my bedroom in the attic.

Joan was often tense but I put that down to work pressures for their fruit and veg business had taken off and was thriving in fifties Britain. Her input was needed, or more accurately, demanded by her husband.

I began to be aware of a sense of being watched. This was not the same as being studied to see if your clothes were clean or your school books were ready to go. Instead, there was a vagueness in the feeling, certainly a foreboding as if there might be a return to the explosions of rage engulfing me and

I would be back in my father's world where he could be found over-turning a table as he detonated himself with fury.

This vagueness began to materialise. I would see Fred staring at me over the kitchen table. His questions became endless, inquisitive ones, prying into my private life at Ackworth. Why did he want to know what I wore? Why did he query who I mixed with? What boyfriends did I have? What were their names? And always ended with, '...did they have a lot of money?' Much of what he said had a sexual connotation with the classic idiotic phrase: 'he fancies you,' spoken with a leer, which Joan attempted to push aside with a wave of her hand as if it had never been said.

Any feeling of unease is hard to describe with certainty. I could not define it, let alone interpret what was behind his words. To try to explain how Fred felt about life in general, it might be an idea, to give you one example.

Fred had learned he had a wealthy married cousin who lived in Maidenhead, a long way from Barnsley, one hundred and eighty-two miles in fact. He took it upon himself one day to take the family and me to visit his relation, no doubt to see if anything might rub off on him. We piled into his shooting brake, I think today we would call it an estate car, and began the long drive from Barnsley to Berkshire on the Thames, eventually stopping off for lunch.

'What's the address? Queried Joan while we ate.

'Not sure. It's down by the river. The Thames. Big house, I expect.'

'Do you mean to say we have come all this way, driven almost two hundred miles with no idea where we are ending up?'

Fred looked dangerous. He knew he had made a mistake in not finding out the address before we left. 'We'll find it,' he replied through gritted teeth. 'It's a very big house. Can't be too many of those.'

Joan shook her head in despair at his ignorance. Maidenhead was not Barnsley, not by a long chalk. I stared out of the window at the lush Berkshire countryside with its neat houses and clean streets. It was a world away from Doncaster Road with its sooty slate.

I had no idea why we were there nor what Fred intended to do if we ever found his cousin's house. He had been unable to tell them he was coming as he had no address to write to them, nor a telephone number for the same reason. It seemed daft to me and a total waste of time, and petrol.

We drove through the streets of Maidenhead looking for large houses of which there were many until we came to a very nice area overlooking the Thames. I could imagine parents of some of my friends at school living here.

'There! There it is! It must be,' hooted Fred swerving dangerously in his excitement. There was indeed, a very large house in a leafy glade. It looked right if nothing else.

'How do you know? You can't be sure. There are dozens of big houses here.'

'Not as big as this one though,' he retorted, 'and it is right by the river.' He was now convinced he had made the right decision. 'Come on, all out.'

Fred marched confidently to the front door, manicured lawns lapping the drive as if it was a calm green sea, and rang the bell. He turned around and smiled at us as if to acknowledge how clever he was. And, with such a big house, surely something good would rub off. 'I can just smell the money.'

The door opened by a woman who was clearly a housekeeper for she wore a spotlessly white apron.

'Ah, good afternoon. My name is Fred er, Frederick Ward.' He began to explain who he was and the connection with his cousin. He was just passing (from Barnsley!) and felt it was right to pop in and say hullo.

'I'm so sorry Mr. Ward but your cousin is away with her husband at present in France.'

Faces fell, for differing reasons. 'But,' the woman continued, 'I am sure they would want me to invite you in. At least I can get you a cup of tea and I have been baking this afternoon so I have a home-made cake. Perhaps a slice of lemon and walnut?'

We needed no bidding, now we knew Fred had been right all along in finding the house.

Inside, the rooms were quite beautiful. It quietened Fred and Joan as we walked through the hall on Indian rugs. Fred winked crudely at us. We were led into a withdrawing room. You could not describe it as a lounge.

'I won't be a moment. I have the kettle on anyway.' Our unnamed house-keeper disappeared towards, I assumed, a kitchen bigger than our house, as we sat in whispered conversation, matins in church before the vicar arrives, studying pictures and a grandfather clock. The room smelled of leather and oiled oak and the clock tocked with accustomed and metronomic regularity. Alongside the garages was a boat cradle but no boat.

The tea arrived in a silver tea-pot and matching hot water jug, as one might well expect in such a well-heeled mansion. The smell of the newly baked cake tickled anxious noses after our bowl of chips in the town. The slices looked large enough even for Joan.

It was during this delicious tea I saw Fred's eyebrows go up in his face settling into a grimace. He was quite clearly stressed. Eventually, he gesticulated to Joan, then back to some silver framed photographs on a side table. The house-keeper had just pointed out a recent photo taken of his cousin at some resort or other.

Fred rose. 'We mustn't keep you any longer. You must be a very busy person,' he said, surprising us all. He had a dozen questions yet to ask so it was most unlike him to leave before he had started. He signalled with his hand for us to get up, his fingers flapping up and down in his palm with some urgency. We all said goodbye and walked swiftly down the drive to our car. Meanwhile, a mystified house-keeper waved us off wishing us a safe journey northward.

'What was that all about? I wanted another piece of that cake?' demanded an equally mystified Joan.

'Jesus. That was the wrong house. That was not my cousin

by any stretch of the imagination.' Fred chuckled, away his embarrassment. 'They can't help us.' We drove on wondering what the owners of the house would say when given the news their cousin had turned up with his family for tea.

It was this need to pry and Fred's complete disregard for the niceties of life which began to breed in my mind. I began to see a very different side to my brother-in-law. There was a creepiness about him as if he had to know everything about a person, what his or her weaknesses were and how he could exploit them. He stuck his nose in everywhere he went, even turning up at their doors only to find no-one in. He would then walk round to the back of the house and peer in through the windows pressing his nose against a pane of glass the better to see if anyone was still there, or hiding. Sometimes they were, bending down below the windows so they could not be seen, for it meant inviting him in for a drink and a long tirade on life if they did.

The weirdness of his actions continued. His cellar at his house was always filled with whole stalks of bananas ripening, ready for the market. He would come down the steps leering at me to see what I had achieved, for it was my job to cut the hands out forming the familiar bunches. Then I had to pack them into twenty-eight-pound cases and lug them up the stairs. His eyes would follow me all the way.

To get away from the deprivation of our own house, was, you would think, a blessing, but it was very soon to turn into a nightmare. It became difficult to separate the cruelty of my father from the eeriness of Fred's ways. Both were horrid, though many people simply did not understand why I was so diffident when asked, 'Aren't you lucky.'

For starters, there were the three holidays we had in Blackpool. Fantastic you might think to yourself. Isn't she lucky (again). Three times I went to Blackpool, each time staying in a seedy hotel currently ranked eight hundred and seventy-seventh out of nine hundred and fourteen hotels in the town. Before this, Fred and Joan had stayed at the Redman's

Park House which has certainly improved since those two-star days, but, after the first few years of their marriage Joan left Fred behind and took a woman friend instead. It became apparent as to why I was brought along for it was here I became useful. Joan could go on holiday with a friend provided always she took her three daughters with her, and this conflicted with her desire to dance. She would dance every night until the dance floor closed at eleven. I was a most useful baby-sitter. Joan's obsession with dancing meant that the day Jack, my epileptic brother died, I had to remain alone with the girls in the hotel while she returned to Barnsley to attend the funeral of her eldest brother who was only twenty-three years old. It meant I could not go to see my brother off. I wasn't even asked if I wanted to go and have no clear picture of the service and how the family reacted to his death. Joan returned that night and off she went again as the waters closed over the sad affair and life returned to normal.

She would always choose the first or second week in September, before Ackworth went back for the winter term. Her friend Betty would always accompany her and the two of them would dance the evening away. Because I was left alone so often in the hotel, the owners, along with some parents who were attending their children's National Swimming Championships clubbed together for my last night and took me to the Pleasure Beach. To my tearful thanks, they also gave me some money to take home.

Fred's prying nature led him to drive over one year to call unannounced at the hotel. I do not believe it was because he was suspicious of his wife, he just needed to know everything which went on in his tiny world. Finding his wife not at the hotel, he went on to the dance. It was a wasted journey. Joan was a faithful wife needing only to get away from the stifling atmosphere created in the home. I was not party to the conversation when they met at the Tower Ballroom but it was probably phrased in words of one syllable. This obsession extended itself. It was as if he needed to know the exact whereabouts and the precise words spoken by his entire family whatever the time of day. It was his paranoia which led him to suspend a microphone over the house telephone so he could listen in to conversations made by whoever answered the call.

So, the end of school term saw me travel back to Joan's house, fuller in face, very fit and dressed in clean clothes. When I went to school I weighed 4stone 4pounds when the average girl at the time was 7 stone 4 pounds. My accent, also, had removed itself to the far corner of the room, replaced, not with posh, but with smoother vowels and less accented phrases. Nonetheless, the original could be resurrected at will if I wanted to tell a funny story in fluent Barnsley.

Being away from Mam so much, I realised she would also have liked to listen to my funny stories and explain to her what I was doing at school. She would have wanted to have listened for it would have driven away the demons in her life for a few minutes and made her understand that her daughter was going to make it in life. It would have brought a smile to her face. The hardest part of this small story is that she never had the opportunity.

I had been lucky that Christmas holiday. Against their better judgement, Fred and Joan, maybe through embarrassment if they had refused, had agreed for me to spend three days with a good school friend at their house in Harrogate to see in the New Year. I took a bus from Barnsley, excited at the idea of being away from the town, with a good friend to chat to about things we wanted to discuss, without Joan or Fred chipping in.

I was picked up in Leeds by the Broomheads, my friend's parents, and we drove back to Harrogate to what I was told were fifty-three rooms in their house. On arrival came my first embarrassment; it showed up the huge gulf between our two families. I did not have the clothes with me to enable me to dress for dinner, and by that, I mean dress. It was New Year's Eve and everyone dressed for dinner. Tactfully, carefully, Prudence, my school mate, suggested I wear something of hers and I came down to dinner in a dress I could only dream about. Her father was a successful surgeon and owned three cars including a Daimler which was positioned on the forecourt declaiming to the world that right here, was a success story. 'I've done well.' The beautiful house included a library of books: in Doncaster Road, we had never had a book in the house. The point did not go unmissed by me. For the girl who had never owned a book in her life came a clear message: 'you could do better.'

We had a marvellous time, with the whole family being so kind I could have wept, that others could be so caring. Prudence was removed from Ackworth a little while later and sent to Cheltenham Ladies College. I often wonder if it was because I, a coal miner's daughter, was forming too strong a friendship. Perhaps that is totally unfair but whatever the reason I have been trying to contact her ever since to thank her. I haven't found her yet but I am still trying. And maybe, there had always been a plan to send her to Cheltenham. I do not want her parents to think I was ungrateful for that wonderful weekend.

It was the day after New Year's Day when I left. I was collected by Fred in a grim mood who said: 'There's been trouble at your Dad's house. It caught fire over the holiday. There's a terrible mess.'

I sat, unsure how to reply. I was no longer living with my Mam and Dad but how was my mother? Was she alright? When I saw the house, it was ruined with smoke and water. It stank of charred timber. The floor was covered in broken glass and filth; water was everywhere. Mam merely stared into the distance, all hope gone.

'Cigarette,' she said. 'A cigarette down the side of a chair.' Her ravaged face told its own story of a party gone wrong, beer having got in the way of sense. The dog, a Peke had been killed by the smoke.

I was driven off by Fred back to their house and the next day thrown into non-stop chores, rising in the middle of the night to climb onto Fred's lorry to drive to the market where he had an open veg. stall in Barnsley. Sacks of any vegetables are heavy, let alone potatoes, which all had to be carried to the stall by hand before being manhandled up into place. There were no fork lift trucks in those days. This would be followed with the need to tackle the washing of the three children's clothes, the ironing and the cleaning; sort of Cinderella syndrome without the glass slipper, the ball, the coach or the waiting Prince. At the end of the day I had to stay in, baby-sitting, to allow Joan and Fred out on the town. It was lucky that I only had another week before I went back to school. Dad's house was repaired eventually but whether there was any insurance to pay for it all I have no idea. I don't think house insurance would be too high up Dad's budget.

*

One week back at Ackworth, settling in again to the tranquil routine of the school I was called to the Headmistress's study, an occasion which always drummed up nerves, never quite knowing the reason for the summons. The door closed quietly behind me and I was told to sit down, again in a quiet voice.

'I'm so sorry to tell you Veronica, that your mother has had a stroke-'

'Is she-?'

'Yes, she is still alive but she is very ill. She's…. paralysed.'

'Can I go and see her?'

The Headmistress paused. Her conscience seemed to be troubling her. 'Your father says, at the moment, there is no point in visiting.' She placed a hand on my shoulder for she had not sat down with me. It was a strangely comforting action, not one she was used to applying to her pupils. 'I will keep you up-to-date with any news I get.' She looked up and returned to the business on her desk. I went back to my class.

It had to be the fire, the loss of the few, yet precious possessions she owned, the continuing break-up of the family. There was not a single light at the end of the tunnel for her. Poor Mam. And now, paralysed? What did that mean?

It was February. The days were becoming a bit lighter when I was told to be down in the Hall in half an hour. Fred arrived to take me to see my Mother. At the time, I did not understand she was slipping quietly away from us and this would be my last chance to see her. I had been told, and had believed, that for the want of an ashtray this might never have happened. Years later, I found out the real reason behind the fire. It was nothing like the story I had been given.

The fire had started at three thirty in the morning well after the revellers had gone to bed. Mam had nudged Gordon at half past three in the morning, waking him as usual to go to the early shift. As she did, she said, 'I smell smoke.' Gordon could not smell anything but had to get up anyway, so he went downstairs in his string vest for none of us had any money for pyjamas. As he arrived at the bottom of the stairs he could see a chair on fire which was spreading up to a wooden cupboard over the kitchen sink. The room was full of choking smoke and the dog, a Peke and the budgerigar were already dead.

Gordon smashed the kitchen window and shouted upstairs for the boys to pour water on their floorboards for the fire was immediately below their bed. Meanwhile he threw water on the chair. There was no point in ringing for the fire brigade. We had no telephone ourselves and the nearest telephone box was several hundred yards up the road. Gordon would have had to get dressed first and as he ran up the street the house would have collapsed into a pile of ashes before the arrival of the fire tender.

Mother had been awake beforehand. It had been easy for her to creep out of bed before going downstairs, and in some desperate *cri de coeur* had lit the fire herself. A bit of paper on the chair and a match was all that was needed, nothing too big so it could not be put out. She must have known that her son would have rushed downstairs as soon as he smelled smoke and he could put the fire out. Maybe it was post-natal depression that had led her to such desperate action, who knows, but the cigarette was invented as a cover. Whatever the real truth was, Dad could not be blamed this time. He was at the mine on a shift so he could not have dropped the cigarette. Working in the mines where he had to be so careful of naked flames, Dad would chew tobacco. I had wrongly assumed he or one of the members of the party must have been the real reason. But, it was a close-run thing. Five more minutes and they might not have been able to get out at all. It was a terrible thought, for one read of these horrors in the papers, so easily dismissed at the time with a slight frown and a sigh.

When I arrived at the hospital, Mam was lying in a hospital bed, the smell of antiseptic and other chemicals tainting the air. She was being fed by a nurse. She was completely paralysed and could not use her hands or arms. It was a mind-numbing sight, seeing this gentle but frail woman brought to such a low level. She had never had a chance in life: it seemed so unfair. To a twelve-year old, it was a turning point, for my only life-line was contained within the sad shell which had been my mother.

I had to go back to school, but the crisis was far from over. There was a telephone box at the school which we could use and I had telephoned for news. It was a month after my visit and I had heard nothing since from any of the family. It was as if I had ceased to exist to them.

'Don't go out to day Veronica, Mam is not good.' It was Joan who had answered the telephone. Why today, I wondered? Was it just a coincidence, me ringing, and bad news, possibly arising? At two that afternoon, Gordon, my brother, arrived in a car and I was spirited out of class to go back home. As we parked outside my old house, he told me to remain where I was. Strangely he said: 'Stay in the car, I can see the doctor. He's still here.' In fact, he had gone in to warn the whole family who had gathered with my Father, to let them know I was back from school. I had not been told my mother had died that morning at eleven. Maybe Gordon was, in his muddled way, trying to protect me, though it was too late for that. Mam was dead. He could not change the fact she had given up the struggle to live. The pain of the moment, the idea I could have been excluded from my mother's dying moments has stayed with me. I never forgot he had attempted to pull the wool over my eyes. She was my mother also.

I was eventually told, and was taken upstairs to see Mam lying on her bed, the mountain of cares and worries smoothed out of her face. No more would she have to endure her awful life which, no doubt, had started well in nineteen twenty-eight with so many promises and plans. She was just forty-nine years old, no age, not even in nineteen fifty-five, and we had all failed her, every one of us. I drew some comfort from the knowledge that before she died she had retained an abiding image of her daughter, Veronica, who was doing well at school.

I stayed away for a week, ending up with the funeral at Carlton where she was laid to rest alongside her family. On the Sunday, I was driven back to Ackworth. The countryside was sane, the trees still waved at me and my friends welcomed me back. No-one, as far as I could tell knew why I had been away and I didn't enlighten them. The Headmistress kept the knowledge to herself not even telling her staff what had happened to me. Much later in life a teacher saw me on television and took the trouble to ring me up. I invited her to come and see me in the prison (not very well put but you know what I mean). She told me she was never told why I had been away for a week, for the Headmistress never shared this sort of information with any of her staff. Quite a change in today's demanding social media environment.

At least, poor Mam never had to witness the new shock, five months later, as Dad did, coming home from his shift to find Jack dead in his bed. Jack's attacks had often been scary, usually with no warning as the tremors often ended with him on the floor foaming at the mouth. We would have to turn him onto his side so he did not swallow his tongue and he needed watching carefully until the attack subsided. Jack had been lucky to have had a good job in Woods Glass Company, for by this time companies were encouraged to help epileptics. They were taught to apply their first aid training and were aware of the fits and how to treat them. This time, he was alone when the fit came upon him. There was no-one to help free him in his contortions, for his brothers were in the Forces and lived away from home. A blanket had wrapped itself too tightly around Jack's neck into which he had gasped out his life. He too had gone to a happier home. In less than half a year our family had gone from eleven to nine, two nice people, erased from life who had made neither a mark nor even a scratch on the surface of the world. It was as though they never had existed.

I have an image of Gilbert in his National Service uniform who was deeply upset at his mother's death, so much so that after a plea to Roy Mason our M.P. with a strong mining heritage, (ennobled to Lord Mason of Barnsley) a compassionate discharge was arranged for him and he was released to sort out his life at home.

About a year after Mam died I was told Dad took in another woman with her own children, but my brothers and sisters, who remained in the house, refused to come to terms with the new arrivals and it was not a success, so she left to go where, I have no idea, nor do I know her name. It was an incident in Dad's life. Perhaps he was lonely for company even when surrounded by the rest of his family?

*

You did not have to be a sooth-sayer, just clued up to life, to see a pattern emerging. It was just too convenient; I was just too valuable a commodity to be allowed to continue at school. It was annoying, was it not, for me to keep disappearing at the end of the school holidays for another thirteen weeks, when I could be struggling with the next sack of potatoes. Fred was not stupid, he could see he did not have to employ further help, the baby-sitter was free and his wife could be released from the house-hold chores to spend more time on the stall, and all for a pound a week. Besides, his business, which had flourished, was beginning to feel the cold light of reason as the Supermarkets began to bite into his profits. It was just the excuse he needed and the option was a great deal cheaper than Joan having to bring in expensive baby-sitters and staff for the stalls. There I was, in my school uniform and my posh accent, an hour's ride away, frustrating Fred's carefully made plans.

I received the dreadful news the day I returned for the autumn term. I was called in to the Headmistress's study again, not even having had the time to unpack my trunk or gabble with my friends.

'This will be the last term at school Veronica. I'm sorry but I have had notification from the Education Authorities that your *family* is no longer wishing to keep you here.' She used the word family carefully, not sure who it was who was keeping me at Ackworth or who did not want me at Ackworth. 'I'm so sorry.'

She might as well have thrown acid in my face. 'But, I'm taking my GCE 'O' levels in June,' I replied, not understanding, not believing what she had just told me. 'Besides, I have a grant-'

She cut me off. 'It is final Veronica. I'm very sorry but remember, you have done well here.'

I was to lose, not only my beloved school, but would be prevented from taking my crucial exams without which I could get nowhere in life, at best, I could look forward to a factory job or a bus conductor. Having taken my Art 'O' level earlier and passed I knew that I could achieve several more in the summer and I was entered for eight subjects. It was also shaming for neither Fred nor Joan could face telling me directly.

I could not help it. I burst into tears. I thought the unhappy days were far behind me. Sure, I had to work long hours in the holidays but they were soon over and I sped off back to school and my friends with joy in my heart, able to forget the drudgery as I pulled out my hockey stick.

I was stunned. I walked out of her study, my face streaming, other girls and boys wondering what on earth I had done on the first day back to merit such a telling off: and Veronica of all girls.

What had it done to my carefully planned life? I had wanted to be a PE Teacher at a school of my choosing, far away from Barnsley. I knew that as soon as I left Ackworth I would be put to work, employed in the market for a pittance with no hope of ever gaining a better job. Of all the dark days in the past, there was none so black, none so despairing as this complete dismissal of a human being. And I would have given up the pound a term I received. That was not important. What other reason could Fred want than to exploit me for his own ends? The school fees were paid by my scholarship. I could get by with the clothes I owned. There would have been no cost to him.

What I have never told anyone until this book was agreed, is that a few weeks later I returned to Ackworth at the end of January, having left the school at Christmas to meet with a person who had helped me the first time. I was desperately unhappy and lonely and without my beloved sport. We discussed my predicament and, after careful thought she suggested she might be able to gain a bursary for me allowing me to return to the school and take my 'O' levels. She told me to go home and think about it very carefully. I left with my hopes high but then began to understand just what I was doing and what could happen to me. I would be unable to return to Barnsley in the holidays; no-one to return to. I would become homeless; a condition I am sure the school would never accept. No money, no home, what on God's earth could I do? The plans died before they had had time to form. I returned to Barnsley with not a single light in the future.

*

That last term I existed only. I was as low as I could recall. Each day I woke, my pillow was damp, my eyes red, filled with nothing.... nothing at all to look forward to, no future, the *cheap option* to satisfy a greedy man.

I was to be denied a proper education and a chance to make something of my life. If you are able to look back yourself to nineteen fifty-five, think what you were doing in that year? What hopes and aspirations you held, and what successes you eventually achieved? Perhaps I could have matched your achievements, who knows, but we *will* never know because of the incalculable greed by one man. We would have been living in the same country yet as far apart as it was possible to conceive.

I had had my own hopes. Then, and despite my wretched family, I was on the edge of starting off in life myself but I was powerless to stop time or reverse it. Instead, the term went, passed in a flash as if I was sitting in a train gazing out the window, none of which I can recall with any certainty, until the day came when Fred arrived at eleven in the morning, when most of my friends had been picked up at seven, and collected me. During the drive back and when I got home I was told nothing, there was nothing mentioned, no apologies for my lost schooling, my lost life, and the next day I was back on the stalls serving customers and restacking.

Despite the growth of Tesco, Fred's business was huge in those days. He and his brothers did not sell, as you might think, five or six boxes of apples and a similar number of bananas on a Saturday but a hundred boxes in a single day. Eventually, I was detailed to look after Joan's three children on a Saturday to keep them out of the way of the parents. All I did was feed them in front of a television set, lay the table and clean the house ready for their return.

I dropped into a routine. I was not going back to school, so I had to accept the new situation whether I liked it or not. This meant being told to remove the children on a Sunday morning from the house with instructions not to return until one-thirty for lunch. As soon as the meal was finished I was placed in charge of her children and took them to Sunday school to allow Joan to retreat to her bed. This routine would run into the following day when I would often have to be up at three in the morning to climb on a lorry to go and pick up or deliver fruit and veg. to their other stalls. I was expected to pick up the heavy sacks just as much as the men, for which I was still paid one pound a week.

My sister Susan had joined us and was living in the attic with me and the three Ward girls. Even in those early days she was filled with a holiness I could not match, and she could be found anytime armed with a bible. Unkindly, I wondered if it was the only book she had? But, neither of us had an option in life. We were told what to do and when to do it, such that neither of us had any control on our futures.

After both of Fred's parents died, leaving the family their house at Flamborough, we were all sent there for what was termed a 'holiday'. We were to be without an adult, unchaperoned in other words. It was an ideal excuse for Susan and me to be sent with the three girls for three weeks in the summer, giving the parents a break from the hassle of the children at home. I was now seventeen, growing up with responsibilities thrust upon me whether I wanted them or not. One could say I was just another ungrateful awkward teenager, but five of us together in a house with food convoyed in at the weekends by Joan, was not a great holiday despite what you may think. It hurt that Joan would always arrive with beautiful, clean clothes for her children but my clothes had to be washed by me as part of the eternal routine. After the first day together we had run out of ideas so we stayed in most of the time, watching television. Ghislaine, the eldest of Joan's girls was always good and helpful, not reflected in the second sister Isabel, her mother's favourite. When disciplined by me, which I had to do from time to time, she would wait for the weekend and pour out her sorrows to her mother leaving me with much less control during the long week ahead. The third sister, Katie was a beauty with blonde curly hair who was thoroughly spoilt. I, in the meantime had to wash, cook and clean for the four, before turning to and ironing a mountain of girls' clothes. At the end of the 'holiday' we were driven back to Barnsley on the assumption we had had a wonderful time, and weren't we lucky? (again).

But Susan couldn't settle. Although she didn't work in the market as I did, she often had to care for the three girls when I was on the stall, being held responsible for washing and feeding them. So, despite the news she had received, of the continuing drunkenness at home, Susan left and went back to Father. Later on in life she talked a great deal about the drunken rages but, by then I had moved on and my mind had wrapped and packed the nightmares together and stored them away in a dark place.

Chinese restaurants from Taiwan finally came to Barnsley. The Chinese island at the time was then known as Formosa. It had a need to raise money urgently for their beleaguered new state, separated as it was from the mainland, so they built restaurants all over the world, much to the delight of English diners who had never experienced such food. The Taiwanese families running these new style restaurants, received the main elements of the menus from Taiwan sending any profits back home, but needed fresh fruit and vegetables on a daily basis. Fred quickly stepped in and set up agreements to deliver to their back door. It became my job to take trays of mush-rooms over at lunch. I would always find six or seven Chinese sitting on the floor noisily eating away with their chopsticks, surrounded by piles of vegetables, some strange ones I did not recognise. They would be mixed up with raw chicken legs and exotic smelling spices. Sitting on the floor to eat, in Yorkshire, was about as alien as this new food was to us.

Tomatoes were another fruit which were seasonal in the Sixties. They were very expensive especially when the first of the year's crop arrived from Guernsey. If I put just one tomato too much in a bag I was scolded '…. that's a penny wasted' but when you were adding up in your head in pounds, shillings and pence and weighing the next item at the same time, it could be difficult to get it right every time. I would nod my head in understanding, trying to remember I had got to four shillings and fourpence, and smile at the customer. It made me good at mental arithmetic.

Neighbours and family saw I was living, or staying might be a better word, in Fred's vastly superior house. 'Wasn't it nice to be there? Wasn't it so much better than being with Dad?' There was a sitting room which held the much-prized television, a three-piece suite and a carpet (yes, really) and some very nice curtains but, naturally, I was not allowed to enter this room, the Front Room, at any time. Attendance, instead was to Fred's daughters. When he took them swimming he took me also so he would not have to bother about putting them in their costumes. I was there, and I did it well, to remove, from his shoulders, the annoying parts of having children. He simply did not want to have a tearful daughter near him when I could do the job of comforting a half-drowned child. And of the television in that Front Room? I have a memento today, for I bought the cabinet it had sat in for years, from Fred, and I use it today to store my shredder. Quite an apt use.

It was just as well Joan pushed us out to play, for she was always irritable and critical of my work on Sunday mornings. It was hard, knowing I had not made many mistakes – I was always so careful in doing what I was told for fear of stirring someone's wrath – but I stayed away walking alongside the canal path in all weathers while I attempted to keep the three girls in a reasonable mood when it began to rain.

This canal almost proved calamitous one day, which had started off quite normally. I was washing up in the kitchen keeping an eye on Ghislaine, now aged five who was playing in her toy jeep in the field behind us. Distracted by the other girls, I had taken my eye off the window for a while. And, when I looked out again there was no sight of my charge. Panic-stricken I dashed outside but she was nowhere in sight.

I knocked up as many neighbours as I could and their shrill, increasingly alarmed voices began to bounce around the houses. Fred arrived in his lorry some fifteen minutes later. Taking in the high pitch of voices he roared off towards the canal, our greatest worry, where he soon found Ghislaine sitting in her toy car alongside the canal's edge but talking to a stranger. Seeing Fred, the man disappeared and the day ended in firm words all round but no harm done. It can be as quick as the bat of an eye. A sneeze almost, a glance to find the time, a few seconds to open the oven door and then, one falls into a pit of pure terror. But, we cannot keep our children in cotton-wool all their lives for if we do, we take away their natural defence mechanisms such as I had learned at home. There has to be balance.

We ran into Christmas at break-neck speed, our busiest time of the year following which Joan, as every year, almost like clockwork, took to her bed complaining how ill she was. This meant I would be driven to work in the Mexborough shop to help unload the dozens of boxes and sacks of potatoes being brought in from Hull, Covent Garden and from the farmers directly from their muddy fields. There weren't any of those spotless King Edwards in those days.

Back from the market did not mean a rest, for I was now made responsible for the washing and ironing for the entire household. Fred's very large garage held not only a loo but a twin-tub, one of those old top-loader models. To get through this pile of laundry would take most of the morning so if I was lucky and the wind was in a drying mood, I would be able to start the ironing by the evening. Fred's clothes stank in the washing basket from the heavy inhaling of *Players Please* but it was only for him as Joan never smoked. She was a sweets person; sweets replaced the desire to smoke.

While I laboured, Fred would leer and jeer but, when challenged would say he was just being protective. I became fed up with him saying, 'That's all men want.' He managed to reduce everything in life to sex.

My own sex-life though, did not advance, but it did not stop Joan attempting to pass off a young Woolworth's manager who she knew, suggesting to him he might enjoy a date with me. I found her idea unusual but accepted to go out once or twice. A short time later Michael the manager, came around to wish me a Happy New Year. Fred and Joan were preparing to go out for the evening leaving the children with me while I was talking to Michael. Fred left for the dance with a sideway glance at us both. A few minutes later Michael also said goodbye and I returned to entertain the girls. They were well tucked up in bed when at about quarter to midnight I heard someone shuffling about in the outer porch followed by the crash of a flower pot being knocked over. Terrified, I rang 999 and was told to put all the lights on, on the first floor but I was too frightened even to move out of the kitchen. The police arrived; three motorcycle units and a car (nothing changes, does it?) but they were very good and searched all around outside the house. The broken pot was there lying in pieces so they knew I had been telling the truth. After they left, explaining they would be close by on call, I grasped what had happened. Fred, suspicious of leaving Michael with me alone in the house had sneaked back from the dance and, having knocked the pot over and found me alone, I presume, had returned to the dance with Joan. I could quite understand why Michael could see no future in taking me out, and the whole thing fizzled out before it had even started. Damp and squib are two words which framed the affair in those days.

CHAPTER FOUR
SOME LIGHT AHEAD

I simply had to change direction and towards this aim I began to read the advertisements in the local newspaper. One caught my attention. Marks and Spencer was looking for Trainee Managers. I had often been guilty of day-dreaming through their stores, studying the clothes racks for older women as there was little for my age available in those days. There was also the minor point I had no money to buy anything anyway. The idea of becoming a manager in a Marks and Spencer store appealed and I wrote off asking to be considered. After all, I had several years in front of the customer, had a nice speaking voice and I understood retail selling. One has to pack out one's c.v. as much as possible these days, but I believed I had several attributes of value to such a great company though you shouldn't get carried away with the idea I wanted to become some Captain of Industry.

I was told my letter was passed on to Leeds who sent it on again to Baker Street, their Head Office, and I received back a letter asking me to attend an interview in London. I had passed Ackworth; I could do it again.

I must detour for a moment to explain how I got to London for the interview. By this time, I had passed RSA English and Typing at night school which I had had to pay for myself but, with some money left over, and telling no-one at all, I took some driving lessons, together with putting in some hours reading through the Highway Code. Did you know, because

I didn't, the Code was first published in nineteen thirty-one surprisingly? It has grown to contain three hundred and seven rules to learn. On the carefully managed day of the Test, it being a half-day closing for me, my Instructor arrived in his car to take me down to the Test Centre. It coincided exactly with Joan's return.

'What's 'e doing here?' She demanded.

I had to come clean saying I was taking my test in the next half hour. I felt deceitful under her withering stare.

'Well, you won't pass that,' she said as she pushed past me to the front door.

Not a good start when my nerves were already exceeding the limit where I could keep my hands steady and calm.

But I did pass. And, not only passed but was lent Fred's Mini to go to London for the interview. Astonishing turn-around you might well consider. There was, of course, an horrendous quid pro quo and one I had to accept. I was to take the girls with me. There was to be no option for I had to continue with my home jobs whether I had wanted to or not. My interview was quite secondary to Fred.

'But, I'm going for an interview in the Head Office of Marks and Spencer,' I wailed. 'Baker Street.' What else could I say?

'That's alright. They can stay in the waiting room. They must have one of those.'

I could have tried to go by train as my expenses were going to be reimbursed, but the point was, and it was made very clear, Joan could not look after all the children all day.

Fast forward to the day of the interview. I drove the girls down the Great North Road to stay with a friend overnight. My first impression was of the smell of polish and the shine on the furniture but I don't think she was expecting three small girls to be put up as well. I had to share the bedroom with not only my friend but my nieces as well, but it was a free bed and I could not argue. In the morning, we went in by tube and found the Head Office in Baker Street where I spoke to the girls very carefully, keeping my voice low-key but deadly serious. I was going to have to leave three young girls on a busy road while I attended the interview. I simply did not have the nerve to take them inside the lush offices. When I came out of the office having stumbled through the interview I learned that the children had been taken into a furniture store after they had been seen by the staff leaning on the wall. They made them sit down by a window so they could see when I was coming out. To leave them like that today would be an offence and probably then too. Needless to say, stressed beyond words, waiting for a scream or a crash of a car against a soft body, I failed to impress and my life was not to end up as an executive manager with a smart brief case, climbing up the ladder towards the Marks and Spencer Board. Raging against the unfairness of life, I took the tube north to where we had left the car, and drove back but, so exhausted by the whole event, I had to stop in a motorway station to rest up, getting back eventually at eleven in the evening. What a waste of time, what a waste of effort and, for nothing. I was still in the tunnel with not even a gleam of light at its end. I had no idea of its length or whether I would be able to recognise the end if I saw it coming.

*

I had to leave. Having planned before and failed, I knew it was the only hope for my sanity to try again. It might be thought, rightly so, the use of the word 'sanity' was a bit powerful, a bit over the top, but these stresses in my life were to build until they became uncontrolled later on. Fred and Joan's suffocating interference in my life, especially from Fred, swamped me. He was everywhere that I was, prying into every aspect of my life, 'suggesting' other ways to do something, preventing me from cementing even small friendships. Let me colour this in for you.

On Mondays, I would have to take the week's takings to the bank, several thousand pounds in total, a great deal of money in those days. Sunday evenings would be chaotic as Joan would bring in Monday's cash contained in a brown paper bag; it might be stored in a drawer all week with one or other of the family taking a fiver here, a fiver there for purchases needed. Then would come Tuesday's, a separate bag in another hideaway, and so it would go on. I would walk to the bank, blissfully unaware of being the subject for a snatch, if only my routine had been studied, for the same streets were always followed. Arriving, I usually engaged in friendly chat with the same young cashier over the counter before going home. It was all very innocent, just a break from the routine. Fred got to learn through his friend, the same bank manager, of my smiles and chats. He moved quickly and it did not take him long to insist to the manager he should remove his member of staff to another branch in the shortest possible time. He did.

As I say, I had to leave.

*

I was more than usually depressed, one day when a neighbour, meaning to be kind and seeing my face stopped me in the street. We chatted for a while until she pursed her lips together in anger.

'You've got to get away Veronica. You are nothing more than a little slave.'

I knew in my heart it was true, and I was beginning to morph into something lower than a service maid, unable to apply my abilities to any worthwhile future. (Have I written this before?) There had to be something I wanted to do. There is nothing wrong in being a service maid but I wanted to do something which would stretch my mind and, out of that see a change for the better. Up until now I had worked and looked after the children solely to keep the peace. My neighbour's comments struck a chord; they became my tipping point.

Determined this time, when I read an advertisement in the Sheffield Evening Star, I kept it to myself and told no-one. A couple were seeking a live-in nanny, a mother's help if you like, where there was one young son and another on the way. The new nanny would be required to start immediately with £3 a week, three times what I was getting from Fred, my own room and all meals provided. It was a roof over my head, I would be 'warm and fed and, free. I telephoned as soon as I read the advertisement and was, amazingly accepted. Thrilled if shaking, I went upstairs and packed my entire life in a small, overnight bag and waited for the return of Fred and Joan.

'I've found a job. In Sheffield. I'm starting tomorrow,' I declared, spilling it out before I had time to lose my nerve.

'Tomorrow? What about the girls? After all we have done for you. I've put pounds in your pocket,' said Joan, visibly angry. Joan was shouting as she knew there was nothing she could do about it. It dawned on her she would have to look after her own children. You see, I was the *Cheap option*. Nothing would be cheaper or more convenient than me.

I could not stop myself. I screamed back. 'Yes! But I've worked for every one of those pennies. I am going to be paid three times what you pay. Three times,' I repeated in my anger,' storming back to my room knowing I had made a giant leap forward in breaking the fetters which bound me to Barnsley.

The next morning, early, I left without a backward glance, my tiny case held protectively in front of me as I headed for the railway station. Joan took years to forgive me and returned all the children's presents I bought them for Christmas. It hurt, for the girls had grown up with me and I had grown very fond of them. We had forged close bonds. Like most nannies, they knew me better than their parents. When I had been sent to Flamborough Head to stay in Fred's parents' house, I was alone with them all day for three weeks. So, they knew me well and would not have understood why I left so suddenly.

I arrived in Sheffield Station to be met by Mrs Grainger who drove me to their house, chatting all the way. I cannot but wonder what she thought of my small bag, though at the time all I could think of was, I'm free.

I was showed to my room where I was to sleep with David. One of my duties was to take him for a walk every afternoon in the park. I helped, willingly in the house and formed a warm, comfortable relationship with both Grainger's who really took an interest in my welfare. Once I had had supper with David in the kitchen I could go to my room to listen to the radio. I rarely went out, there was no point, and it meant I could save money.

It was a happy time. Mrs Grainger was a very good cook; her home-made soups were delicious. She and her husband could never thank me enough showing their appreciation for looking after David while Mrs Grainger was in her final months of confinement. She was to have another boy, Jonathan, and both boys went on to do very well in life and who, magically were reunited with me later in life.

It was like a pantomime. Like the ubiquitous 'baddie' in whatever show you want to think of, Fred re-appeared from the wings, on stage, not perhaps to audience boos and hisses but certainly to raised eyebrows from the family. A knock at the door one day revealed Fred standing there ostensibly asking after my health. 'How is Veronica? Is she getting on alright?' I had not told him where I had gone and had to assume one of my family had given this crucial information away, probably under constant badgering. I explained to Mrs Grainger he was a brother-in-law and where he fitted into the sorry picture. She nodded politely but she was an astute woman and I could see she was far from convinced he was the right person to pass on any information about his young sister-in-law. But Fred called again; strange questions for no apparent reason and I knew he was going to cause trouble. He told me *sotto voce* that Mr. Grainger fancied me, a ludicrous suggestion. I knew and had experienced what a loving family they were.

*

In the depths of my despair the conclusion was clear I would never be free unless I moved completely away, somewhere where Fred could not follow. Joan had mentioned to me on several occasions she would have liked to join the Police Force which only marriage had prevented. In a uniform, in a police station, surely, I could be free of interference? Joan's words now acted like a stage prompt and I wrote off for an interview. Women in the police force were few and far between in those days, it was, after all, still a male orientated society. These were the years of bobbies on the beat, of television's George Dixon and 'Z' cars. This could well be a job I could manage well for a few years, even just two years, until I had sorted myself out. I had to have a job with a roof over my head if I was to move, as Fred would never welcome me back to his house in Daleswood Avenue unless it was on his terms.

The only alternatives for me were to be a bus conductor or work on a factory line, both jobs which I could learn in a week after which boredom would set in. Neither did the Armed Forces appeal to me.

The Police have an entrance exam covering English and Maths. With RSA English behind me I was lucky in my maths for it was all standard stuff, not Geometry or Algebra with which I could have come unstuck. I was told to be ready for an interview that afternoon which implied, at least, I had passed the written papers. There were only four of us up for the interview but Doncaster Borough Police Force was very small in comparison with other cities.

Having been called to '…enter' I examined the eyes of each of the examining board seeking assurance, approval, rejection or plain disinterest. There no signs of immediate dismissal nor a look of 'next please' about them. It was an encouraging start. Whatever the men thought of women being involved in their work, they did not reveal it to me. The questions were searching but fair and I began to see a life filled with interest and one where I would be taught to look after myself. This idea I liked very much, being told I would hear shortly by mail.

It was not long before a letter arrived in Sheffield one morning. I had passed.

The Grainger's were devastated, for they had said, very kindly, I had a natural gift with children (I had had years of experience) and they had hoped I would have stayed on. Being intelligent people I am sure they realised there was an underlining force driving me away and it was not of their making. I kept up with their two boys for some years but, as I was moving so much I eventually lost contact. What they did do for me was to remind me there were good people in this world, where kindness came before seeking a profit, people interested in me and what I wanted to achieve in life.

*

The Force allowed me to join at the age of twenty-one. It was but a short time until, in February nineteen sixty-four I reported for my first day of a two-week induction course at Doncaster. Success there would allow me to progress on to my training at Warrington, I was told. Within half an hour of shaking hands with the CID Officers they started briefing me, explaining patiently to a young woman slightly bewildered at the pace of things, they had been trying to catch a purse thief. A woman who operated in the market was quietly removing purses from the open baskets which shoppers used in those days. Before I knew where I was, I was handed just such an open basket and a purse and told to walk around the market to see if anyone might take the bait. This was a very long shot to me, having just arrived that morning; surely no thief would just happen to be there when I turned up out of the blue armed with basket…and purse? I had a lot to learn. I was to notify the police if the purse disappeared at which time they would arrive on the scene waiting to pounce. Oh, so that's alright then.

'We will be following you,' they said reassuringly, one officer seemingly being almost half again taller than me.

After just half an hour, trying to act as a choosy customer, unbelievably I saw the purse had gone. I made haste to signal for the police to close in, but, nothing happened. No sign of a burly man in uniform as promised. Turning, I could see a woman walking quietly away, heading for the toilets on the lower ground floor where she disappeared. At the same time one of the officers did arrive. He ran down the steps to find her. But, the delay had been just enough time for the woman to vanish with her basket and my purse, or rather the property of Doncaster Police. We had to return to the police station not a little frustrated. I tried to give a description of the thief, but being untrained, and first day confusion, I fear the likeness was nothing like a real person.

After discussion, more training, I suppose, I agreed to return to the market where, by a million to one chance the same cheeky woman had returned to try her luck again. This time there was no mistake, and we closed in and the woman was arrested. We found several other purses on her. It was my first arrest and on my first day; that could look good on any future c.v.

Two weeks of induction followed where I came to terms with strange machines such as a telephone switchboard and general duties in an office. I also spent time, up to ten in the evening – we were not allowed as women to work later – checking all the shop door locks, before being driven home by a male colleague when my shift was up.

At the end of this I went to the National Police Training Centre at Bruche, in Warrington. Much later, there was a national sized scandal centring on racism within the Force at the Centre, when ten officers had to resign and twelve more were disciplined. When I was there, however, there were no signs of such issues amongst us.

I was there to learn how to be a copper over a thirteen-week period. A five-day week meant there were no lectures or courses over the weekends and my fellow trainees disappeared home. I remained, swotting hard to keep up with the others, being given a sandwich on Saturdays and able to partake of the Sunday buffet in the evening when the weekenders from further away returned ready for the Monday.

There were lectures in theft, traffic, sexual attacks and police law and for the first time in my life I came top in the results. I was twenty-one. Mind you, I had been lucky, for I had read up on Judges Rules and I was given a question directly on the subject. There were also fitness tests and we had to gain life-savers certificates. At the end of it all we had a memorable black-tie dinner where I bought a long (they were all long in those days) white ball gown costing three pounds, (£42.50 in today's greenbacks) which I don't think I ever wore again. All students made a small donation which went towards the purchasing of the cut-glass, the silver and the candelabra. Over time there arose a magnificent array of dinner ware and silver for these special evenings. We had a passing out parade to demonstrate our well-rehearsed skills in drilling, with parents clapping enthusiastically as we marched by, eyes right. None of my family attended, what is called *par for the course.*

Passing out meant I could concentrate on my new career. I was aware women could not go further than as a Sergeant and the Equal Pay Act only came into force in 1970 when I had moved on to a different service. I became skilled in knowing what to do in motor accidents, Point Duty and marvelled at the professionalism of the Force. Today there are great changes in the way Police are trained, as all lectures are videoed, allowing students to return later to a booth where they can replay the lecture as many times as they wish. Now that would have suited Veronica, very nicely.

We were advised, admittedly with a smile on our lecturer's face, that comfortable as we were in our new knowledge, this training period would be the happiest time of our career. His words turned out to be quite true, and it was with colleagues who never minded that you were a woman. We all helped each other.

So, having graduated and at last a WPC, I began to walk

the beat in my uniform, monitor cycle proficiency tests and chase shop lifters and prostitutes but, maintained my naiveté. I was so naïve I did not know I was naïve. In many ways, I had been sheltered, cut off from the real world beyond Doncaster Road, and Ackworth. There was no-one to answer my questions when they arose. I had been told to be good, I was. I had been told to keep quiet and keep out of the way. I did. Further than that remained a secret. Until, that is, one day I arrested a prostitute and brought her as I was instructed, into the Station, where the woman was asked to empty her bag on the sergeant's desk. Out spilled, among other things some square flat packets.

'Hullo,' said the sergeant to me,' thankfully, he did not say, 'ello, 'ello, 'what are these?' He directed his comments towards me as much in conversation as asking a direct question.

'I don't know Sergeant,' I replied mystified. I had never seen a condom nor had any idea what you did with them. The sergeant gave an exaggerated sniff, eyes cast, as it were, towards heaven.

'And what might this be?' he asked. This time his face was more serious and it demanded a reply.

'Don't know Sergeant. Could be a nail file I suppose.'

The Sergeant sniffed again as he glanced sideways at me. 'This is a tool used by abortionists. You have found one of the nasty people in this world. This case will now have to go to CID. It's a crime.'

So, I learned and was kept busy. I arrested one shop lifter who had already stacked three large bags outside the shop when I caught her with a fourth. Unable to march her, and her stolen goods to the Station, I called for help. On arrival, the CID recognised the woman and knew of her family who were all crooks. They made the decision to raid their house straight away. It turned out to be an Aladdin's Cave stuffed with random stolen goods from soap powder to food. Her sons had been stealing in the market to add to the pile.

While the pay was a great deal better than being a nanny,

eleven pounds a week (£201.0 per week in today's money) it had to go on accommodation and all the other usual costs of living. It was not going to make me rich I realised, as our queue formed up quietly while the Sergeant received our signatures, handed out pay packets in those familiar brown envelopes with the notes, such as they were, sticking out of the end flap, Because I needed more cash to save for the future, if my career was ever to change as I had planned, I opted for every single chance to earn overtime like weekends; Bank Holidays were nice and Election Days at a Polling Station from seven in the morning to ten at night were even nicer. These were big treats for me, which, re-reading this seems a bit sad to note I had written it down as if they were luxuries in my life.

But, I had a job, nice colleagues to work for, interesting work, paid if poorly; and an all-important roof over my head. I was becoming more settled as I began to see a future spreading out on a calm sea with a clear horizon. I was also, away from Fred and Joan. I had enough to eat, I wore a uniform so I was never cold. What possibly could go wrong?

There is an old adage which goes: *'everyone is given the same chances in life'.* In nineteen sixty-eight it did not seem that way to me. Some people maintain their good luck all their life. Others have an up and down sort of life, not bad if the ups outweigh the downs. I had chances too, just out of reach of my fingertips to grab; they just slipped away as if they were pieces of soap in the bath.

One night I was playing cards with three friends. I was concentrating hard, annoyed only because I was being disturbed at the extreme edge of my eye by some movement or other. It was coming from the window. I threw out a ten of diamonds and looked up. I should have known what or rather who framed the glass as he peered at my friends attempting to see if he recognised any of them. It was Fred. Prying, peeping Fred. It was outrageous and frightening for I could see he was never going to stop stalking me. I should have known for he was a close friend of the Chief Superintendent of Doncaster

Police. A few words in his ear would soon have elicited enough clues for the address. It made him come looking. He slunk off like a fox in a car's headlights, when he saw me peering through the window.

It was quite hopeless. What on God's earth could I do? I could try to emigrate to Canada, as had some of my friends, but I had no qualifications other than as a nanny and how could I raise the fare to cross the Atlantic even if I was offered a worthwhile post? Surely there was somewhere in the world I could go, safe from his eyes where I could get on with my life, but where? And how? And more importantly, when?

I rose from the card table, surprising my friends and stormed to the door, but he had left as he had arrived, skulking away into the darkness. My family could never understand why I did not like my life to be under Fred's microscope every day. They considered me to be a snob believing Fred was not only funny but generous and had no idea of what he was like away from the family.

I was trapped, desperate and very unhappy having been in the police force for four wasted years.

PART TWO

CLIMBING

CHAPTER FIVE
CHAMBER POTS AND CHAOS

Do you remember those iconic images of the Ascent of Man? You might not even have heard, or wanted to know the name of the man, Professor Clark Howell, who first displayed a series of apes and men in one horizontal banner. On the far left was an image of a knuckle-dragging ape with a low forehead and bone swellings over the eyes. Through a series of transformations, the ape begins to stand so, by the time of the far-right illustration, having travelled past the extinct Homo Erectus, we arrive at Homo Sapiens, upright and not too hairy and quite a bit brighter.

I saw my past life as that shuffling ape with my hopes and aspirations focussed on getting, at least to Homo Erectus even if it was going to take a great deal of effort to travel along the line of progression; it was all a question of straining one's back to make it move to the vertical, like the rest of the tribe; painful but possible.

It was a short while later, when Fred's presence had made itself known to me in Doncaster, that I found myself talking to a woman in a shop. She was wearing the uniform of the Prison Service, quite a rarity in those days of nineteen sixty-eight. She knew me for what I was, for I was in my Police uniform. As we chatted, allowing other shoppers to swirl past, making comparisons in the two Services, it became apparent she was much better paid than me and her wage was all found, for it appeared everything else was paid, such as accommodation, furniture and bedding.

An idea formed like a speech bubble above my head, though I didn't pass it on. If I *was* to become a Prison Officer, there was no way Fred could come and interfere. He would be locked out behind secure gates – and I would be, literally locked in – and he would have no chance of being able to see what I was doing or who I was seeing. And, Prison Officers and Police Officers must have many similar skills. This fact was supported by my new friend in the shop. I realised I could be backing myself into a corner if Fred managed to ingratiate himself into Leeds prison but at the time it was an alternative and an attractive solution to the ever-present subject under discussion. I had argued that I was running away from the problem, which I knew was perfectly true, but when one is on one's own, the alternatives are reduced; the upside was, there were good chances of fast promotion within the Service. My time at Ackworth had shown I could lead a team as Captain in most sports. I could do it here.

The woman was still talking and broke into my thoughts. 'And you would get in very easily. The Service is very .... keen (she might have been going to say, desperate, but was too polite) to have more female officers. There's a great shortage.'

We said goodbye and I thanked the woman, not realising my career path had just changed for ever, and walked back to the Station.

This would turn out to be the real tipping point in my life. I thought it had happened last time but, in retrospect I had already made the break from Barnsley; this was to make it per-manent and not as a nanny nor as a police officer though I had enjoyed both. It would mean another exam, another interview, but I had passed out of police training, top of my class. This surely could not be more difficult?

Such a move could enable me to drop any nascent ideas of emigrating to Canada or anywhere else in the world. I could save money without having to pay out on an expensive Atlantic crossing and I would be able to hold onto my ever-widening circle of friends. To make the decision to change was, all at once, not difficult, and I had nothing to lose. If the interview for the Prison Service went horrendously wrong there was still my current job which I could continue.

Within a few days, I had filled in an application form to join Her Majesty's Prison Service. Again, the response was quick, almost eager I sensed, as I sat down to another, by now familiar exam, this time at Askham Grange, just outside York. Askham Grange to all intents and purposes was a stately home, built in eighteen eighty-six for a Knight of the Realm. It certainly looked like it with its sweeping staircase and sunken garden, a ballroom with a swimming pool below the sprung floor, stone fireplaces and surrounded by an old kitchen garden wall in brick. New ideas in the prison service proposed that prisoners should be gradually freed up, gearing them to come to terms with the world outside the walls which had contained them for so long. as they came towards the end of their term. Institutionalised as so many were, the plan was to merge them carefully back into society without too many snorts of rage from the uninformed public. Three meals a day, a heated cell, no work pressures and a radio to listen to was as good as it gets to many. Mary Bell, an infamous killer who strangled two young boys when she was eleven years old, ended her sentence here for this very reason. What I did not know at the time was that within five years, the youngest Governor in the Prison Service, at twenty-eight, took over here; and she was a woman, Susan McCormick.

There were only four of us up for this exam, no doubt reflecting the unattractiveness of the job to women. I was to be tested upon English and Maths as I had done for the Police; similarly, I was comfortable with both. I must have passed, for I was asked to stay on for the afternoon to attend the interview. There I met a Chief Officer, the Head of Administration and a Governor. The three of them sat in line in the Governor's beautiful office and asked if I wanted to specialise in catering or perhaps in nursing as a hospital officer. Promotion possibilities were endless due to the shortage of staff. They were there to grab hold of.

'Why, Miss Bird, do you want to enter the Prison Service?'

'I want to help other people in difficult situations,' I replied with some fervour. I believed in the idea.

I had had considerable experience in looking after children and was aware of the mother and baby units in prisons. I also had four years in the police force which had to add up to something useful.

'Quite so,' they concurred after I had told them everything about my short life. They studied the diminutive figure in front of them, one sucking his biro as if to draw some sense into his words. 'And, could you stand up to the harsh environment of the prison regime. Some of these women can be very tough.'

'Yes, Sir.' I was as clear with that as I could be. A woman prisoner could be no harder on me than my father had been and this time I could resist the blows on my body. I would be trained to do so.

Following the interview, I felt sticky on my back from the strain of answering questions. I wanted to be believed. The next department I was being sent was to attend a stiff medical but this was no problem bearing in mind all the sacks of potatoes and carrots I had lifted onto lorries and my sports career at Ackworth had kept me supple. The Board would not accept overweight women applicants; they also had to be a minimum of five feet three inches, which I was able to clear by two and a half inches. Another question was thrown at me across the table, one which I hoped would be raised. I was ready for this one.

'Are you, Miss Bird, prepared to move away from home? Promotion comes faster if you are totally flexible on this score. Is there anywhere you would not want to be?'

'No, er yes. I would like to be far away from Barnsley, oh, and London. Anywhere else I would be happy with. But, essentially, I will go anywhere in the country if I am wanted. I have no ties. None at all.'

Fred lived in Barnsley and visited London each week; Holloway was a short journey by tube.

A few days later, I received a letter in my room in Doncaster which stated, unequivocally that I had been accepted into Her Majesty's Prison Service. It was nineteen sixty-eight and I was twenty-five years of age.

*

I informed my boss of my decision to accept the post which raised a few eyebrows, as if to say, 'you'll be back,' and took a train to Risley via Warrington which I knew from my police training days.

Grisley Risley as it was known to some lags was a new (1964) prison purpose-built remand centre for both male and female inmates. Its architectural outline was very different from the forbidding Victorian structures which our great grandparents had liked to justify, many of which were still operating. Much of the building work at Risley below ground was in concrete which had contracted 'concrete cancer' meaning whole areas of the prison had to be rebuilt.

I arrived at the main gate and was met by a lady called Mo who took me straight away, to the female wing to show me around. This was on two storeys and contained twenty-five cells each with just one prisoner. I soon noticed that many of the inmates were mentally disturbed. How did I know this so soon? My first images were appalling. I had landed in hell. This could have been Dante's first vision before he painted his Apocalypse. Prisoners were screaming at the top of their voices, banging on the doors, howling like wolves. The stench was horrendous as the women queued up with their full chamber pots whose contents were to be dumped into the sluice. It was as if Bedlam itself was taking a peak at me.

The first and foremost impression was not the ideal image of prison life I had drummed up in my mind. There was an abrupt belief this was a very long way from my idea of what a prison should be, and my heart sank as I realised the foolish and trite words I had uttered to the Chief Officer at Askham

Grange when I had suggested I wanted to help those more unfortunate than myself.

Having determined the layout and limits of my new world, I was driven three miles to my accommodation leaving me more dismayed because I had no transport. I was left at the door with my tiny case and told to report the next day.

I walked into the room and from right to left I had: a door, a wash basin, a wardrobe, a small bed and a chair. That was it. No more, no less than the cells I had just seen. I placed my bag on the bed and gazed out over more prison officers' houses. My introduction to my new life could be summed up in one word: grim. My thesaurus adds *forbidding* and, I would attach *lonely* from my own lexicon. The room was hollow, totally devoid of warmth. Any sense of homeliness was immediately challenged by the echo in the room.

I was left for the rest of the day to unpack and told I could walk to the village if there was anything I needed.

By six that evening my mood could have been described as 'anxious'.

'Have I made a mistake Veronica?' I said aloud to the bare plaster wall; the small mirror over the basin sneered back. 'You wanted to make money. You could have stayed with the police.'

'But, it's only two years,' I snapped back. 'And think of the money I can save in that time.' The mirror nodded reassuringly, pacified.

Because I was a trainee, I did not have a uniform but was provided with a dark-blue overall so I could be identified as a staff member. The uniform came when I was fully qualified. All these niggles were still with me the next day when another prison officer drew up in her car. The two of us were on duty by ten to seven to oversee the prisoners' breakfasts at seven. These were served before our own. (I remembered that army cavalry officers always fed their horses before themselves) The ten-minute gap was filled by the staff discussing any issues arising from the night before.

The prisoners had a small, measured cup of cornflakes and

a dessertspoon of sugar. This sugar had to last all day so it could be hoarded by those with a less sweet tooth and it could be swapped for other goods as if it was a currency. There were two slices of bread and a small pat of butter. Tea, only, arrived in an enormous urn with the milk added, some time before. Not nice. Try having your breakfast like this at home to see the deprivation you might go through if you were to challenge the law some day on a mindless indiscretion.

Amazingly, after the inmates had had their meal, we had to go through the whole palaver of locking them up again while we sat down to our own breakfast. There was, to my untrained thought process, a further lack of sensible logistics when we went through this whole routine again at eleven-thirty for lunch which was too close to their first meal. It was further compressed at tea which came at half-past three. This left little room in between for other activities. A bun and cocoa were provided later in the evening.

All prisoners had one hour's exercise each day, pacing round a concrete yard which many found boring and pointless but to me was fresh air and sunlight falling on the many bleached faces starved of vitamin D. Without it, prison life for children had often led to rickets and other deformities. Then there was Association. This was when all prisoners came together from half-past six for an hour where they could watch television, play cards, chat amongst themselves. (I am reminded of porridge, the T.V. comedy series when I think of this activity).

With the arrival of the night-staff we could leave, having recounted again to see the numbers tallied. This meant the night-staff, who did not have keys, had to ensure they had the same number of prisoners, for it required a day officer to be brought back to unlock an area of concern and sort it out if the count was different.

One of my first duties was to learn how Reception ran and how to make up the 'bundles' ready for each new arriving inmate. Reception was where new prisoners were processed into the prison system. It was extraordinarily degrading especially for first-timers. It was their first real experience of what life was going to be for the foreseeable future. Each bundle was made up of two sheets, a pillow case, a tiny towel which had to last the week, like all laundry; a winceyette nightdress and slippers if there were enough to go around which sometimes there weren't; a comb, a laughably small piece of soap carved up from a block, a toothbrush and some powdered toothpaste. On the top was a Reception letter with postage paid to allow arriving prisoners to inform some relative or other that she had arrived 'safely'.

Meals broke the boredom. Meals provided a discussion on something tangible, for there was a shortage of real news. Many could not read, so food filled a large gap. The food for the women was prepared by the chefs in the male wings and brought over in all weathers to be deposited at the back door. The menus were varied, say for lunch, a casserole with cabbage and a rice pudding. The only fixed meal was fish and chips on a Friday. Chefs would seek to set aside a small amount of the prisoners' daily allowance for food, so at Christmas and for New Year's Eve, a special feast could be cooked. For Christmas Day inmates, might have had a grapefruit and orange cocktail followed by roast turkey, stuffing, roast and creamed potatoes, Brussel sprouts and carrots, Christmas pudding and mince pies while for tea they would easily find room for Christmas cake, crisps and a salad. It was so good that one well-known lady would ensure she smashed a window in a street some-where making certain the police knew who it was. She would have previously handed her cat over to a neighbour and off to prison for the holiday period she would go, acknowledging the officers' smiles with a wave of her hand. She managed, to my certain knowledge, to have twelve Christmases inside.

When a new prisoner arrived at Reception she would be locked into a small wooden cubicle to remove every article of clothing and jewellery. Painstakingly, we had to record every item on this pile and, to prevent fraud, would describe, say, a gold watch as 'yellow metal' and silver as 'white metal'.

Clothes, likewise, were carefully described. From Reception, the women would be weighed, measured and issued with their uniform. They would be examined by a nurse for nits, bruises and signs of self-harm, before being bathed and led to their cell measuring twelve feet by six feet. It was eight feet to the ceiling. There was enormous impact on arrival for the first timers at the solid door with its inspection port. Inside, was no better. It held a metal bed with a thin mattress, a pair of sheets and a pillow. In winter, the bundle would be formed of three blankets and two in the summer. Over the bed was draped a very thin cotton throw either in red or royal-blue. There was a chamber pot. Plastic cutlery had to be carefully guarded for if a fork or knife went missing it was just hard luck. There wasn't a replacement.

I have used the word chaotic above. To my ordered mind, honed through stocking up stalls and loading up delivery lorries with the correct requests it appeared as if, for very little outlay in terms of money, fights and festering arguments could have been avoided. With only two brushes and mops to clean twenty-five cells, conflict would easily arise with impatient women. Surely, there had to be a better way of planning all of this?

Spending time in Reception early on in my training, I was fascinated to study the faces of the women who came through those doors. There were the first-timers, appalled and distraught at the bundle, and the sheer exposure of everything physical and mental in their presence. Nothing at all was sacred; privacy was gone out of the window(barred). There were the old-timers who waved a hand at you as if to say, 'Hullo, I'm back'. And there was me, in my blue overall who could walk out at the end of my shift and wave also, but from outside the wall, a free woman. It was indeed, a life of contrasts and yet certain similarities as well for we all, staff and inmates were locked up together and breathed the same air. Deep inside of me, though kept private from others, was the knowledge I was away from Fred during my watch.

So many images were retained in my mind from the very early days. Stark, tragic pictures like the three new prisoners who walked in from the van one day, none of whom had been inside previously. The first was a woman, quite superbly dressed in a mink coat, leather boots and handbag and gloves. She breathed money and bazz-azz into that dismal space; undeniably we could tell she was from the family of a very successful businessman. Her problem was, she had killed him.

Because she was a murderer, she had to go to the hospital wing to be assessed to see if there were any psychiatric disorders which had led to the actions she had taken. This was sensible and in this lady's case she was found to be mentally unstable which led her to being held in a mental hospital. When she was found to be safe and stable and had completed her term she was released back into society.

I mentioned three new arrivals. The other two were seventeen-year-old twins. You could not have found a greater gulf between them and the other woman brought to the same reception on the same day and given matching bundles. Every prisoner was boiled down to a lowest common denominator. The twins, from somewhere in North Wales had been found guilty of theft and each given three months. Both only had the dress they stood in, shoes but no socks, no underwear not even a cardigan. (I was very mindful of my own past which was hardly any better). They had no knowledge of how to use a bath – they had to be shown – to comb their hair, clean their teeth or eat with utensils. In fact, they were close to being feral; they could neither read nor write.

Desperately thin arms received the bundles but they had to be shown how to wash in the bath provided before being taken down to separate cells to be left to their own devices.

Although they were given uniforms, it was at a time when prisoners were for the first time being allowed to wear their own clothes. There was a catch, naturally. For to wear your own clothes you had to provide three sets rather as I had had to do in Ackworth. The twins hardly had one set of clothing between them, but, as in the nature of things, help was at hand in the form of the Mothers Union fairy godmother. They provided the clothes which were kept in a store and could be drawn down to make up the requisite stock for each prisoner. It did lead, in the early days of transition to those with and those without, clearly marked out by contrasting uniforms and everyday dresses. More fights would break out until, eventually, all prisoners were dressed as they wished. The days of the broad stripe or arrows was gone. The arrow had denoted it was Crown property. Until this was all sorted out convicted women under twenty-one were obliged to wear incredibly uncomfortable black shoes made by the prisoners, massive bras and bloomers, a grey skirt, thick stockings and large suspender belts. There was a blouse in red or royal blue spots, whatever was available. Women over twenty-one wore a mulberry coloured blouse.

When the night shift arrived to make a count, peering through inspection windows to see if they had a 'body,' it was to their surprise that first night of the twins' incarceration to find the first twin missing. No keys meant a day officer had to be called and the cell was eventually opened. The twin was found, under the bed screened by the throw, lying on the freezing concrete floor dressed only in the nightie. She had no other idea of what to do but lie on the floor as she always had done. The second twin was found to have gone to sleep also on the floor under her bed. And this was in 1968!

When the twins left three months later having been taken under the wing of the other prisoners, they were fuller in the face from good food, clean, better dressed and had both begun to read and write. This is not a story one associates with prison life and I like to think they were able to make a new start in life formed totally out of their time inside.

My three weeks' induction was completed before I had time to draw breath. My next destination was beckoning, Holloway.

I would be at Holloway for a period of eight weeks before the start of my proper training. It was strange. Why not stay at Grisley Risley? Why Holloway all the way down in the south?

The reason became clear soon enough. If Risley had been an eye-opener with its stench of fresh urine and its mad screaming to stretch every one of your nerves throughout your shift, now you were to be tested as never before. Holloway was to be far, far worse.

*

All new recruits were sent to Holloway for one reason. So as not to waste valuable training time and costs by trainees resigning half way through the course, we were to be sent to a 'clearing house' to weed out those who were not going to make it through to become a prison officer, and those whose sensitivities would otherwise have been numbed, those with no backbone for such a life and those who simply had '.... made a tremendous mistake.' At the end of eight weeks those left remaining in the sieve would almost certainly be able to weather most storms and make good officers.

Old Holloway was opened in 1852, (that was the year Kings Cross Station was opened) built by Victorian builders for males and females with one wing set aside for juveniles. There were four hundred and thirty-six cells in all. Due to the improvement in catching wrong-doers, a further three hundred and forty cells were added and a hospital wing constructed. But between nineteen seventy-one and eighty-five the prison was reconstructed, in so doing, it lost its famous battlemented facades. To the outside world, a passer-by would have seen the grim stone towers and walls with its massive gate. From inside, for the women prisoners to whom it eventually became exclusive, as more female only facilities were needed, pigeons could be seen flying about, spraying their guano with abandon which gave rise to the millions of cockroaches in every crevice. It was, as I say, much worse than Risley and in nineteen sixty-eight, was to be our workplace to test our resolve.

Counting prisoners filled my days; counting and reading letters. Every single letter had to be read, a custom which went back into time when officers, suspecting a gaol break, would seek clues in the hand-written notes to the outside world. Whatever the origin, it was still our duty to check. Murderers, serious offenders in special units of their own had all their letters copied which then formed a complete history. Thus, Myra Hindley in Holloway had an entire file devoted to all the letters she ever exchanged. The authorities always lived in hope they might find some indication in her words of where she had buried Keith Bennett, the poor little boy, still left on Saddleworth moor. He has never been found.

These special units were there to divide prisoners up into categories of risk for not only was there a unit for the likes of Myra Hindley and others like her, but mothers and babies were in their own unit, equipped for the very young children; there were also units for Remand prisoners as were women on Trial and convicted criminals.

During reading letters time, I called a young prisoner to my attention and told her that the Royal Mail simply would refuse to deliver her letter with such an address on the front. The letter was addressed to Mr F OFF, badly written I agree but the message was there. 'It's too offensive.'

The girl, who was working out a drugs sentence of six years, a long time for anyone, frowned as she studied the envelope in my hand.

'But, Miss Bird, you don't understand. My boyfriend's name is Fred. Fred Foff. Mister Foff is his name!'

For each letter received a prisoner was allowed to send one back in reply. It made for a great deal of reading and some illuminating results.

Naturally, there was counting. We were taught to keep a diary which would get us acclimatised to counting prisoners. Like sheep, they would occur in my dreams, so important was it that the numbers balanced. I would count them out and count them back in (I recall a similar phrase during the Falklands War), so everyone knew how many prisoners were in a specific unit at any one time. I would have to phone ahead to say that 'x' number of prisoners were coming through. Each roll check had to be balanced. If not, it would have to be made right before the officers could have, say, their own lunch following which, day shift officers with keys, would have to remain until the numbers tallied as required.

Although our inmates, by the very reason they were with us, were villains of one sort or another, it could often be hard on their families travelling from all over the country, to arrive in time for visiting hours at one thirty. With many fewer female prisons than male, family and friends were far worse off than the men who had prisons over most of the country. Visits for remand prisoners could be every day though just for fifteen minutes. If you had been sentenced, visits were only for half an hour every twenty-eight days. Borstal girls had to go to Exeter Prison or Bullwood in Essex which is almost off the map, was often too far for a mum to travel from the north of England to meet the time and might not be able to make any visits at all.

Prison visits could prove interesting as it brought together two people who might not have seen each other for some time. A visit could be very strained as no-one knows what to say. A young girl was waiting for her boyfriend to arrive at one thirty after lunch; opening hours lasted until three thirty so there was a two hour window. At three fifteen he finally arrived, quite drunk. She was not unreasonably, annoyed, but her anger manifested itself in the form of attacking him with considerable force. I, being on duty, waded in, being the near-est, as I attempted to separate the furious couple. It was at this moment the Governor decided to make an inspection of the room, (timing is everything) and, seeing the fracas and never one to hold back, climbed into the affray. However, my police training had clicked in and, in the melee of sixteen arms and legs, I managed to bang her quite hard, well, very hard, well, very, very hard, I suppose, with my own head. It almost knocked her out and she had to retire to let me sort it out.

In her report on the incident the Governor, amongst other comments stated that 'Miss Bird is a confident member of staff but bloody hard-headed!' And added a foot-note 'you can be on my staff anytime you like.'

One of the not so brightest prisoners had a photo of her dad in drag; not a funny party picture but a serious posed portrait. Told to hand it in with her bundle she managed to keep it. At the first visiting time, her father arrived before his estranged wife. He was dressed in stilettos and a silk dress, lipstick and handbag, looking remarkably like Dick Emery but, he was perfectly serious. Later his wife walked in and passed by not recognising her ex-husband. Came the time of the next visit, staff and prisoners would wait for him to arrive in the after-noon. But his daughter loved her dad and she was allowed to keep the photo.

There was no doubt that although Holloway was a scary place it did have its softer moments especially in the mundane jobs all prisoners did to occupy themselves. They would make pullovers for the prison population rather in the manner that shoes were made on site, and they also made jam. Plum jam, for example where the prisoners would pour plums, stones and stalks, some leaves as well into the pot and boil it all up into a red gloop. The jam had a certain cloudy consistency and parts had to be sieved between one's teeth before any attempt could be made to swallow. From jam-making it was a simple matter to take on a major company's request to have hundreds of thousands of those wooden spoons you find with your ice-cream, slid into a paper sleeve. Aware of where those hands had often been, I refused to eat ice-cream with a wooden spoon ever again.

The jangle of keys is a sound redolent of slamming doors and iron-barred windows beloved these days of television doc-umentaries. It defines the profession of a prison officer more than anything else. As a trainee, I was not privileged to carry my own bunch, but for some newly qualified officers this could be the end of their short career. So powerful was the totem, some were known to be unable to insert a key to lock up a woman prisoner.

'I can't turn the key,' one might say. 'It just won't turn in the lock.' But of course, it always did.

I can understand why it happened. One day, our Training Officer herded us all together into a cell, left us and locked the door. The impact on us was immediate and quite horrifying. A solid door, solid walls and solid bars on the window; the room resisted every time we made to place a finger on a surface to touch some part of the cell for whatever reason. The space appeared to be shrinking, closing in on us as if to squeeze the very life out of us. And I was with my friends and colleagues. Alone, I would have felt a terrible despair as the door clanged shut behind my back. It was an object lesson in understanding the mindset of some of the more sensitive prisoners especially first-timers. It was also much easier to understand the mentality of those potential suicide cases which occurred all too frequently in jail.

I was always shadowed by a prison officer, not only to see I was learning the ropes correctly, but for my own safety. I was young, naïve. Though the police force had straightened me up in many ways, I was still quite vulnerable. Events would, all of a sudden leap, out at you. A peaceful afternoon could be shattered in a blink of an eye when vicious fighting might break out as a prisoner was attacked, possibly serving time for sexual offences which had included children. There were many mums inside who had their own children cared for by grandparents but aware there were often unguarded moments in their young lives. This led to worry building up in their idle moments making it a dangerous place for such offenders.

In my four years in the police force, I thought I had seen and experienced life fully in the raw. Not a bit of it. Holloway opened my eyes to a much darker world where we, as the supposed guardians of safety, strolled its perimeter and occasionally looked in. It was a world I wanted to understand better and, as I came to the end of my time there, I knew the future would lead me down a path of seeking ways to improve conditions but I was fully aware I was still a trainee and not yet a prison officer with a voice.

While all this intense training was continuing, I was living in a Nissen hut outside the grounds. It wasn't much but then, I had never had much, so the changes were not so acute for me as to some of my friends and colleagues. The officers were friendly and some had never moved, having been there for years. The Governor, a big woman in all respects, did not wear a uniform so she was always in her everyday clothes. Below her grade, a Principal Officer wore two silver stripes on her cuff and a red background to the cap badge. Me? I was still in my blue overall yearning for the day I could put on that uniform, look the part and jangle my keys.

Respect from the prisoners was surprisingly high. They would, for example, always stand when I entered a room. Now that was because they had been taught to do so but there are two ways to stand up as someone enters the room you are in and it was always with a smile rather than a surly half-rising from a chair. We would address women prisoners by their first names (men were by their surnames – hence, Fletcher) while I was always addressed as Miss Bird. It is nice to reflect, now I am retired, some Governors hold me in sufficient respect today by continuing to call me *Miss* Bird. That is a long, long way from Doncaster Road. One of these Governors, Bob by name, was appointed as an investigator during the escape from Armley. He was in a position to extinguish my career if he had wanted, but instead he was very supportive at all times and one could see why he was so respected in the Service. He was, quite simply, a very special Governor.

I had determined not to let Fred's name pass my lips or to divulge any of his antics to anyone. I had made a clean start and wanted it to remain like that. However, I had been warned he had called on several occasions while I had been working. Fearful again, fearful of the future, I took one of my training officers into my confidence and told him of Fred's history. I could see, vaguely, a career in front of me but if I decided only to go the two years I had planned this could still end in embarrassment. She was as good as her word and helped me to keep away from returning to Holloway after I completed my training.

Before I leave Holloway, I want to describe impressions of Myra Hindley I gained in my time with her. There were women murderers as evil as Myra Hindley but it was she who is remembered today for her depravity, being elevated in the Press over a long period almost as a celebrity. There is plenty of evidence to suggest she enjoyed her notoriety in her early years.

My first brush with her did not stir my consciousness at all and I had no idea who she was when I first saw her. It took a prison officer to say to me, 'Do you know who that was?' Prisoners would go out of their way to point her out to me as if she was a bus route or a 'D' celebrity.

There was no doubt she was an extraordinarily evil woman. She was born in nineteen forty-two to a father labelled a 'hard man'. He taught her to stick up for herself and to use her fists but continued to beat her regularly in his drunken rages.

The history of the killing of five children with Ian Brady is well-known and will remain as a dark chapter in Yorkshire's history. When she was finally caught, and sentenced to life imprisonment, the presiding judge declared she was 'the most evil woman in Britain'.

What came to light, thereafter, is astonishing? Myra abandoned writing to Brady in his prison, for she had fallen in love with Patricia Cairns, a former nun and now a prison officer in Holloway. Cairns was a lesbian and had fallen frantically in love with Myra where they had first met playing table tennis in Association time. An affair began, lasting three years which eventually became common knowledge among the Holloway staff.

Now comes the first extraordinary part of the story. The two women planned to escape to South America where Myra thought she could become some form of a preacher, no doubt led by Cairns' vocation as a nun in her former life. Myra moved forward, while the plot developed, being permitted to change her name by deed poll to Myra Spencer and applied to have a driving licence. It is not clear to the authorities how she would have found any use for such a document bearing in mind she was in for a minimum of twenty-five years before consideration of parole, but she was allowed to go ahead with her requests.

The movements of prison officers were noted and soap and plaster impressions were made of three separate door keys. Pink Camay soap was, apparently used for the moulds, using the kitchens as a convenient workshop. Of course, Cairns, the ex-nun now a Senior Officer, was not only able to get hold of these three keys but managed to secure the master key for D-Wing where Myra was being held. The planning proceeded with help from another inmate, Maxine Croft. Passport photographs were taken with both women wearing wigs.

The final plan laid out the escape in detail, though without a date in mind, scaling the perimeter wall where, once over, Myra would be met by Cairns in a hired car.

It was in November nineteen seventy-three, the police began to pick up news that Myra, the most hated woman in Britain might be planning an escape. Cairns was arrested, talked and as a result was jailed for six very difficult years for her part in the plot but eventually adapted to prison life and, on release, was given a new identity. The prison returned to its normal routine.

Or, did it? There is a second narrative to this sorry saga. Myra had been locked up with some of the most dangerous women in the country. During the investigation, it came to light those same keys, put together as a package could have been used to unlock the other cells on the wing where many of the inmates were extremely dangerous. Detective Chief Superintendent Frank McGuiness from Scotland Yard and a highly-regarded officer was placed in charge of the investigation into the attempted escape and began to make the links. Dolours and Marion Price, the IRA sisters who are mentioned in this book, were due to be imprisoned in this same high security wing following their sentencing. In Myra's cell block also resided a member of the Angry Brigade, you might remember the title, who had direct links back to the IRA who, in those days were fighting the British with a long drawn-out programme of terror bombing.

Here was an association with bomb-blasted Belfast, McGuiness was looking for. There was a special irony. The key impressions which had now been found looked remarkably like a bomb in their package. The connection to the south of Ireland was made by chance, for on opening the suspect bundle, the link back to Myra was made. A second farce arose earlier when Cairns attempted to leave the package in a left luggage locker at Paddington Station only to be told she had to go elsewhere due to an IRA bomb threat and nothing was being stored in the Station.

Frank McGuiness summed up the result as a brilliant piece of planning right down to the driving licence in Myra Spencer's name.

It might have been thought this was the end of an alarming episode in Holloway's long, sordid affairs but at the time, due to the IRAs' continuing impact on mainland Britain, McGuiness's report was buried, sealed for one hundred years. It was only when Myra Hindley died that this file came to light, now released into the National Archives Office in 2002, the year of her death. If the escape had succeeded it would have been one of the worst and certainly the most dangerous jail breaks, in history. It would have caused resignations at the highest level in Government.

The real end of the story was dismal. Myra, after trying everything in her power to have her sentence reduced or at least, be given parole, retreated into her cell for the last eighteen months of her life. If she had been paroled she would never have survived outside in what, to her would be an infinitely more dangerous world of reprisal.

When she died, the prison, as usual, approached the local undertaker to cremate her body, but on reviewing his future clients, made the decision not to undertake the work. He would have lost a great deal of future business based on the continuing hate and venom local families attached to the dead woman. The prison was then obliged to approach twenty other undertakers before one brave company raised its head above the parapet and agreed to deal with the problem. Such was the mood of the country and the almost, everlasting spleen directed towards the Moors Murderer.

There was a sequel, of course. I was often asked by the public and the Press, later in life, if Myra had really died or had she been released under cover at the end of her sentence. 'We want to have a picture of her dead body,' went the clamour. 'Prove it to us.' But she had died and that was the end of the affair.

Myra's reputation was powerful as all truly evil people impress, in a sick, sad way. Outside the prison, following the escape plot, children had to be reassured it was safe to go outside, and mothers would glance across the street as they waited for their children to come out of school. There was no way they were going to allow them to walk home alone despite being told she was safe inside her cell. Such was the status she 'enjoyed' but remember, she was not a celebrity, manipulative, yes, evil very, but don't let us fall into the trap of giving her a cult status.

I write in some detail about Myra Hindley's time in Holloway. Although she was carefully moved about the country from prison to prison, a fellow prisoner was able to get to her in an unguarded moment. The prisoner's name was Judith, a dangerous psychotic. She was apt to flip from eating out of your hand at one moment to a sudden and unsafe rage. This day, for whatever reason, Judith launched herself at the Moors murderer and managed to throw her over a high balustrade where Myra landed on the security nets strung across the light wells to prevent suicides. Such was the force used, Myra's head was smashed in and she had to have plastic surgery to repair the damage. These incidents occur in the flash of an eye and those eyes need to be in the back of one's head.

This protection of prisoners, from prisoners, was an every-day requirement particularly if a woman was inside for sexual crimes which had involved children. There was little clemency for such people especially where many of the women had their own babies with them. Such dangerous women had to be moved very carefully from one unit to another which meant the other prisoners had to be locked up prior to the transfer. Today, it has become even more important as it is within pris-oners' rights – those Human Rights again – that all-encom-passing shield they use, to sue if they are hurt by fellow pris-oners. Ian Huntley, the Soham murderer did sue the Prison Service twice after he was constantly attacked and hurt badly.

Let me stay with Judith for a moment. When she was at Styal prison she climbed one night out of her cell window which had no bars, urged on by the knowledge it was New Year's Eve. She shinned down a drainpipe (yes, really), into a workman's yard where there was a conveniently stacked set of ladders. (You cannot make this stuff up). Selecting one of the long ladders, Judith climbed out before walking off holding out her thumb as she went. Who should be the first to stop and help her but an off-duty policeman. (I told you it could not be made into a film – no-one would believe it). He said good-bye to Judith, a dangerous psychotic, at the start of a motor-way and drove off secure in the knowledge he had helped a lady in distress. Having enjoyed a night's celebration through into the New Year, she finally turned up at a friend's house in Swansea at three in the morning. She had managed to remain unchallenged for over twelve hours as a friendly inmate had signed the register at seven in the morning for her. This meant she remained unnoticed until lunchtime when the duty offi-cer saw her name was not in the book. The alarm was raised; the hunt was on but Judith was well gone. The police finally apprehended her in her friend's cellar and took her back. *Red* and *faces* were two words which probably came to mind several times that day with the prison officers, and no doubt, those ladders were securely locked up.

This checking was all part of the eternal need to know how many prisoners there were at any one time in any part of the prison. To do so, numbers were checked four times a day, at seven in the morning, when Judith's friend stood in for her, at lunch, in the afternoon and when the night duty staff arrived. When prisoners were moved around the prison or had to leave to go to a trial for example, chalk boards were constantly updated. As one prisoner left, the number was rubbed out and a revised figure inserted. When they came back the number was altered again. The boards were divided into sections, such as Remand, Trials and Section the last was where a prisoner had to be transferred to the hospital section. Pretty low- tech in those days but it worked, usually.

As I came to the end of my eight weeks I was skilled in controlling fighting prisoners, night patrolling, interpersonal skills, gate duty, the switchboard and.... counting.

I was ready for Wakefield.

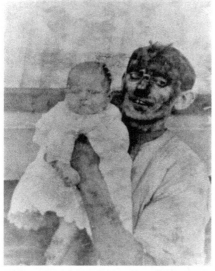

1929. George Bird with
Joan. '...finished with shift'

1965. Joan Ward '...with
thermals' on the stall

Early Sixties – Fred Ward.
Joan, left in picture.
'Party boy!'

1954. Ackworth '...like moving from hell to heaven'

1955. Only known photo of Kitty Bird – 'happier times'

1965. Me, testing cycling proficiency Doncaster police

1965. First proper job – working for the
Bill. Doncaster

1968. Trainee at Holloway. No-one
wanted to be locked up in Holloway

1968. Roger Kendrick
'…he literally, saved
my life'

1972. Principal Officer in the old uniform '... I like the red blaze on the cap badge

1976. This time in the new uniform at Styal. Something like an air stewardess

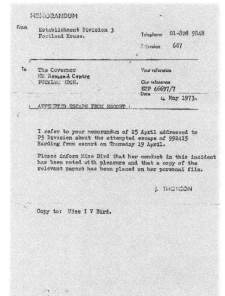

1973. 'Bum' biting incident, '...noted with pleasure'

1973. God's office, Risley '… I felt hot under the collar'

1976. Styal prison workshop. '…could be in any factory in England'

1976. Me, modelling new uniforms for the Service. 'See what I mean about air stewardesses'

Baron Brittan. Styal '…I met all the
Home Secretaries, all clever, all seeking
questions, all in a hurry

1988. 'Know
what I mean,
'arry.' Frank
Bruno with
suit

1988. Frank
Bruno without
suit. 'Lovely
man'

1989. Sir Douglas Hurd at Thorn Cross. Me as Deputy Governor

2000. First Governor to receive the Butler Trust award. 'Fairly proud, I think'

2001. Ivanova team plus blonde Russian support

2001. Women's prison. Ivanovo.

Inside Butyrka prison, Russia

2002. Fred Ward's lorry preserved for a museum

2002. OBE. '…from Doncaster Road to Buck House'

With John Major at the Dickie Bird Foundation

CHAPTER SIX
EVERYTHING ALRIGHT, VERONICA?

I was going back to learning again, the first time in nine years with the exception of night school. There were close reminders of my last school at Ackworth as I arrived at Wakefield for the start of my thirteen-week course. Wakefield was a college, like a University or sixth form school, but at least our earlier experiences in Holloway and Risley had given us a firm base on which to understand what we were about to embark upon.

Wakefield was fresh air, space and sanity, the absence of smell and noise, rather, you sensed the aromas of chalk in the classroom and the lack of clamour and echo assailing your ears while you were on duty.

Those with me on that course had all passed the first hurdle of Holloway. Those left in the bottom of the strainer, so to speak, had a more respectful and dedicated approach knowing now they could come to terms with this job. Of course, as in every avenue of life, there were those who did not make the grade during progress Sometimes, on a Monday morning we noticed an empty chair where a trainee had been told on a Friday night, when most trainees went home, not to come back the following week. Some indiscretion had arisen such as a criminal record from the past which was not *spent,* that is, it had not run the course of five years. In those days, even motoring offences were deemed to be criminal. Some POUTS – Prison Officer Under Training – might change their mind as they began to focus on a life in the future, literally in prison, albeit they were on the right side of the bars. Meanwhile, to those of us left, we were subjected to a wide array of topics some of which I was already familiar with, having been a police officer; other matters were brand new.

We learned about Categories for prisoners. Category A was for the worst and most dangerous prisoners such as terrorists and drug barons, and in the past, IRA prisoners. Category B covered rapists, murderers; C was for run of the mill offenders and D was for white collar crime such as motoring offences. Geoffrey Archer would have found he ended up there.

At the time, there were only two training centres in the country, the other was at Leyhill. We lived on site and absorbed our lecturers' pleas as they sought to train us in keeping ourselves safe at all times. It was easy to forget, in the evenings, just how dangerous some of these inmates were. Many had nothing to lose at all, and knew that an attack could bring them, albeit briefly, an overwhelming sense of power and control. We all had to listen carefully for it was a salutary lesson in the art of self-preservation.

After the practical work at Holloway, we were involved in written work, alternating with fitness training. We became skilled in how to control and restrain a prisoner, the care one had to take at the main gate and what to do on night duty if a prisoner became ill. The course was wide, and deep and very professional. Two weeks before the end I was called into a tutor's office.

'Veronica. You are to be posted to Pucklechurch when you leave here. It's about eleven miles from Bristol and will take you half an hour to get there from the city centre.' He had forgotten I didn't have a car. 'It's a small, happy prison and I think you are going to like it there.' He paused and looked up to see if I was paying attention. I was. 'I'm sending you there with Elaine. I want you to look after her.'

It was my turn to query. 'How do you mean Sir?'

'In confidence, Veronica, you must know that Elaine now has the results of her check-up at Pinderfields hospital and she has been told she has an inoperable brain tumour. There's nothing she can do about it but, of course, neither can we. She is to take leave to tell her rather elderly parents the sad news, and will then come on to Pucklechurch.'

I hesitated. I knew Elaine had gone to the hospital following her collapse at Wakefield one day but had not heard the result. 'I'm very sorry to hear that Sir.'

'We have allocated a room for her next to yours, so you can keep an eye out on her. It is the least we can do.'

And so, I said goodbye to Wakefield, a fully-fledged prison officer in my new uniform, though no doubt I would be carefully watched for some time as I shoe-horned myself into the routine.

Pucklechurch was a community (now Ashfield Prison) and community was, strangely, the right word to use. There were only twenty-eight women prisoners imprisoned on the site of a Second World War RAF balloon site. Building had commenced in 1963 and was duly opened in 1967 so both the prison and I were very new together when I arrived in 1968. The place was designed to take both male and female inmates on remand with the male units larger than those for the women simply because of the greater numbers.

While I am quite comfortable to write that when I was at Pucklechurch, it felt and was a happy prison to work in, by 1990, only twenty-two years later a vicious riot destroyed many of the buildings. It is the nature of the beast that tensions can arise out of almost nothing and, when fired up, it is very difficult to stop the destruction. It happens so quickly.

I still remember my first day in my first job in the Prison Service. I had already been given my uniform for the passing out parade at Wakefield and I was very proud to wear it. In 1968, it was of a much higher quality of design and material and trouser suits had not even been invented for women. So, we wore a skirt in royal blue, a blouse without a tie so we could not be strangled (though men wore a tie, it was a pull-off type) I was given the option of being given shoes or take an allowance to buy my own, which of course I did, as I presumed I could save money that way. Not soon after I joined, all shoes were provided by way of an allowance and I settled for a court shoe with a low heel. This would, we were told, save on the administration costs of sorting out all our shoes sizes and trying them on. So proud of the outfit, I spent a great deal of time making myself smart in front of just about everyone; finally, this was recognised and I became a model for new uniform designs. (yes, but not on a cat walk).

I had travelled the day earlier with a rail warrant to Bristol. It was followed by a taxi for the last ten miles where I was met at the prison and shown around before being taken to my accommodation – well, a bare room in fact. I unpacked my worldly goods comprising a dress, a skirt and three blouses which took about two minutes. I had been advised to buy some food in the village at the only shop, as there were no meals set aside for me at the prison until the next day. This I dealt with, carrying my supper back to a cheerless room, but looking forward to the morning.

Day dawned as I walked across a grassed square to the main gate to be duly signed in to a register. I could see this grass from my window and further across to the prison itself. They spelt out the boundaries of my life quite clearly; during my time-off they connected back to the prison. This was my world.

Below, you can find a typical day, though it did take some time to learn all the ropes. Unlike another prison such as Holloway which was so much bigger, Pucklechurch was small enough for me to have to carry out any and all duties required of me. This was not to be a place for specialism.

06.50	Check in at the main gate
06.50–07.00	Discuss any issues arising from the night before
07.00–07.30	Unlock cells, prisoner slop out. Wash.
07.30–07.50	Supervise prisoners breakfast
07.50–08.00	Lock prisoners up
08.00–08.30	Staff breakfast

08.30–11.00	Unlock cells. Prisoners to workshops or laundry
11.00–12.00	Prisoners to exercise yard. I supervise
12.30–13.30	Prisoners locked up. Staff to lunch
13.30–15.30	Supervise visiting families
16.00	Prisoners to tea then locked up
1830–20.30	Prisoners unlocked and to Association. I supervise. Prisoners locked-up.
20.50	Night staff arrive
21.00	Sign out at main gate

OR: I might escort prisoners all around the country to attend Court or transfer to other prisons when I would get back by 2000 for supper.

Each night during the week, one prison officer would have to sleep in, in case of emergencies. It could be a long day but I didn't mind. I was going nowhere. I was safe, watered, fed, housed and making friends. Because I became known as dependable I received good reports. It would help me in my promotion prospects in the future.

Pucklechurch was a small village in 1968, now expanded out of all recognition. The builders started construction in 1963 and took four years to complete with the surrounding village growing alongside so it could accommodate the prison officers housing. They needed to be close to the prison in case of emergencies. It had been built to take young male offenders under the age of twenty-one but now the site was shared with a woman's unit. Arriving prisoners, having been checked in at Reception, would walk down a magnolia painted corridor carrying their bundles to the cell block of fourteen cells, seven either side facing each other. There were a further fourteen cells called the hospital unit. An area contained a sluice for chamber pots and basins where an enterprising Architect had located the office, correctly as it turned out, on the opposite side where it was engulfed, trapping the appalling smells. But the office was there for a reason. If there were going to be any fights this is probably the place where they would brew. There is nothing worse than a grumpy prisoner who has had a bad night holding a chamber pot in a queue which seems especially slow that morning. Apart from a pint of urine dumped on you, accidentally on purpose, the pot itself could give you a very nasty blow, but officers in the office could arrive very quickly to sort it out. Early mornings were the worst time of the day for us.

With space at a premium, a portacabin was craned into the site but it had no bars on the windows and the walls and floor were flimsy to say the least. I imagined on more than one occasion the idea of prisoners, at the dead of night, digging down through the floor to the space below as if they were P.O.W.s' in a German Prisoner of war camp. No-one would have been the wiser – until roll-call the next day. Luckily my fantasies were proved to be groundless while I was there but there was one escape through the floor after I had left.

Close-by was the dining room, a multi-purpose space with a highly-polished wood block floor. It became a church for Church of England use on Sunday morning and after lunch the Roman Catholics would use it. As the boys came over on Sundays to attend a service from the male units they would be put in the front so they would find it difficult to ogle at the women, most of whom were under twenty-eight years old, but kept at the back of the room. The girls were able to watch the boys enter the room, to judge if there were any new arrivals better looking than the others. By evening, after supper, it became the Association area where they could engage in Bingo or play board games or just chat. The tables they played on were metal framed with Formica easy-clean tops but were dangerous missiles in a riot as were the wooden stacking chairs. Just these items of furniture could batter a room into pieces.

These fights and arguments came, seemingly in waves. A week of total calm could be followed by days of screaming arguments as prisoners would fight over a particular chair in a particular position – 'armchair syndrome' we called it. Having been to some extent, institutionalised at Ackworth to living in close contact with many, often noisy girls, the new environment sat more easily on my shoulders than some of the new arrivals having had less of a Spartan regime in their young lives. I found I accepted the *status quo* and got on and dealt with the issues one by one as they arose.

At meal times, prisoners would sit at these tables waiting for me or another staff member to call them, table by table, to the servery where women doled out the food into metal trays with depressions to contain separate foods. It often produced cold, glutinous dishes and was unappetising to many. The food had previously been cooked in the male kitchen, carried over to us and left at our back door thus further cooling the meal.

Whether it was at mealtimes, or cleaning out cells, escorting them around Britain or watching them in the exercise yard, the most difficult issues were always with the high proportion of psychologically disturbed women. A psychologist said at the time, and this was in nineteen sixty-eight, she believed that up to eighty percent of our female inmates were mentally unbalanced to some degree or other, a percentage you might want to argue over when you have more time. But, these irrational moments could manifest themselves often without warning. One such woman had an issue every time she saw glass and wanted to smash it into pieces. This meant whenever we had to move her we would have to go to the laborious task of locking up all the rest of the prisoners as it needed three or four prison officers to keep her under control from damaging herself or another prisoner. Another woman smashed an arm through a pane of glass so hard she cut her wrist very badly. I was detailed to escort her to the hospital, a task I loathed as I hated the sight of blood. Luckily, the surgeon probably recognised my fear and talked through the operation describing the layers of skin, the torn tendons, while I concentrated on the sky, the grass and the trees I could see, anything to keep me from looking at the gory mess. The prisoner might have been unable to use her hand again but for the skill of the surgeon. The woman recovered completely and was able to return to her cell in due course. I ask you, should such people be locked up? Is there not something better that could be done?

Writing of unpleasant and painful experiences, many of the women were heavily tattooed. To try and get them going for interviews for jobs when they got outside, they were encouraged to have the tattoos removed, at least on the hands and wrists. There were, however, no lasers in those days and scouring was the only way of removing the purple and blue marks. Scouring meant extremely painful treatment, so bad for some they had to take to their beds. Painkillers were few and far between and for obvious reasons could not be handed out like sweets.

In my daily roster described above, I mentioned the need to travel around the country. Pucklechurch had twenty-eight staff in the woman's wing and a further ten nursing staff, so the staff to prisoner ratio was above 1:1 and significantly better than crew to passengers on a so-called luxury cruise ship. Despite this it still meant I had to take what I considered valuable time out each week to escort prisoners around the country to attend Court. As we were at the whim of late running cases and judges summing up, I had to spend many hours, usually in a cell knitting or writing letters, of which I wrote many, to pass the hours. It was a waste of time but the system did not have the flexibility to change until, at last, these duties were contracted out to companies such as Serco, G4S and GeoAmey took this time-consuming task away from us, allowing the prison to get on with one of its tasks of training prisoners for life after sentence.

I had arrived feeling I wanted to get on with my job while knowing I had to keep an eye out on Elaine. She had had a painful reunion with her parents to tell them there was nothing they could do, and returned to work as best she could. But, it could not last and three months later she resigned and died shortly afterwards. It was a sad time for me for I felt so helpless, not being able to do anything to relieve her distress. It was an uncomfortable edge to my new horizon and the incident sobered me up for a time.

I try to summon up my feelings of that early time in my career, the year of 1968. Those two London thugs, the Kray Twins, were at last arrested and Enoch Powell made his notorious 'Rivers of Blood' speech the day before Edward Heath sacked him from his shadow cabinet. The floods in the southwest of England made no difference to the home-coming of Sir Alec Rose returning from his round the world sailing non-stop which made banner headlines at the time. Coal mining came to an end in the Black Country as Baggeridge Colliery closed after three hundred years. I was not home to hear what my father would have thought of the news but could imagine his surly retort against all governments, if asked.

Back in Pucklechurch, you might have noticed, if you picked up an AA roadmap, that the site is almost eleven miles due east of Bristol and I mention this location for a particular reason. In nineteen sixty-nine on a May morning with nine months of my time at Pucklechurch under my belt, I brought all twenty-eight women prisoners together and with help, escorted them down to the exercise yard. It might have been any old exercise but, that exact day, Test Pilot Brian Trubshaw flew Concorde on his first British test flight over the prison at eleven in the morning. I don't suppose he had singled out the prison as an item in his planned trip nor even to use it as a turning marker as they still do around Windsor Castle, but to the women it was a day to remember as the wonderfully sleek aircraft flew over in seconds, but the roar of its engines was enough to vibrate your rib cage. It caused much chatter and animated faces during that lunchtime. It was a break from the stifling regime which prison life holds for everyone and I was not unaware of how well received my action was that morning.

This notion stayed with me. I had joined the Service to help those less fortunate than myself. With just a small effort, I had been able to give my charges an insight, however insignificant it appeared to others, into another, better life, one where hopelessness could be replaced by hope, where despair could be traded for confidence. There was a chance I could make a difference with, at least, some of the prisoners, a difference which they could hold up to the light and see there was always an alternative to back-to-back confinement.

These impressions would often run through my mind while I was on night duty. I would leave my colleague on the main reception desk, so I could stroll on my rounds. The lights were always turned off at ten along with all radios, leaving just the emergency lighting to illuminate my path. It was spooky at times, listening to the women asleep, or crying out in a nightmare. Some must have had worse dreams than others, if they had possibly killed someone. The brand, a 'murderer 'was a hard one to accept at times, thoughts likely to surface from the slime in the darkest hours of the night.

Psychiatric reports and self-harm accounts meant I had to inspect a specific cell every fifteen minutes, the suicide watch as it was known. Having seen all was well, it was back to the other prisoners who needed a check every hour. In those early days of mine we had a small key to turn in a box – the pegging system – to ensure we checked everywhere we were instructed to cover. Today, it is the digital age which means the Prison Officer has a tracker attached so his or her whereabouts can be checked by an oppo in reception.

A problem which could arise in the night-time was when a prisoner might fall ill. Night staff did not carry keys, so if they found a prisoner seriously ill or saw a fire for example, they had to open a sealed package to obtain keys, such an action had to be carefully explained the next day in a report. Cautious judgements always had to be made when a cell needed to be opened in the night, for it was very dangerous to do so on one's own. Breaking the key seal meant a good explanation had to be forthcoming. In Pucklechurch and Risley it was somewhat easier for we could call over a male officer as back-up to help out if trouble was brewing, or I had to escort a prisoner to hospital, which could leave the remaining night staff without a back-up member. As further help, there were always nurses on call.

This danger of fire in prison never went away. It might be hard to understand how a fire could take hold in a cell built of concrete and steel. But, these cells often held seriously disturbed women. Smoking was everywhere, so matches were readily available. Put the two together and fires were not an abnormal event.

I was walking down a corridor where the cells were separated into two banks when I saw smoke curling from under an inmate's door which held a pregnant woman. It was undoubtedly a cry for help but at this moment all I could think of was to get her out of her cell and go for the nearest fire extinguisher.

'Fire! Fire!' came the familiar cry from my own lips, this time as I pulled the woman through the smoky opening while searching for an extinguisher. As luck, would have it, another prison officer was close by and hearing me, dashed forward. She was, let us be kind, a bulky woman, a woman from Wales no less, formidable in size though perhaps, less well trained in fire-fighting. Well, thinking about it now, not trained at all.

'Bang the knob down...on the floor!' I yelled at her. The volume of my voice rose a smidgen with frustration but, in the end, it did communicate to my compact colleague who threw the offending instrument at the floor, eyes closed, knob first which started the water coming, good and proper. Regrettably, I had failed to tell her to keep tight hold of the extinguisher during this operation.

Have you ever seen a fully inflated balloon at a children's party being released into a crowd of excited party-goers? This can bring much mirth but, when it is a solid object of considerable weight, it can be as dangerous as a loaded weapon. Safe to say, and to reduce embarrassment to those involved, the bloody hose, having wriggled around like a green mamba trodden on by a water buffalo, discharged its total volume of water in encircling arcs of spray, dousing everyone who attempted to reach it.

The burning mattress was put out I am pleased to report. So were we, so to speak, wrung out, soaked, sodden and water-logged were words which go well with the end description of this soggy day. We studied the, by now, useless extinguisher with baleful eyes but it was empty, no use to anyone until it had been refilled and instructions relayed, possibly in Welsh, explaining how to hold one in an emergency.

*

Dealing with fires was one situation we were used to and which would break the normal routine of the day, not that we wanted a fire anywhere except on the village green on November the fifth, but it did keep us alert and on our toes. We needed this adrenaline to help us be watchful in case of escape; our *raison d'etre* was to prevent escapes and keep the public safe as a result. So important was this to our credo, that an escape could mean loss of one's job and, for me that could mean loss of my home. I could not allow a prisoner to escape on my watch. It just could not happen.

It was on such a premise I found myself having to escort a new remand prisoner, a young woman, more of a girl of seventeen years old to Court. She had stolen a baby and then, thinking twice about it, had left the child in a Ladies lavatory, luckily bringing no harm to it when found. It was, nonetheless, a very serious, and emotive case and I was detailed to escort her in a taxi to the Court. The driver and the two of us set out entering horrendous traffic holdups due to road works, delaying us quite badly. The Court, in its wisdom had pushed the hearing into the afternoon and we eventually arrived. We had spent hours getting there only for the young girl to spend just six minutes as she answered to her name and date of birth and the other standard questions required. Finished, we had to return to Pucklechurch a long, tiring day with little point. There had to be a better way.

My prisoner, as was standard in those days for non-violent cases, was not handcuffed and I provided the only escort officer disregarding, of course, the taxi driver in his London cab, embarrassingly, a white Mercedes. My prisoner's mind, unbeknown to me, had been calculating distances, widths and timings even as we travelled back caught with more hold-ups, caused by lengthy road works. Sure enough, when we came to a red light my prisoner, quick as a speeding bullet (well, at the time it seemed to be) with one jerk managed to lower the window sufficiently to dive, head first for the open space. I lunged after her knowing I could not let her go for all the reasons I have given you. I screamed through the small gap left in the window still available.

'Help! Escaping prisoner! Stop her!'

A bunch of navvies who had caused the holes in the road in the first place, goggled at us as the taxi driver leaped out of his seat; they laughed as they sat back on their shovels to see what would happen. To them there was a taxi, a head sticking out of a car window, a massive queue building up, horns blaring by those who did not know what was going on, and a woman prison officer trying to pull this, to all outward appearances, dummy back inside the cab. The taxi driver became distracted, not sure what he could do to help. A very smartly dressed gentleman climbed out of his Jaguar behind us as he could not go forward even if he tried, and walked towards the prisoner unaware of the real situation, until she let fly at him with such a stream of foul invective I could see the colour drain from his face. 'What on God's earth have I got myself into,' was stitched across his eyes but, brave man, nonetheless he kept coming towards us.

Seeing her possible escape route about to be closed off, our prisoner struggled further and broke her zip, causing her jeans to slip down to her ankles. I was going to lose her along with my job and my home. She slipped out of my flailing arms. There was only one thing I could do. I clamped my teeth into her bottom in the nature of those school pictures of sabre-toothed tigers, and hung on, possibly a terrier with a bone is a better description. There was an enormous yell from in front of me, while the navvies looked uncertain for the first time as events began to unfold in front of their shovels. They were now most unsure this was the correct procedure for an arrest of an escaping prisoner of this nature or, let's face it, for any arrest. This certainly wasn't Dixon of Dock Green and it had never been witnessed on Z-cars.

But I had her. I couldn't talk, of course, with my mouth full of bum, but the smartly dressed Jaguar owner had her arms by this time, and the taxi driver helped to push the woman back inside. Gradually we brought the situation under control much to the amazement of the bystanders who had grown in number since the lights had changed from red to green many times over.

We drove slowly back to Exeter to an unmanned police station to await back-up which duly arrived. We never knew, particularly with new prisoners, how reactive they would be, being escorted to a Court and a rather frightening judge for the first time. Plainly, our remand prisoner had been put off by what the judge had said, and wanted no more of it. In mitigation, we would have had another officer in the taxi if it had been a serious offender and even a nurse in the front at times.

When I finally got back that evening, Roger Kendrick the Governor asked me to tell him what had happened.

'Everything alright Veronica? No-one missing?' This was the key point of his enquiry.

'Yes Sir. All present and correct'. This allowed everyone to breathe again.

But in his report to Headquarters which always had to be drawn up in such situations, he added a note. It was titled: 'The bum-biting Officer,' a sobriquet I had to live with for many years.

That road down to Cornwall (we covered all the way down to south Cornwall) was a busy one for us. I had to travel down again, this time escorting eight men and three women charged with fraud. It was a big case. Each day the judge saw fit to grant the eleven prisoners with bail at lunch and repeated this in the evening until the next day. On the final day, he was to sum up in the afternoon after lunch and he had made up his mind they were all guilty as charged. This meant he could not grant bail but, by mistake, the practice was allowed this last time. We the prison officers and police of Exeter, released our charges for lunch as we had done for weeks.

Panic, nay, huge panic, not unnaturally, set in with the news we might have lost eleven escapees before they had even begun their sentences. They could be hell-bent on jumping ship....to another ship, bound for South America If the Press were ever to get hold of this, they would have a field day. They did…. anyway.

Every available prison officer and policeman was sent out, dispatched into Exeter town centre.

'Find them!'

As luck would have it, the eight men were found, almost legless, well, blotto is a better word, by this time, knowing they were going to prison for a long time, but enjoying their last hours of freedom.

And, my women charges? They were found, still in the Courthouse, still nattering away to each other, unaware of the drama in the streets outside.

'Well, 'e never did, did 'e?'

'Yeah, I'm tellin' you….and with a rollin' pin.'

'Getawaywithyou?'

You know how it goes.

The sequel to all this was, of course, when we eventually all filed back into the Court room, the Press gallery was packed for the best story in weeks.

*

Funny when I look back on it, but placing me under pressure at the time, as there might have been repercussions from above, happened when I was asked by the Governor to see the reception area was cleaned up. The 'high-ups' were coming for an inspection from Headquarters and good old Veronica could always be relied upon to carry out such duties.

'I am sure I can bank on you Veronica. This is an important visit for us.' No pressure then but an easy one I thought. So, take one prisoner called Brenda; brief her carefully on tidying up reception, especially the planters.

'Remove the dead leaves from the planters Brenda, and remove any mess on the soil of each pot so they all looked cared for.' Simple. Brenda nodded her head affirmatively, pleased to be given the responsibility as gardener for the day. Off I strode and returned two hours later before lunch to see if the work was finished.

Do you remember those old sepia First World War photos of Tyne Cot? Where just the remains of tree stumps rose above the mud? Branches and leaves stripped, the earth blown by shell fire away into the distance? Well, my Reception was a miniature Tyne Cot. Brenda had removed all the dead leaves very well. Good. Brenda had also removed the mess off the soil in each pot. Even better, *'However,'* as Winston Churchill was wont to say, Brenda had also removed all the healthy, green leaves and the clean soil in the pots. This left a small forest of nude, naked, upright stems each threatening to fall over, as their roots were unsupported by soil. Brenda, it turned out was not a gardener. The Governor, luckily saw the funny side of it.

Gardening often has its funny side. A good friend of mine, a prison officer at Drake Hall Prison in Staffordshire, quite scruffy in appearance but with a heart of gold told me she had been put in charge of gardens after she had suggested that she should take over at her interview. She duly received the appointment to be in charge of the prisoners who would tend her gardens. Being slightly madcap, her charges decided it would be nice if they helped her out with the large planter at the entrance to the village which spelt out 'welcome' in multi-coloured flowers, to brighten the lives of those arriving. It took her a little while to notice they had re-arranged the plants and added some more. The sign then spelt out Welcome – F*** Off.

The same colleague also declared to the Governor that the prison could produce all of its own potatoes, a useful top-up to the always stretched catering budget. Agreeing to the idea, the potatoes were duly planted, and awaited with much anticipation by staff and prisoners alike. This was what it was all about. Growing vegetables for yourself. Back to nature. Healthy, home-grown food, they thought.

Some months later, the Governor enquired when he might expect a potato out of his own grounds.

'Oh, I got bored with that. I've dug them back into the ground.' He was duly informed. As I say again, gardeners, proper gardeners that is, were in short supply.

Smoking helped many in prison whether they were inmates or staff though I have never been one for the weed and thus have never had the need to carry a box of matches or lighter in my pocket. Prisoners had to manage their tobacco and matches carefully, as they had to buy both from the prison shop. They were paid a small amount for the work they did which was not a great deal, so they took to splitting the safety matches lengthways into two some managing to split them into four. The familiar request of, 'Have you got a light Miss?' was a constant in my life having to turn down the requests each time.

It quickly got around our block that by drying banana skins and adding some to the tobacco before rolling it up brought, allegedly, a high like cannabis. Not surprisingly, bananas disappeared off the menu and I look forward for someone to write to me to confirm, or otherwise, the efficacy of dried banana skins as legal highs.

Time progressed, confusion arrived. Decimalisation came to the Prison Service. Anger levels rose when the country, which included all of the prisons, 'went decimal'. Few understood the new coinage which, inevitably caused prices to rise without a subsequent lift in prisoners pay. By such events, misunderstood to begin with, could spread quickly into a riot and attacks on staff.

We were a small women's unit of twenty-eight cells. We had no capacity to take more prisoners if, say, a large trial was on and we had to take three or four remand detainees. We were then obliged to turn around quickly to supply mattresses for the dining room floor, with no additional washing facilities being available. Like tobacco issues, resentment built up by the long-term prisoners unwilling to share with the temporary women. Eyes and hawk would come to mind many days of the year as I had to be a sooth-sayer in many ways to try and calculate if a particular action taken a week earlier, could affect my own unit's peaceful regime. After such an event, the senior prison officers would meet to see how the night had gone and determine if there was any spare capacity anywhere. This problem would only get worse; the pressure on cells was an issue which would remain with me as I sought to reduce the tenseness bubbling to the surface.

I mentioned there were no washing facilities for these newly arrived prisoners who had to be supplied with metal bowls for their ablutions. They were not amused with such a basic facility, but they found another use for them.

The Governor had the good habit of patrolling the prison, inspecting every nook and cranny of his domain. Fed up with no facilities to wash properly, nor any in sight in the future, one or more lags, all unknown, placed a metal bowl, full of water, on the top of the door leading into the dormitory. Enter, one dry Governor, depart one very wet and very annoyed Governor. But, the point had been made. Things could only get better.

*

I had been asked on several occasions if I was beginning to settle down in my new life, to which I was able to endorse with a positive – yes. Everything seemed rosy, I thought I was relaxed; I knew I was enjoying myself despite the grimness of my surroundings. But, I was hungry for promotion and worked every minute given to me on my future exams. Sometimes I, with some colleagues, might cook a meal together and laugh at life but, often I was late finishing work and would go to bed straight away. I could see a future in the Service and I wanted as much as I could be trusted to take.

As before in my life, how wrong I was.

It was eighteen months into my time at Pucklechurch, soon after Governor Roger Kendrick had taken up his post with us that things went wrong; not to put too fine a point on it, my world exploded into a black pit of hell. There is no better way I can describe it. I have no idea of what caused the trigger to be squeezed. Maybe it was the years of stress which had built up like autumn rain behind a dam; maybe it was the news, Fred had found out where I was, for he had sent a friend around to the prison enquiring after me. The man said he knew some people in the tiny village! It was nonsense of course, but the knowledge was there. Perhaps it was a whole combination of things.

What I write below is information relayed to me by several friends, for I have no memory of it now. I fell into a serious mental breakdown and was rushed to Doncaster hospital. I was in such a state that, after trying various other alternative and less harmful treatments, the decision was made to place me on ECT, Electroconvulsive Treatment. Today this would involve placing the patient under a general anaesthetic, injecting muscle relaxants following which a surgeon applied electric currents directly into the brain. With the muscles relaxed, the spasms were much less than if the patient had been awake, so the convulsions were considerably reduced. It was as if I had suffered an epileptic fit, repeatedly. These days, ECT is well documented with two expert groups ranging themselves for and against applying such dangerous action. The only difference with me was, that in those early days, the patient was not given a general anaesthetic and was not given an option. As a result, I had to be strapped down to a bed to prevent the convulsions throwing me off the bed. It sounds prehistoric, barbaric and extraordinarily dangerous and was certainly a worse treatment than any prisoner might have undergone.

It caused me a loss of memory for a long time and the absurdity was, that during the treatment I had the symptoms of epilepsy from which my brother had succumbed to the disease.

But, I did not die, and, after a while could continue to work, though it took several years for me to recover fully. What was much more frightening, was that convalescence might cause me to be dumped by the Service, out of work, without a roof over my head. It then got worse.

Fred and Joan came to collect me from hospital after the treatment had been completed and took me back to Barnsley, they, pleased no doubt they had me back under their roof and after a suitable period of rest I could be called back into the market.

I was, quite literally trembling on the brink when, about a week after Joan had taken me home, a real hero came to my rescue. Roger Kendrick, my new Governor must have read up on my file and noticed, among other things I had asked to be placed anywhere in the country so long as it was not near Barnsley. Putting two and two together he came to call and insisted he take me back to Pucklechurch where he said, he could ensure I was looked after all day. Fred did not like this at all but, neither could he argue the point and I was driven off to Bristol greatly consoled to be away from my sister and brother-in-law. More so, I was relieved to learn my job was still intact. Roger had me placed on light administrative duties for six weeks before I felt fit enough to return to normal full-time service.

Roger saved my life. I owe him everything. Later, when I was up for promotion he learnt that I had a future plan to leave the Service. I had put aside sufficient money to try elsewhere but he wrote me a hand-written letter in which it said he had heard I might be thinking of leaving the Service. He went on say that although there were many things still wrong, it did provide me with a home and security and I should stay and go for my promotion.

Like the cleverest of psychiatrists, Roger had pinned down my problem and then did something about it. Some of the staff might have been jealous for the amount of time he put into seeing me back on my feet. He believed I had a future with the Service and resurrected my career when it was seemingly at an end. Roger and his wife became very good friends and even asked me to their daughter's wedding. That was a kind and personal thought, so typical of the man.

He was that good he was transferred to Northern Ireland in 1973 to become Governor of Magilligan Prison near Londonderry, to run the special category of prisoners comprising IRA and UVF terrorists. In 1985, the violence came and brushed up very close to his family when, one night a gang broke into his garage and tried to place a bomb beneath his car which he had imagined was safe. It turned out that the dog, hearing noises, barked so much the men retreated without completing their work. His son, Johnny summed up his father with apt words during his funeral.

'Dad was larger than life, a true gentleman. He was a fighter, remaining determined to "beat the buggar" right up to the end.'

Roger died of cancer after a long fight in 2009.

It was Roger's letter, his constant support and his declared belief in me did what no ECT could ever do. It brought me into 'a sunny world' – sorry about the cliché – where my innermost fears were banished forever. I knew I could handle my job. All I wanted now was to get on with the rest of my life.

I had been at rock-bottom during my breakdown and it took years before I finally found myself not only fit but retaining my memory. A dam had broken, somewhere inside. With the water having drained away I found myself on firm ground. Joan must have seen the change for she began to re-establish her links with me. When she learned I was on show for the Service at the Badminton Horse Trials, promoting ourselves from a very nice tent, Joan arrived; she was clearly attempting to make amends for the bruising past years. She recognised what I had been put through. I was happy to listen for I was far enough away from Yorkshire and Barnsley in particular, for it not to matter anymore. So was my father. He was so engrossed in his drinking and smoking with his mates he had become known not only for leaving his front door unlocked but leaving it open to passers-by. But, of course, who would have wanted to break in? There was nothing to steal.

Other than Joan, no-one else in the family ever wrote to me or tried to call me up, share a cup of tea and talk about their children. There was no interest in making contact, for in their eyes I had moved up to a different level of society: Veronica was going somewhere. As Fred put it when he learned of my house in Wilmslow. 'What does she want with such a bloody big house?'

It wasn't that big, but compared to my shared attic space, it *was* enormous but it was jealousy which made him say what he did. He simply could not come to terms with his sister-in-law doing as well as him. And not a potato in sight to do it!

CHAPTER SEVEN
STYAL- FIRST TIME AROUND

I got into a bit of a pickle when I went for my promotion interview in London for Styal Prison. I wanted the job but the timing was wrong.

I was in the process of putting in a bid for my first house in Pucklechurch, nice but not pretentious in any way; it would be my very own place in which to stamp my own authority.

As I did, Headquarters called me up for an interview.

I was well aware that when one was put forward for promotion you only had one chance to accept a new job. Otherwise your name was removed from the list of officers who wanted to progress through the ranks. Refusal meant a life in the back waters of the Service and I needed to experience what it would be like at a higher level in the Service I had chosen.

Refusal was not an option I could contemplate even for a moment. I wrote the date in my diary, swotted up what I thought I needed to say, hoping I would not have to juggle. When the day arrived, smart outfit in place, hair (short) brushed back out of sight, I knocked on the door and was told to enter. The familiar questions began, almost as a routine. I could reassure them I was now fully cured from my illness and ready for any challenge placed in my path; you know how the story goes at these interviews. They are the same wherever you go. I sounded blasé, do I not, during this third interview (four counting Marks and Spencer) but I wasn't, I was nervous as hell for I wanted the promotion badly because I was absolutely certain I could hold the job down.

At the end of my allotted time I was asked if there were any questions I wanted to ask. No, I answered, only kicking myself as I left and had closed the door behind me. My new house. I popped my head around the corner of the door where the interviewing panel, deep in conversation, looked up.

'Can you tell me please, when you will be making a decision?'

'In two weeks' time,' they replied believing that to be a very short time to wait. I nodded my head and withdrew. I had been thinking it would be much sooner, allowing me to come to a judgement on whether I bid for the house or not. I might not get the job and I could lose the house as well. So, I made my bid and sat back to wait for the results.

They came together; sod that is, and a new posting I wanted. I was appointed to Styal Prison and my bid for the house accepted. Sod and law were applied in equal amounts. At a stroke, I had bought a property which was going to be one hundred and fifty-four miles from my work place. It would never have worked, of course, and I never did live there, but I did go to Styal Prison, to work that is.

What was completely unexpected was the level of appointment I was given. I had applied for the next step in the promotional ladder, that is, to be a Senior Officer. The powers to be around that interview table had decided to allow me to leap-frog the post, promoting me to the level of Principal Officer; Styal being a much larger prison than Pucklechurch with considerably more responsibility was just what I needed, they believed! This was a big jump in my life but, nonetheless, I was very pleased. It was indeed, just the challenge I wanted. I should mention, to avoid confusion, that this position has now disappeared in the reorganisation and no longer exists.

There were moans from the prisoners that spring, while I waited for the transfer, for the heating supplied by coke boilers had been turned off as usual on April Fool's Day, only to see a protracted cold snap arrive to invade the already chilly corridors. The inmates only had heating pipes in the cells. The fear of trouble meant the least amount of equipment possible was installed so it could not be pulled from the wall in a frenzy; normal service could return quicker because of the inability of the prisoners to do too much damage. Riots could be frightening places to be, the land of the uncontrolled mob, where reason and sense disappear out of the window. Thus, the idea of introducing any new piece of equipment or furniture has to be very carefully thought through before going into mass production. We had the same heating restriction's as the prisoners, so we all had to wait until November First to get the heat moving again in the pipes and bringing a welcome return to warmth.

And so, to Styal.

*

Styal was unlike one's standard image of a prison as we might imagine, in its design and layout, unlike also, the familiar ideas of forbidding walls and massive doors. In eighteen ninety-eight, several cottages had been grouped together to create an orphanage for destitute children. It was the sort of facility the Victorians loved to show off to the world. Styal was located at Wilmslow just south of Manchester Airport and endured until nineteen fifty-six when it closed. Up until this time the houses had been named after flowers. Someone came up with the bright idea of using the derelict buildings as a woman's prison. This meant we lost the flower house names and substituted them with well-known prison reformers such as Fry and Gaskell. Perhaps, with reflection, we should have left the original titles as a point of cheer? The women would come from Strangeways, a name recognisable as a grim reminder of the past in British prisons. Over a hundred prisoners were to be executed there over the years.

As a women's prison, Styal was transformed into an important hub, for out of four hundred women prisoners in the country two hundred of them were in Styal. (today there are four thousand). Of this total, it had been calculated by the powers at Headquarters, that women under the age of twenty-one were more susceptible to radicalisation than those over this arbitrary dividing line; the idea being that the older you were, the more wicked you were: and what nonsense was that? Styal's unique layout of individual houses meant that a high fence had to be installed, as if it were Jerusalem, keeping the under twenty-ones on one side and those over this age on the other. Surprisingly, the only thing it proved was the older women were only too keen to keep away from the younger intake as they were '…. too noisy, too brash and quite unsettling.'

Such a mix was always going to bring problems to staff to sort out.

A Borstal sentence was handed out to offenders with a maximum term of two years. This could be reduced with good behaviour. Likewise, it could be reinstated up to the maximum if no progress was being made.

With lifers' close-by, both types of offender generated differing characteristics and placed opposing demands upon the system. Our job, my job, was to prevent Borstal prisoners from re-offending and coming back to Styal on the other side of the fence later on. Perhaps reaching these girls early enough, we could instil in them enough belief in themselves to keep them away from crossing that line?

As I continued along in this enclosed world of mine, though with growing awareness of the issues which needed to be tackled, Edward Heath, Prime Minister of the time saw fit to put the whole country on a three-day week caused by striking miners wanting a better life. Where ever I went, mining followed me, memories of early days, of a blackened face and staring red eyes. They might well fade away from the day to day job until, a headline, or a news item brought it up to the surface as if it was a bucket of coal coming up in the winding tower. The newspapers had a ball, while the Prime Minister struggled to keep on top of the crisis. To us, though, prisoners came and went as regularly as clockwork. Not even the Government could stop the even tenor of prison life.

Early on in my life at Styal, I was sent on Detached Duty for four weeks to Brixton. I was needed urgently to travel down to Brixton Prison along with eight other officers Detached from regular duties, all of us were deployed in four weekly tours. This is a male only jail and the reason we nine officers, all female, were sent there was a decision made at a very high level, to hold the Price Sisters on remand in a totally secure prison. Having seen the operation in action, I can confirm, to any doubters, there is no way in which a prisoner could be spirited away from under the noses of the Brixton staff. (So saying, two IRA prisoners did escape in 1991).

We were there at Brixton, as no female prison facilities were secure enough to hold female prisoners and it had to be a top security facility due to the extraordinary danger the two sisters posed.

In 1973, Dolours and Marian Price were part of an IRA unit who placed four car bombs in London which injured over 200 innocent people. It became known as the Old Bailey bombing. The sisters were caught even as they tried to board a plane to Ireland. They were tried and sentenced to life imprisonment, though this was subsequently reduced to twenty years. Meanwhile, as they waited to go on trial, we had to look after them as best we could. It was a scary time. We had no facilities to occupy their minds so all they could do was to read books and write letters which were very carefully scanned for information hidden in the content for clues leading to the IRA units.

They were permitted to attend Roman Catholic services, albeit heavily guarded. They spent most of the time playing up the Priest saying he was wearing sandals which they found funny. To us, though, there was not even a smidgen of humour in our days. We were proven right for when they were eventually released, Dolours, still active politically said of the Good

Friday Peace agreement, 'It is not, certainly not, what I went to prison for.'

With such statements, there was no way we could turn them towards peaceful ways. The past hurts of Ireland and the British were embedded in their psyche too deeply.

*

I settled down to learning about being a Principal Officer for, until then I had assumed I would be engaged only on tasks covered by a Senior Officer. At least there had been time enough to absorb a good working knowledge of the prison. I was more than lucky to get this promotion for there were not many female Principal Officers posts, perhaps thirty in the whole of Britain.

Styal's fundamentals of having houses, separate blocks if you will, meant each type of prisoner was allocated a specialist unit designed to keep particular types of inmate apart. So, the houses, held between twelve to sixteen women. One would contain dangerous lifers, Mary Bell the child killer and Carole Richardson connected with the IRA bombing in Guildford were here; mothers and babies in another; short termers, those deemed mentally ill or, as we put it, inadequates. There was, of course, a punishment block singularly named, *Bleak House.* This last unit was where the Governor could send a recalcitrant inmate for a fixed term, say three to seven days. Cellular Confinement was its politically correct label. The implication was that a prisoner so charged would spend twenty-three hours a day locked up, for the term handed down. There would be just an hour for exercise and time out for toilet visits. Meals were served in one of the eight punishment cells. Alongside this there could be loss of remission, up to twenty-eight days though the two punishments might not be necessarily linked. To top this, the final straw as it were, was to lose earnings, meaning loss of tobacco which stored up trouble as smoking was endemic in the prison and as familiar as placing fish with chips. There was no special kudos in being housed in a particular block though each house was tailored to the needs and demands of the inmates' offences. Progression through their sentences, allowed us to begin preparing them for open prison and thereafter for the big, wide, and often, just as frightening, world.

Supervising in Bleak House was, well.... to be accurate, bleak. There was very little to do and it took a pair of officers, always in twos, who would read the letters as normal and chat to each other. The necessity to move these prisoners was much less frequent. The one hour of exercise became a welcome break for them as well as our inmates. To supervise in Bleak House needed staff who were well-balanced, with a calm nature and who could deal with the special environment they were placed in. They were, in fact, as securely locked up as the prisoners. Think about that, when you next listen to a moan from a prison officer.

When I reached the grade of Principal Officer and my turn came up for night duty, it was my task, amongst others, to patrol between the various blocks set in the grounds of the prison. Black shadows everywhere could hide a dozen escapees. Rats scurried back into the darkness, owls hooted and a fox would often slink away on my approach. Although the outer gates were double locked with a second key, I was always pleased when I completed my tour and could come in from the cold.

The pressure on staff from their charges was constant and morale sapping. You, the layman tends to receive all of the information on prison life from the more lurid red-topped rags, often widely distorted or simply untrue. It could be frustrating to see some of the most infamous prisoners almost glamorised by having associated with some D celebrity or other.

Where ever one worked, in whatever sector, and however funny a situation might be, to soften the day there came a time after work when many of my colleagues would need a drink, to push the demons back into their box. These after work drinks could be what I would describe as 'substantial', as though some staff *had* to have a drink rather than just enjoy a drink after work with a colleague, to laugh away a particularly anxious morning or afternoon which could have arisen out of nothing. I did take a drink from time to time to be sociable, but I didn't join in every day. You might well label me as a prig or a prude in some way, elevating myself above my peers but it was not for that reason I often declined an offer of a drink. Still locked painfully in my mind were the oft-repeated scenes of my drunken father lashing out at us when he got home from work and all because the potatoes were not yet cooked. Drink had stained his daughter's wedding when he had become legless in front of Joan and Fred. So many chapters of so many incidents were stitched into my mind and I had no intention of hurting others by going down that same road. It was easy to do.

Sometimes, there might be a real reason for a drink, such as a birthday or a christening. I would lift a glass with my colleagues, anxious to toast the new child, or the success of the promotion of a colleague. Otherwise, I would smile and shake my head. They got to know me well, but I knew I was doing the right thing as I found out the dog, living in the flat below me was an alcoholic, which says a great deal about its owner.

Although I didn't enjoy my midnight patrols through the grounds, it was a different picture during the day, particularly in the summer and on a fine morning. The women had a common room for wet weather, otherwise they could walk outside in the sun and fresh air, far away from the tobacco contaminated smoke of their cells, the high fence and concrete exercise yard. The past was separating from the future at an ever-increasing speed.

At the beginning of each day, after breakfast, the women would walk across to the workshops, being carefully watched by two prison officers to prevent the passing of contraband or letters. It was a familiar sight to see the women going to work, chatting, dressed in their own clothes as if they were off to the

factory down the High Street. The change from prison uniform to their own clothes was a new relaxation to help improve
their self-esteem. The next step was a hair dressing salon which
we opened and it worked. The women began to take an interest in themselves and with that came a desire to get home as
soon as possible.

Sundays, though, was the nail-biting day. Our prisoners
were entitled to attend church each week. The church at Styal
was outside the prison boundary wall. It had no secure bars
(stained glass and iron bars do not go together very well) and
there were several exits which needed guarding. When handling dangerous criminals, this caused much worry when they
declared they also wanted to attend a service. (Perhaps that
is why they did it?). Two officers were placed on the road to
prevent a runner but, if there had ever been a pre-arranged
escape by a group of detainees with a well-thought out plan
we would not have stood a chance to catch them all, if they
had scurried in all directions at the same time. It would have
caused wide-spread panic once the Press had got hold of the
story, and heads would almost certainly have rolled.

This church caused me to reflect on life when two women
with their children arrived one day for a service. Before the
arrival of the vicar, they began to point out various features
of the interior as if they knew the place, though we had never
seen them here before. Intrigued, I went over to them after
the service and asked them if the prisoners had behaved themselves even though I knew the women had every right to be
there.

'You seem to know the church very well?' I enquired.

They told me they had both been orphans in what had been
the orphanage before it was turned into Styal prison. They had
been there at the time when the British Government had con-
nived with the Australian Government to take ten thousand
children in what became a shameful episode in British and
Australian histories. Both countries had agreed to send thousands of children who were orphans, illegitimate or just too

poor for their parents to hold on to them. They were 'exported' over a period of twenty years from nineteen forty-seven. It took until nineteen ninety-eight for the House of Commons to recognise 'Britain's shameful secret,' causing the practice to come to an embarrassing international halt.

But, for these two women, it was a joyful day. They spoke very highly of the Orphanage Superintendent who had brought care and sensitivity to his role. The women could even recite the words over the altar, *suffer little children to come unto to me.* Apt words, particularly *suffer,* when you knew what so many of the children had had to go through when they arrived in Australia., for they had often been beaten and half-starved as they were forced to build their own housing to live in. Many were only eight or nine years old.

With all this walking around in the fresh air, it is easy to forget there were negatives. Moving to Styal meant my pay grade had improved by two leaps which made me pretty pleased until I realised there was to be no overtime. So, my take home pay was actually lower. Having this in-built paranoia to save, I found there was now much more need to be careful in what I spent my money on. My accommodation too, came under scrutiny. It was a prison service quarters which the Governor and the Chief Officer saw fit to inspect from time to time. It was an unpleasant sensation that, despite knowing one's room was neat and tidy one was aware also of the Governor's fingers which might have been sneaking their way through one's most personal possessions.

In those days, I had long hair, in fashion, I suppose, but there came a time when I decided short was good, long was out. I ended up at the hair-dresser with my long hair on the ground and a breeziness around my ears. I had always kept my hair up tidily under my tricorne hat so when I was wearing it there was very little difference in my looks; or so I thought.

The world exploded when the Governor, possibly a foot taller than me, walked past not recognising me. I assume she had thought I was a new intake who had not been introduced and surprised when the recruit answered her with such a familiar, 'Morning ma'am.'

The governor eventually recognised me and screamed out in front of her staff. 'How dare you! How dare you! How dare you have your hair cut without first applying to me for permission!'

I kept quite quiet. You do not argue with an angry woman, at least, not in those days. The Governor was close to God after all, as was the Chief Officer. On second thoughts, God was just below Governor level. The Chief Officer therefore, sitteth on her right side.

Months went by. I had been in the prison service for five years. I was advancing. I knew I could hold down any job I was asked to do yet, not once did I receive a note or a letter from my father or family. To them, I had disappeared off the face of the earth. Fred, I learned, was still in the fruit and veg. business, their three girls growing up fast and not needing so much care and attention as when I had been there. It would have been nice to have spent my day-off with them occasionally. We could have had a laugh at the times we spent in Flamborough Head. Joan, I heard from a friend, had softened and was impressed with the direction I had taken in life. It had to be soon a time for reconciliation. She must have concluded that everyone moves on eventually. I was no longer a charge on her shoulders.

It was conceivable that the responsibility of taking me out of Dad's way had been a burden for her too, for she had three children as well as a difficult husband, adding Susan, my younger sister, to the load as well for a time. Whatever the issues, I was content to allow time to do its bit and wait for a home-coming one day. Dad, though, had not changed his way of life, at all He was spending most of his time and most of his earnings on booze and tobacco. It must have been killing him, if slowly, but there was absolutely no-one who could make him see reason and tell him to ease off and have some sort of treatment.

*

The Prison Authorities decided, in their wisdom, as the prison population continued to swell, which was a source of constant irritation to the Government, let alone the planning nightmare for us, that some alleviation could be achieved by moving all the women and babies out of Exeter prison and convert the whole place to male accommodation. To put this into action I was sent down to Exeter to collect twelve mothers and their offspring together with the enormous amount of kit which accompanies babies. (Just as Caesar's baggage trains took a day to pass a point). The Exeter Governor wanted a clean sweep and saw no reason to hold onto anything connected with children. The accumulated junk of decades, that only a unit such as mothers and babies can collect such as push chairs, cots, clothing, pots in various stages of decay and filth were piled into our vans instead of just dropping it into skips in Exeter. It would have been better if we had refused the piles of rubbish for there were many good organisations only too happy to help us start again in re-supplying the nursery. The women might be rogues, criminals or purely evil but they had some completely innocent children with them in their dormitories. It was part of our job to see they had as good a life as possible that we could arrange. The taint, 'I was brought up in a prison, (remember Javerre's speech in *Les Miserables?*), is a difficult one to remove.

No-one liked change from the routine, ground in month after month until it became automatic, and the arriving mothers and babies caused the familiar wave of unrest. Eventually, after some spats, the ripples subsided and everyone got back on with their lives.

By the very nature of the job, prison officers are shut away from the real world on the other side of the walls and fences but it did not stop the impact of the country's general malaise of holding strikes. During my time at Styal, the Prison Officer's Association became over-active in its disputes against what they perceived to be an uncaring Government. These actions escalated enormously throughout the Seventies. They became militant. Power was recognised; they began to flex their muscles. The claims made were of overcrowding in cells (which had led to 'threeing up). Abolishing the death penalty meant prisoners would now be on long term tariffs meaning turn-over was slowed. Pay did not keep pace with inflation which was at a ludicrously high twenty percent, nor were reasonable requests for conditions to improve for staff who had to work in one of the most dangerous jobs in the country.

Disputes rose in number and temper. Surprisingly though, the first national strike of the P.O.A. was not until two thousand and seven, well after I retired, though I hold no claims the reason was to do with me being in the Service! I could see both sides of the argument. I was not married and my expenses were a fraction of those officers who had a wife and children to keep, but strikes disrupted the even tenor of prison life and it belittled us in front of the prisoners who could jeer at the exploits of their guards. I also go back to my earlier comments. This is an incredibly hard job to hold down; there is little respite as one is locked down with criminals all day or night. There is little colour in the job – it is formed of greys and blacks, often of an abandonment of hope by the people one is charged to look after, so, go easy on the men and women of the Service. If not, come and try it yourself for a day, as I did. It is the second day when it becomes difficult.

CHAPTER EIGHT
GRISLEY RISLEY

I never did find out when my father first contracted Motor Neurone disease. It was not something I knew much about. It is a progressive disease which attacks the motor neurons, or nerves, in the brain and spinal cord. As if it is a mouse, nibbling away at a lump of cheese, ultimately there is little left and the messages to the muscles become moribund and eventually come to a stop. The sufferer finds his body becoming weaker and can feel the muscles shrivelling up and casting off from the body, leaving one dangerously isolated and unstable. It is progressive. It can affect a patient in how he or she talks as well; also, drinking and finally breathing are affected. There is, currently, no cure.

It was with this brief information, I went to see Dad several times in hospital having been told he was ill, if not what was wrong with him. He had been placed in an annexe of Worsborough hospital for the past six weeks, a place set aside especially for long-term patients, having been moved out of his awful house on a dreadful estate. It was difficult to get over to see him for I had had a recent hysterectomy, which meant I was not allowed to drive, so I had to resort to kind friends who found the time to take me over on my day off. It was Gilbert, the caring member of the family who had arranged for father to leave his shoddy estate bungalow in Kendray, supplying him with pyjamas and sweaters. I slipped in when others were not there, in considerable pain myself as the operation had not been a success. It remained like that for four years until, returning to a new job back in Styal, my old doctor sourced the problem and quickly corrected the issue.

During my first visit, I had no idea any of these arrangements had been put in place and had not been told the degree of seriousness to which Dad had arrived, nor even that he had left his house. It was so typical of our family that communications with anyone else was at a zero. Nonetheless, I was able to brighten his day with a bottle of whisky, which, I felt, he might as well enjoy.

On the last visit, I found him sitting in a chair in his room in what appeared to be new, or relatively new clothes. Dad had rallied as so often with dying people, some inner last strength to make a point and he was quite bright. But, he began to complain as soon as I entered the room.

'They are always smoking. The lads that is, behind the nurses back. And they get so angry with me. I'm supposed to stop me mates from smoking. Might as well tell them to find me a pink piece of coal. The nurses are getting at me as a result, so I want you to tell me mates not to come again. Can you tell them for me?'

'I don't have a pink piece of coal Dad.' He smiled grimly with understanding. I was, for the first time in my life, in control of my father. He was a beaten man.

He grunted, then sniffed. 'Listen,' he was going on. 'I know I've not done right by you and some of the others.... with anyone for that matter.' He was tiring fast. 'I want to change my Will. I need you to get another of those blank Will forms for me...so you can benefit.' He looked up, believing he had said the right thing to me. 'Things went wrong...since your mother died,' he added. 'I want you to get something.'

I let the wall clock second hand sweep downhill and did not reply until it was climbing up the other side. 'No. You can't do that Dad. Whatever would the rest of the family think, knowing I have been coming here and then you go and change your Will to benefit me. Life would not be worth living with them.

Besides, I'm doing well, better than the others. I don't need it.'

Dad looked round at me and studied my face, not something he had done when he had been a fit man. I think he was seeing something in me for the first time in his life. His face cleared eventually and he nodded his head in a tired but resolved way. After all, it was him and him alone who had created this dysfunctional family; it had not been my mother. His mind was now clear, made up.

His hand dropped to the arm of the chair. 'You're right. Doesn't seem proper, though.' I had never heard him speak like that before. He was exhausted, I could see, both physically and mentally. The fight had gone out of him.

I thought of all those years of pain, the dread, the sadistic attacks on all of us, the sheer bloody-mindedness of his attitude to life. Above all, there was his complete detachment from fatherhood, of providing a loving household. I was silent. *It's too late father,* I said to myself. He could not put right the thirty-nine years of wrongs and I had no intention of exacerbating the family mood by Dad changing his Will in my favour. Nor did I ever see the Will, nor learn of its contents, nor did I want to. It didn't matter. I was free.

My father died the next day. Gordon organised the whole funeral, for he alone knew everything about the man who linked our family together for all the wrong reasons. There had been no family pow-wow on what Dad might have wanted for himself and he had told no-one where he had wanted to be buried. The funeral was very low-key, just the family and four or five other friends. There was a certain irony burying him with my mother as was decided, which was achieved after he had been pulled past the Stairfoot Working Men's Club where he had been drinking in the final years of his life. His ashes were interred ensuring he left this world without having marked it in any way with the exception of the indelible scars lacerating his family's memories.

Was anyone upset at his passing at the funeral? Perhaps. Guilt? Yes. Could we have stopped Dad becoming the laughing stock as he stumbled down Doncaster Road – probably not? With the funeral over, we all melted away across Yorkshire and, as water covers the sand at high tide leaving no further marks Dad shuffled off his mortal coil. The chance to come together as a family unit for the first time was lost. Gone.

*

Father died in my fourth year when I was Chief Officer at Risley prison, which encompassed Birmingham Female Unit. I had known it in 1968 when I was a trainee and not much had changed in the ten intervening years. It is about twenty-three miles due east of Liverpool and was known in the circles as Grisley-Risley, a reputation which was well earned. It was built as a Remand Centre for both male and female inmates with several wings each with a specific purpose. But, as time progressed, conditions for women were found to be deteriorating badly. The prison had been built for 83 women and while I was there, circumstances meant we increased to two hundred women prisoners. It was bursting to the seams. This, inevitably sent out anxious waves from me to Headquarters and we received a visit from the Director General of Prisons who made a trip up from London. On his arrival, he shook me by the hand.

'I often wondered how you have progressed since I last saw you,' for we had known each other years earlier. I explained the reasons behind the serious overcrowding and the lack of facilities. He threw his eyes heavenward, an action he must have done many times before as he tried to stem the flow of funding requests from one prison Governor or another.

'I know all this,' he said but promised to look into it.

There was a growing belief in me that I needed to find new ways of giving chances to the women which they had never had in their lives outside the prison walls. I wanted to find a solution to their eternal calls of '…no ma'am we don't want to do no learning.' The experiences of many at school had been bad, or non-existent in some cases, and anything to do with education was deemed to be degrading. Yet, they needed to have jobs when they left here or they would find themselves back inside within months. I learnt quickly to hide any suggestion of tutoring, of learning, beneath carefully couched phrases such as, '...let's have a cooking session.' Slowly, the women in my charge began to understand it could be fun to cook, with the added bonus as they realised that on getting out they had a much better chance of having gainful employment as a chef or a cook. We spread this to other types of work. A woman with computer skills could earn considerable amounts of money and could be a major contributor to the household funds. And above all, there was their self-esteem. Remove any suggestion of 'learning' and my inmates wanted to learn. Confidence in themselves rose dramatically.

This was all a far cry from my arrival where I had been shown the punishment block housed in the strangely named Rule 43 wing which was on the ground floor. Mayhem abounded, screaming as only women can scream, and at the top of their voices, shouting out abuse so that one Anglo-Saxon word was strung to the next, Doors were constantly banged with whatever object they could get hold of – it was appalling, and very sad. Into the air rose the aroma of warm urine, tobacco smoke and B.O. in equal parts. This was arising from the sub-human practice of slopping out into the sluices, having inhaled the stench in their cells from eight in the evening to seven in the morning.

There were two punishment cells, each containing only one prisoner. These were cells within cells to reduce the level of noise which could rise to the landing above. Some of these screams would start at the entry of one or more cockroaches invading a woman's space and on one occasion a prisoner, terrified of the insects went berserk. That time, the prison officer opened the doors and scooped up the roaches and lined them up suggesting she might like to bet on the winner. This was not the way to form any relationship with the occupant of the cell and her eventual reduction in tariff. The landing above was quieter, for the cells were kept open all day which allowed sweeter, fresh air to flow through the space. It reduced the complaints from these women not in punishment.

As I have described earlier I have never had a warm relationship with rats, mice or cockroaches. Spiders could be added to the list with ease, so the day a mouse popped out of the wall into my jacket sleeve was a day to be mentioned in my diary. I had been interviewing a particularly dangerous prisoner, necessitating being surrounded by prison officers, well-trained, strong staff members there to see I got up to no mischief. The mouse had by this time decided it liked my pocket and I was concerned it might now make a meal of the lining. My colleagues had taken on board what had happened and were updated by me through much grinding of my teeth and a voice fit for the film *Ice cold in Alex*. (when the team were attempting to haul the ambulance up a sand dune). Some officers eventually exited with the prisoner, the rest, out of sight of any witnesses, sought out coats and gloves – gloves for god's sake – being the toughest staff in my team, and proceeded to work through my clothes in a manner which could be described as 'gingerly but frantic'. De-moused, I shook like a leaf, recovered, and dismissed my staff promising myself I must learn how to control such events. There were many mice and many cockroaches and all seemed centred on my office. And, I had to remind myself, I was now a Chief Officer.

It had been a shock to reach this level, for the usual route took sixteen years of steadily climbing the prison service ladder, making grade after grade in turn. That was the way. When my turn for interview had come around, I told my colleagues, I was up for a job as Chief Officer. They were quite rude. 'not a bloody hope Veronica. Bloody waste of time.' So, they were not too pleased when I got the job…. as Chief Officer. It took a time for them to settle down to the fact someone was directing my career and, perhaps it wasn't fair but Veronica was the boss directing their careers, and the boss had to be listened to.

Early life at Risley enabled me to compare conditions, not only in the women's wing but in the men's' wings as well. Curious as to why there was so much rubbish piled up outside the prison under the cell windows, it began to seep into my mystified mind that prisoners were dumping their pots and any other refuse they didn't want, out through the windows at night, to mitigate the smell which otherwise might remain until the morning unlock. No-one appeared to worry about it, but to my Yorkshire eye it was an offence.

I detailed cleaning teams, inside and outside the prison to scrub and polish, to remove all the rubbish piles from the women's windows and allowed them additional time to sluice out in the evening. I needed to bring back some pride and I did it by suggesting to the women, their wing could be much cleaner and tidier than the men's, a simple competitive edge inserted, which was as effective as my ideas for education. The men continued to dump through their windows everything they did not want until the contrast was so great I was summoned to the Governor who asked me to work with the men in the male wings. (not in the cells, of course, but to move over entirely to the male side). He wanted me to improve the living conditions.

This was not for me. Equal opportunities were not yet a factor of our lives, for it could mean a man losing his job and I was not going to be branded by his colleagues as a troubler-maker. Better, I get on with my job which was eternally busy anyway.

As a Chief Officer, I did not have to work at week-ends but I was in charge of all uniformed grades and I had to ensure the twenty to forty prisoner escort movements each day were organised and staffed to keep the Courts running on time. Judges did not like to be kept waiting. This delicate logistical problem was on top of the need to listen to the grouses on pay, duties, leave and accommodation. Prior to leaving for Court appearances, each prisoner on remand had to sign for and collect their belongings, be booked out, leaving the whole operation to reverse itself if they were returned that night to the fold. All this had to be done by hand, no computers of course It created a great deal of paperwork. Nowadays, prisoners can appear by video-link removing many of the demands placed on us; men and women are moved together in secure vans rather than private taxis. All efforts to reduce costs which would include no more bum-biting or jeering navvies for me.

The graph became almost vertical as I learned the job on the job, so to speak. Jumping up another grade but being so busy in the meantime had meant there had been less time to train up to the position, read books on theory, listen to other Chief Officers with care and ask them questions. It made me nervous. I could not afford to make a mistake and the adjudication procedures were either right or wrong; there was nothing in between. Being wrong meant you rattled the Governor who was wholly dependent upon your actions to follow the correct routines, but the prisoners would also be upset when their own private orders of the day went astray. What the hell, you might say, does it matter if they are a bit put out? Well, a happy prisoner is one who is no trouble to you, so you tended to see their own small worlds were kept on an even keel. I was learning. If I was fortunate enough to become Governor grade in the future, I would have that balance between finding the support I needed from my staff, while keeping the lid on the potential furnace which would always fester in any prison.

It *was* a furnace. It is easy to forget when the prisoners are all locked up together, to assume that is the end of the story. But prisoners yearn for freedom as much as any passer-by in the street. They too would like to sit on a beach on holiday, sipping a cold beer and ogling the six-packs walking out of the sea. And sex, the over-riding drive in any healthy woman or man never goes away. It remains in a bitter state of enforced abstinence, growling at an unfair world which manifests itself in sullen outbursts of rage and frustration.

Add to this, the prisoner has to do as she or he is told, non-compliance inevitably meant a punishment cell for them with claustrophobia screaming at their minds. Is it any wonder the lid has to be kept on tightly?

Britain festered in 1981 in the run-up to Christmas. It was the season when Arthur Scargill became leader of the National Union of Mineworkers and Margaret Thatcher rose to the dizzying heights of becoming Britain's most unpopular post-war Prime Minister. It was also, more seriously, a time when the first case of Aids was diagnosed in the country. An instruction, not a benevolent yuletide request, was sent to my desk from Headquarters.

'Veronica, we want you to go over to Thorp Arch with immediate effect. The Governor is on holiday over the Christmas period.'

'Very well Sir. Where is Thorp Arch Sir?'

'Boston. Boston Spa, Veronica. Nice Christmas present for you. Acting Governor. What he did not say was that Christmas was probably the most difficult time of the year to organise and manage. It was known in the Service as a time to get through as soon as possible.

I had no idea where Boston was. On the map, it was clearly sited in Lincolnshire but the instruction had been Boston Spa which eventually turned out to be a large village in West Yorkshire. The prison was built on the banks, almost, of the river Wharfe with a young Offenders facility at one end of the site and an open Prison at the other. (Today it has been much expanded and is a Category B prison). The big issue was that the Governor of the entire prison, the overall boss as it were, had gone on holiday at Christmas. Christmas was the time when all routines came to an end, teaching, which filled the day, ended. Teachers were gone, causing some difficult voids in the weekly staffing charts. How do you fill the day for a healthy if violent youth and keep him occupied? These lads would be moved on to places like Armley once the Courts re-sat; meantime we, or rather I, had to devise ideas to keep the lid on the pressure cooker.

Those who had arranged to send me to Thorp Arch had

also added a written rider, 'Don't do anything silly Veronica.' As if I would? But, it was part of my legal duties to make contact with the prisoners as I had to check each day whether the lunch was acceptable and to ensure that those languishing in the punishment cells were being well-treated. Surprisingly, the men slept through much of the holiday period, for, as New Year approached there came the usual reckoning, the examination of their 'bird', totalling up how many days, months and years they had to go. Some of these calculations brought pleasure; others delivered despair at the seeming endless days to come. It was all feast or famine, a ticking off of the empty days in a cardboard-bound diary.

The Governor, refreshed from his holiday a month later, returned, so I likewise went back to Risley, wiser perhaps and thankful that I could now get back to seeing my charges engaged again in work.

Thankful, I write? Risley held some very dangerous prisoners. Myra Hindley had been here at one time in her sentence. On the other side of the fence were IRA, there were drug barons lording over other prisoners, and the most dangerous of the armed robbers. They were so dangerous a Category A unit was placed inside the Category B site.

There was another snag, perhaps challenge is a better word, to deal with, one which arose every day of the week and one which I would never have given a thought before I entered the Service. I was, I know, naïve, ignorant almost of the association many women made with other women. Of the one hundred and twenty-eight staff under my control, eighty-eight of them were in lesbian relationships. I had to come to terms with the matter quite quickly so I could understand how this acceptance worked inside Risley. The first thing I did was to ensure I always wore a skirt which was like a billboard to the other staff. Officers could be 'husbands' and others were 'wives', some dressed up in trousers to denote their 'gender'. Problems were inevitable as relationships disintegrated into 'divorces' and separations, spats were common and timetables were thrown out when a couple wanted to be off at the same time. Ahhh!

We, as Chief Officers had to lead by example, over-riding these petty arguments by always demonstrating we could do any job inside the prison, and probably do it better. I often showed my ability to take over at a moment's notice, a job abandoned through argument, or sickness, an ability which I think I learned at Ackworth – it is with me today.

Let me assure you, reader, that despite the unusual and high percentage of lesbian relationships, it made no difference, for I retained a very fine force, a dedicated team particularly in the Young Prisoner wing. Such orientation made not the slightest difference when it came to dealing with an issue.

It was in this lighter mood I was advised the Home Secretary, Willie Whitelaw was to make a visit. The Governor put me in charge of organising the day on the Female wing and I read up on the Minister's background which was extensive, and impressive. These were the days when he could make Margaret Thatcher, his boss and Prime Minister, eat out of his hand from which arose her famous maxim, 'Everyone should have a willie'. Willie, as he was affectionately known, was a giant, both physically and in his intellect. It manifested itself in his charm, his calm and his good manners. Somehow, he managed to get what he wanted without raising his voice. His whole demeanour belied the fact he had been a very brave tank officer in the Second World War and awarded the Military Cross. Well dressed, looking every bit the part of the third most powerful man in Government yet well-mannered, he arrived at our Main Gate shadowed by his Private Secretary and a security officer. He had been Secretary of State for Northern Ireland during some of the worst troubles, and he was a marked man, but he managed to maintain his affability with an easy smile while throwing out hundreds of razor sharp questions.

His visit marked a difficult day for me. Working with a full-time medical officer, he had previously asked to check my throat as I had had a persistent niggling cough. He recommended I see a consultant as '…you may have a cyst on your vocal chord.' But as I read the letter he had written out to take with me to see the specialist, I could see two frightening words, *'throat cancer'*. In those days' cancer was a death sentence. There were no cures. Sod's law, of course, for the Home Secretary's visit coincided with my appointment with the Consultant. I had to do both. Of course, Willie Whitelaw was late, such important visitors often were though for no reason I could fathom and, in desperation I had to slink away to find a phone and tell the specialist I would be late. Meanwhile, the fear of the big-C remained while I attempted to answer the flurry of questions.

Eventually, we all waved him off the site and I dashed to my appointment hoping the tremble in my hands was not a sign of something else.

I was told, soon enough into the appointment that I did not have cancer. The relief was tangible and all embracing. Worry had made me paranoid and this expanded to imagining I also had lumps on my breast. This imagination then turned to reality as I was found to have two lumps which were duly removed five days later along with my worries. There was some reasoning behind my concerns, for both my uncle and grandpa had died of throat cancer. I felt better, though restraining myself from kissing the man who also had a smile on his face. It had to have been easier for him giving me this news than the alternative of placing a black cap on his head like a presiding judge in a murder trial.

I left the hospital so light-headed, so ecstatic, I took the wrong road. I found myself on the M6 heading north to Wigan and being unable to turn around, as if that mattered.

The very fact I had seen the prison medical officer was due to Risley having a large hospital wing on the male side of the site. It was staffed with full-time doctors and psychiatrists. One of these doctors commuted on his horse – yes, the four-footed variety – and hitched it up to one of the main gate posts as if he was starring in the *Three Ten to Yuma*. He was one of those medics of times past where the very presence of the man made you feel better – bedside manner we used to call it – so when he was tragically killed on holiday in Scotland on the brink of retiring, it was a disaster for us all. One of the saddest scenes was a forlorn pile of retirement presents piled up on a table uncollected, unwanted, ready for his farewell party (farewell, yes, party, no). Such a loss and such a waste (he was killed in an accident not of his fault) at the very moment he was going to take life a little easier.

Alarms jangled in my ears. A prisoner had activated the fire bell. She was positioned on the far side of a three-sided building containing a courtyard but she was able to see across to the other side to a fire in a cell. The prison officers, however, did not have her vantage point and, abandoning their posts all hurried to the fire which they still could not see, down two sides of the courtyard. They had no idea of the location of the fire as it was just a few yards behind them, much to the mirth of the prisoners when they learned what had happened. It was a lesson in planning for fires and a procedure was put in place so the whole prison was not placed in jeopardy.

It was characteristic of this prison that we never knew from one day to the next what was going to happen. There was always a small crisis which conflicted with the orders for the day. A woman prisoner might slash her legs with broken glass in front of me for no particular reason; another might pretend to be blind – for week after week – until one wondered if she really was blind. The acting could be superb, the ruses more and more plausible though the prisoner who said she was blind, wasn't!

There followed on quickly the case of the great Pepper Order. Norman Lowe, in overall command of Risley was held in great respect by both staff and prisoners with a charm which made one want to do anything he requested. He cruelly suffered from advanced arthritis to such a degree that towards the end of his time with us he had to be driven around various sectors of the prison. He was meticulous in his planning and told the story against himself of a time, soon after decimalisation, having joined the Civil Service. He was working as a civil servant in the prison service food ordering department and had placed an order for 10lbs of white pepper, only to place the decimal point in the wrong place. Hence, his order now stood at 100lbs of white pepper. The market, recognising the large order placed raised the world-wide price of pepper allowing the civil servant, one Mr Lowe, to be congratulated on purchasing his pepper requirements before the massive hike in price. His reputation soared, though he had no idea why. I never found out how long it took to reduce the pepper to a single pot.

Amongst the grimness, the rancid odours and the sheer bloody-mindedness of some of our charges, the country exploded in delight when Charles married Diana. We were determined to make the day as joyous as we could and had agreed plans to install a television in the dining room with lunch as a buffet, just for the day. But, the clue is in the word bloody-mindedness for three of the women were anti-royalist and threatened to cause trouble. It meant everyone had to be locked up in their cells together with their lunch. It was sad to see such bitterness surface, prepared, as they were, to wreck the whole day for everyone else. Such people we had in our care would always take much longer to be won over before they too could be placed on a path of coming to terms with life outside the walls.

CHAPTER NINE
BACK TO STYAL AS A GOVERNOR

There are no exams after Principal Officer. One doesn't apply for promotion; you are called for interview when your performance report recommends you. There came such a day when I was called to Headquarters in London, a request which left me quite nervous. I wanted to do well, I wanted a new job at an improved level and I knew I could hold down anything my masters deemed to throw at me. But, even having the Equal Opportunities Act now making inroads into my glass ceiling, I knew I would struggle to impress against some much more experienced Governors. Nervous was not really the word when, on arrival at Victoria Station I climbed into a taxi.

'Prison Service Headquarters please. I don't think it is far.'

The taxi driver looked back at me through his mirror. He was clearly judging me in some way. Eventually, satisfied, he reached an arm out of his window and opened the opposite door to the one I had entered. 'There you are Miss. No charge.' He pointed at the nearest building. 'Not too far to walk...I hope.' He had the grace to smile and so did I.

Hoping no-one was watching my antics from an office in the building I was headed towards, I marched up to the main entrance shrugging down my new pink suit.

I soon learned there were between twenty and thirty applicants being interviewed though I had no idea for how many jobs. The waiting room had that usual tension, a mix of men idly studying the contents of their wallets, intent on finding some dust in a corner, and those who gazed out of the window as if to determine how many pigeons they could see in one minute. Having counted as many as he could, one of these strolled over to me and studied my new suit with some interest.

'Hullo. Are you on the same caper as me?'

'Well. I don't know what caper you are on.' I replied with a rather asinine retort.

'Governor promotion.' He explained he had had a senior post with ICI but the stress of the job made him look at alternatives. With this sort of quality, I hadn't a chance, but he felt otherwise.

'You'll get it,' he said with great confidence, almost as if he knew the result in advance.

'How on earth do you know that?' Doubt, considerable doubt was writ large on my face. Was I just being chatted up? I was sure the taxi-driver was eating his sandwiches with his colleagues as he retold his story of the day of a woman in a pink suit who.... well you are not going to believe this-.'

'Because you look the part. You look professional. You look as though you know what you are doing. Simple as that.'

I did not believe him but he proved to be absolutely right. I got the promotion along with eight others that day. Returning to work I received a call a few days later from the Regional Director. 'Veronica, we want you to go back to Styal, now you have your new promotion. You know the place.'

On the strength of his words, I had seen a house I liked in Wilmslow and, bypassing the Estate Agent I went in and made an offer. New job, new house. It could not have been better. Naturally, for me, Sod was still keeping tabs on me (maybe you were unaware of this?) but it is not easy to sack or otherwise remove a poorly performing member of staff particularly an out-going Deputy Governor, and it took a year to find a suitable position for him so he could be relocated.

While sorting out this delay, one, strange to me, event took place which was organised by the family – surprise, surprise! It was for my fiftieth birthday and became one of those surreal days with a false gaiety, for none of us save Joan had really made much attempt to contact any other of the family for more years than I care to think. But, it was nice in its way; it was a first step towards a more engaged family. We might never be 'close-knit' but we could take an interest in each other's lives and the progress of children. I returned home, happier, if thoughtful, to learn the Home Secretary, Leon Brittan this time, was to make a visit. His reputation for absorbing facts was legion, so I made a few phone calls to other Governors who I knew had met him in similar circumstances. They soon brought me up to speed with what he might be wanting to know when he arrived.

From the moment this powerfully built, 45-year-old son of Lithuanian Jews (Malcolm Rifkind was a cousin) stepped out of his car, he was ready to go. He was already deeply involved with the Miners' Strike but he managed to maintain his interest as we had coffee together. Then he was off, discarding his security officer and PPS like salt from a mill, throwing out questions whose replies generated even more queries as if he was a many-headed hydra. He roared off alone and found a prisoner working in a greenhouse with whom he spoke, leaving his guard outside simply because he could not get inside as well. Leon Brittan was quite...large. What the Home Secretary did not know was that the prisoner he was in earnest discussion with was Carole Richardson of IRA and Guildford bombing infamy. Carole had been convicted in 1975 and was only seventeen at the time of the trial. At the Court the judge, Mr Justice Donaldson who presided over the proceedings expressed regret that the Guildford Four had not been charged with treason. It was just as well they weren't, for all four would have met the mandatory death sentence in those days. Their convictions were later found to be unsafe. All the greater need for having removed the death sentence from our Courts.

Carole was armed with a spade and a fork, apart from other smaller tools and she could have done him quite a lot of damage but she left him alone to the relief of the security guard. Perhaps with her insight into the future she knew that her conviction was unsafe and she would be released, which she was, but my backbone continued to feel hot until he was returned safely to us. I could not have got into the greenhouse with the Home Secretary blocking the door and no doubt, the security guard would have tried it on before me. It would have made a good cartoon for Matt in the Telegraph.

We went in to lunch which I seemed to remember was fish and chips and strawberries preceded by a sherry, the latter slightly out of place, with a very traditional English meal but it all disappeared down a large hatch, after which we went immediately to a Press Conference in the Staff Rest Room. The subject of the Miners' Strike only took a moment or two to surface leading to discussions which could be described as 'heated,' for the hacks were refusing to listen to his bland replies as they sought headlines which he refused to provide.

Having dealt with the Press, it was a handshake all round, missing no-one before he returned to his car once his security officer had given one of those hard-edged surveillances over the small crowd. His PPS lifted a hand in thanks to me before the car drew away sharply with a spit of gravel. I had learned a great deal that day, which I filed away for future use.

That Christmas, we arranged a carol service for an invited audience which enabled me to put forward my prize singer. She sang a carol, solo without a hint of nervousness, causing more than one tear to roll down a cheek. Most of those sitting there had no idea she was a murderer and, if they had known, it would have astonished them. Mary's Boy Child and child killing could never be reconciled except perhaps, here in Styal where she was serving out her time for killing her two children.

The Governor was to dress up as Father Christmas so he could visit the mothers and babies' unit and hand out presents to the babies. The inmates were concerned that if a Governor was to come calling, albeit in a red jacket and white beard, an inspection might be forthcoming. They rushed as one, to the chimney where they jointly kept their…joints, and various other drugs. Afraid of imminent discovery, they took the lot at one go, so to speak. The effects were rather quick, well, instantaneous is a better word. The prisoners were so spaced out that during Christmas they had no idea the holiday had passed them by and repeatedly questioned why they had missed the big day.

New Year's Eve was no better. It had always placed a strain on the system as Styal could be like a tinder box. The holiday season went by having prisoners kicking their heels each day in utter boredom. With Styal's layout of individual buildings within the grounds, prisoners ran amok outside from block to block, hooting and laughing. Some stayed out until three in the morning, the transgression of which was not entered in the Governor's Journal. Of course, the news leaked out and reached the ears of Area Office. It placed me in a quandary when I was asked my view of the night's events over the telephone by my area boss. I had to remain loyal to my superior governor yet could not deny the reports concerning a riotous New Year's Eve. It proved a difficult time.

This loyalty, having to supervise both staff and prisoners on an equal basis, had to be handled always sensitively. A single mistake can lead to a serious disturbance in any prison. It happened with us. A kind of madness took over one day causing the prisoners to smash everything in sight including their own possessions. It made no sense at all and it still doesn't, and it continues to occur throughout the Service. It was the mob syndrome and it is always terrifying. Logic just flies out of the window leaving prisoners at the end with no possessions of their own and loss of remission to boot.

It made no difference when days were relatively calm, for we had to monitor the leaders who would inevitably rise to the top of the pile to take control of a house. They wielded power, so if they pushed it too far they had to be moved from the prison entirely. A Governor of a neighbouring prison would be approached, at which time I would ask if I could off-load so-and-so and they would usually oblige, and hand one back, for this was two-way traffic and we all had to acknowledge the fact.

One threat which did work in the early days, was to tell a prisoner, who would insist on swimming against the stream, she would have to be moved to Holloway the next day. It usually worked, but if not, off they would go. Moving Rachel to Durham for this same reason brought about an innovative method of restraint, probably not in the manual. Rachel was violent and had injured six nurses in one attack in the high security prison at Rampton. She was known by the doctors for attacking without pre-meditation and with murderous ferocity. The move promised to be a nightmare trip; I could see it in her face. She needed six officers at any one time to restrain her, so we came up with the idea of sitting on her for the entire three hours journey it took to get to Durham. She was unable to move but quite unharmed and we delivered our charge with considerable relief.

At such times, we would take advice from our medical officers who would know the medical history of such women and who became important sources of information for me. I listened to them carefully as they passed on their best views on dealing with unguarded moments which a woman prisoner could seek to exploit with frightening results.

It is the unpredictability of such very sad cases which required me never to relax my guard, not even for a minute. Six nurses at Rampton found that out with a broken arm and hospitalisation for them all. At the time, she needed ten staff to subdue her.

Balanced with such violence was a case of one lifer, a woman who had murdered her husband's 'bit of fluff'. She had been told she had terminal cancer and only six months to live. As a result, she stopped eating and I had to go to see her. Was there anything I could do for her? She replied she would like a Harvey's Bristol Cream. It was not something we stocked in the prison, in fact no alcohol at all was permitted, but, through the medical officers, they managed to prescribe some which brought a fleeting moment of pleasure to her face. I was so concerned for this prisoner I applied for and was granted a Royal Prerogative, the only time I have moved for such a grant and she was released. Before dying, a Bishop confirmed her, causing some resentment among the staff (understandable) but I turned around to them and asked, 'Do we all know the real facts? Who are we to judge such cases? Perhaps you should put yourself in their position sometimes.' This was especially true here, for her husband returned to look after his ex-wife during the last few days of her life.

The importance of the church, in all religions, cannot be over emphasized. Styal had a priest who was particularly strong and he and his church played an vital part in our prisoners' daily lives. There was a priest or celebrant for every denomination, save for Muslims, strangely enough. This was only due to the fact in those days there were few Muslim prisoners and thus no Imam was needed. I am sure these days it is the other way around. Often, stress could be alleviated by the timely intervention of a priest.

Nights could hold as many stresses as in the daytime. I was listening to the police radio one night in the central office when there came an announcement that, for the first time, an escaped prisoner had been shot dead by the police. The bulletin came a few minutes before we received a surprise night visit from the Governor charged with checking us out rather as the banks do with their auditors arriving out of the blue. Stress began to mount as I scrolled through my mind as to what was not in place. I passed on the news I had just heard to a very surprised, and frankly, disbelieving Governor. She dismissed the very idea of a policeman doing such an act. 'You must have heard it wrong,' she said. 'Don't be silly Veronica, this is nineteen seventy-seven, not the nineteenth century.'

I was not going to argue with her, for she still had to inspect the prison. However, after a clean bill of health we returned to my office, where the BBC news, again repeated the death of Billy Hughes. The visiting Governor was now very shocked as everyone else. She believed the police did not do such things. But, let's stand that news item on its head; there is always a different picture to be seen. Hughes was being transported in a taxi and, extraordinarily, he managed to stab one of the accompanying prison officers and injured the other, allowing him to escape. (Hughes had stolen a seven-inch knife from the kitchen). He took a family hostage and over a period of fifty-five hours murdered the family, one by one, keeping the wife to do his chores. It was not, therefore, surprising that, in a moment's lapse by Hughes, a police marksman dispatched him, surely justifying the killing in this case.

Life at Styal was nowhere near as frantic as this episode, but it was never quiet. There was always a surprise, not always violent but requiring urgent action to move swiftly to avert a crisis of one form or another. I was on an overnight sleep-in duty, it was three in the morning when a member of staff ran to my bedroom saying one of the babies in the unit was very ill. I jumped out of bed and ran all the way over to have the baby handed to me by a night patrol officer and I spun on my heel and tore off towards the hospital wing, but, on arrival the baby sadly, died. This was the beginning of December and I felt it my duty to accompany the mother to the funeral of her child, but owing to a blizzard which had blown up from nowhere we were very late in arriving. The mother was quite noisy as she tried to find out where her baby's coffin was located and, seeing no-one, the distraught girl ran to her grandfather's grave where she had asked for her child to be placed alongside. But there was no baby and no coffin; indeed, there was no funeral, for a mistake had been made in issuing the release form to the undertaker necessary because there had had to be an inquest. The troubled girl returned to Styal, causing tension to rise in the prison each day as no news was followed by more of the same. This carried over the Christmas holiday itself, leaving a blot in the air which flowed through the women's dormitories even as we celebrated Christmas. No-one would ever say a baby had died in prison, nor had it, but it took a long while for the stain to disappear with the spring when the form was released and the girl found some sort of peace.

It reminded me of my previous time in Styal when I had been a Principal Officer. I had learned Ruth Ellis had been hanged at Holloway for killing her lover, a racing driver. She was the last woman in Britain to be hanged, the 18th July 1955. The days leading up to her hanging were awful, magnified by the continuous protests going on outside the prison. Inside a prison, you will find a tight community with little penetrating the lives of the inmates. When one of your kind is to be executed, and there is nothing you can do about it, the danger of riot can become extreme. Prison can be like an arsenal. Safe as houses in the right hands until someone comes along armed with a fuse...and a match.

*

As I have described, someone at Headquarters had pulled out my file and begun to read up on how I had coped with my short sojourn at Thorp Arch and, finding nothing untoward to embarrass the Home Office, made the decision to promote me to Governor Grade, at Level 4, the second tier up the ladder. This was the ladder I had been seeking to reach for it led all the way to the top and I knew every rung.

There was a mood about the Service in those days which showed a hardening into something close to militancy led by the Prison Officers Association. Strike action talk which had been unthinkable a few years earlier was now in open discussion.

Trouble boiled to a head when the women Prison Officers at Risley, my old stamping ground, who I all knew well, decided, that with the Governor of the women's sector on sick leave and the Deputy away on secondment, they would stage the first women's Prison Officers strike. Back at Styal, settling in to a Governor's role, I caught the news that Patrick Fitzgerald who was in overall charge of the prison at Risley, was to deal with the strike head-on.

I was at home, undressed and ready for bed when I took a call from Regional Headquarters in Manchester.

'Veronica, pack some sandwiches, buy a pint of milk and come over to Manchester now…on the double. We've got trouble with your women Prison Officers and they are not talking to anyone.'

I frowned. *Your* women Prison Officers? This had to be Mo, a militant officer who had long held grouses about pay and conditions, some of which held some credence. What I knew must be prevented at all costs was to allow the strike spreading to the men on the other side of the prison for there would not have been enough Governors in the country to cover any action if the male officers joined the strike. Leave would have had to be stopped, Governors recalled from where ever they were sunning themselves; minor illnesses would have to be forgotten.

When I turned up at the main gates of Risley, a familiar enough scene normally, it was subtly altered by a group of women gathered outside the entrance. They had been working to rule, but this having failed to make a mark on the Government's policies were to strike the next day. I knew them all, recognising Mo alongside her number two, Angela. With the car parked, I headed through the crowd which parted politely. I did hear a single voice at the back passed to another. 'Bloody hell, we've no chance now she's back. She can find herself round here blind-folded.' This comment was made, I believe, because the strikers strengths lay in the fact there were 120 officers out on strike, mostly toeing the Union's demands, and there would not be enough Governor grades to man the prison. They had not reckoned with Patrick Fitzgerald.

As soon as I arrived I went to see him, having worked together previously. I knew his mettle and abilities. He was busy with a planning chart. 'Ah Veronica. Good to see you so soon. You are going to have to be our ears and eyes at night. If I take the days, there is no-one who knows Risley like you. We will work back to back while we draft in Assistant Governors, and some Administrative staff too. Some of these are still in training but it will be good experience for them. Stand them in good stead for the future. Patrick obviously believed there could be more strikes. How right he was. These trainee governors were following an alternative path to the way I had climbed up the grades. Entrants would take a two-year course at Staff College after which they became Assistant Governors. This was a completely different way from how I had learned the ropes, working in every department in a prison; and then moving around the prisons to get a feel of the differing operations, and Categories of threat. But, this was the manner in which the Service wanted to proceed.

'You are going to need trainee governor grades at night with you to patrol the wing. You are going to have to explain in detail to them what you need and what they have to do. You will find them very co-operative and willing to learn, so you should have no problems in getting them to work for you.

'What about Reception Sir? Women need to be stripped down and given a bath.'

'I've found some women assistants to do that. I'm negotiating some accommodation at the Atomic Energy hostel close-by.'

'No need to bother for me sir. I'll drive back home in the morning, after I sign off to you-'

Paddy stopped me with a hand. 'Thank you, Veronica. You've never questioned my actions once.'

'I know these staff Paddy. They do have genuine grievances – poor conditions, much worse than the men, yet they do the same job. It cannot be fair. That is the area you will have to work on.'

I stopped, thinking I might have gone too far, but Paddy smiled grimly. 'I know. It is not going to be easy. What we do here will be judged right across the prison service, and by the P.O.A.

The Assistant Governor grade staff arrived quickly, so quickly that they had had no time to pack. They were sent out to buy bits and pieces like spare shirts, underwear and toiletries, turning their heads in every direction as they arrived back, as they attempted to gain their bearings. The ratio of staff before the strike had been one and a half prisoners to one member of staff propped up by some admin. support, a high ratio due to the large number of daily Court movements for the remand and bail cases. Each prisoner had to have her breakfast before leaving, so my new team had to be aware of the precise timings of the daily operation. Then, and only then would the prisoners climb into the transport provided, being a taxi most of the time. Luckily, the male wings had always supplied the food for the women so this continued to be delivered on time and avoided any early chance of major problems.

I turned my attention to allocating jobs to the training governors. While the males could not oversee Reception, they could cover the dining room, library visits and the shop, the latter with its tortuous checking of prisoners' credit balances and their spending entitlements. Cleaning was another area but here, surprisingly, the women prisoners helped out. Seeing that we were going to ensure what their rights were, they came up to us and said they would help where ever we needed them. As they knew the system, it was easier for the governors to allocate jobs and sit back and watch. It was almost a war-time camaraderie, a mood hard to find normally in a prison and the co-operation we received helped enormously when the Board of Visitors arrived to see the prisoners were continuing to receive all of their rights and entitlements irrespective of the fact 120 prison officers had removed themselves from the site. And, we had to maintain the flow of visitors; the mothers, fathers, children, boyfriends as well as the solicitors and other legal fraternity; it all had to continue as if nothing was amiss.

The Prison Officers might have been alarmed at the words and threats levelled at them by their shop stewards. Not only did they have to put up with the daily taunts but they were not paid when they were on strike. Some single parent women must have found this intolerable, trying to make ends meet.

Meanwhile, I would have to sign in again in the evening as Paddy was leaving after fifteen very frustrating and stressful hours. I took two Assistant grades to accompany me on my rounds which, they said were helpful to their understanding of the operation. They were there to learn and I had the time to get them up to speed in all sorts of departments with which they had little or no experience. What they were determined to do was to show a united front to the strikers, that they would be there as long as it took to resolve the dispute which was becoming bitter.

My boss was involved in the negotiations which lasted over a period of five days. Meanwhile, I committed myself to seeing the prison would be handed back in a much cleaner condition than when we had arrived...and with the shop sales balancing. In the end, a compromise was struck between the strikers and Headquarters; it had to be, for all involved. Like the Japanese, face had to be saved so each side could say they had achieved what they had set out to do.

The strike was over. It allowed me to go back to Styal, to take up where I had left in such a hurry. I was reminded quite forcefully of Moley, returning home after his trip with Ratty on the river, seeing his paint brushes abandoned as he had fled to the river.

*

Then it was the turn of the two bishops of Liverpool to show they also were concerned. Bishop David Sheppard, the cricketer, representing the Anglican wing, so to speak and Archbishop Derek Warlock on the Roman Catholic team came to call. Such an impression these two men had made on Liverpool that they were immortalised together in a statue on Hope Street. I set up coffee on arrival for them and went down to the main gate adjusting my hat on the way. As our party moved on inside I could see a large sign had been hastily erected over my office door. It read: *God's Office*. Everyone was very excited at entertaining two such well-known celebrities while I was understandably embarrassed, until my two bishops roared with laughter and thought the whole thing very funny. I cannot remember what my Governor had to say on the matter.

After this, it had to be the Hamilton's, the alleged notorious brown envelope MP, the husband and wife team famed later, for pantomime on the stage at Christmas and notoriety in the Press on an almost daily basis. Neil had been making a lot of noise in the more animated newspapers along with his wife Christine, regaling the prison service in general and Styal in particular. What was becoming clear to me was that their comments were based on hearsay and press stories, omitting, or plainly unaware of the truth behind our operation for he had never visited a tough prison such as Styal. It was time to get them educated. With the Governor's permission, I sent them both an invitation to visit, hopefully sooner than later, which they accepted with alacrity. I needed them to understand just how difficult it was to run a prison and what strides we had been making here in Wilmslow.

On their arrival, they proved charming, polite yet firm, believing they had done the research and were in the right in what they had said. But, they were willing to observe and learn and asked to see as much as was possible. They were both beautifully dressed, which was in sharp contrast to the environment into which they now entered, though successfully ignoring the aromas drifting up from the cells. I explained our plans, showed them the difficult side of prison operations, the multitude of van movements, the need to contain the really dangerous prisoners. We visited the hospital wing and answered their questions with as much transparency as was possible. There were frequent nods of a head, a raised eyebrow, a quick smile to a trustee and a number of '...really's?' at the end of an answer. At the completion of the tour, Neil sprung a surprise on me though one I should have expected.

'The Press are anxious to interview us so, if you don't mind, can we go and find them?' I accepted his request though still not having read his mind following his fairly comprehensive visit.

The Pack were there, obviously keyed up to some headline news. Cameras were tilted up, recorders clicked in and Neil straightened his tie.

'Having had a thorough tour of Styal prison and seen the entire operation, I feel I must withdraw my earlier comments which I had applied to Styal. I was speaking from a position of ignorance and my original fears are unfounded. In my opinion this is a sensitively, and well-run establishment, which has a clear, no, a very clear direction for its future. I am willing to learn from my experience.' Neil paused as the Press, nonplussed, peered round from their cameras and Dictaphones, frowning in total unison. This was not the story they wanted to hear, in fact, it wasn't a story even if it was exactly what we needed to overhear. I would forever look up to the Hamiltons who were big enough to admit when they had been wrong and to say so publicly. That takes a lot of backbone. The Press went home writing down smaller headlines and the Governor and I got on with our jobs.

As I said, it was a busy time, always different, always some prisoner or other trying it on. It was 1988, year-end and I always like to remind myself of the year's dramas and humorous events. The pound note went, so did dog licences, so did eggs – that is if you believed Edwina Currie; Colin Pitchfork, murderer, was the first man to be caught by DNA fingerprinting. That was an enormous stride forward in the fight against crime and today, it is an essential tool for the police. Meanwhile, back in January of that year Rowan Atkinson set up Comic Relief. It was probably a time to move on as well.

CHAPTER 10
THORN CROSS – MALES ONLY

It *was* time to move on again, or so my Directors in London believed. They not only considered it necessary but had come to the decision I was ready for a male-only prison. The majority of staff were also male with a sprinkling of female officers. Thorn Cross was an open prison, with no remand prisoners, custom built in 1985 for boys of 15 to 21. The buildings straddle an area on the south side of the River Mersey not far from Warrington. Because it was an open prison there was no over-crowding, the blocks were unthreatening, low-rise, two-storeys in height with very pleasant open spaces in between. There was not a battlement in sight. What astonishes some who like to think that prisoners should be given a very hard time, is that the boys here had carpets in their cells with their own key to their door to prevent pilfering. Outside, they were given everything they could ask for in sporting facilities, trade workshops to learn how to decorate or catering and an interested Governor above me who took an interest in his boys by leading them out for running, football and rugby. He was able to communicate with them at their level. He had one problem however, in that he had, uncharacteristically, almost no inter-personal skills with his staff. At one P.O.A. meeting he became so riled he got up and walked out of his own meeting telling me to 'sort them out'. That was not acceptable to any of the staff and he was replaced by another Governor who turned out no better for he spent a considerable time at Haydock Park race-course conveniently not far north of the prison, leaving me to sort out the day to day running of his prison.

When I am asked, do I prefer looking after men or women, I would say boys, young men as they were. They always had respect for me, were polite and I never had any bother with them. One day when I was addressing a group of them, I over-heard one youth say to another in a stage whisper, 'My, she's class.'

They got up as I entered and stood quite respectfully eyeing me up to see what sort of Governor I would prove. It was not to say they did not become involved with some high jinks. One day they placed a bicycle in the pond with bottles hanging from it as if it was a form of high art but that was just fun. Here, they were away from gang culture and football hooliganism and they showed an interest in being educated. It was a routine, levelled at their disordered lives, and being trained meanwhile in a worthwhile job.

It did have some adverse effects. My brother Gilbert gave me one of his rare telephone calls demanding '….what the bloody hell are you are doing at Thorn Cross?' An old lady had entered his shop in tears saying her grandson, who was at the prison, did not want to come home when released, for Christmas. He had told her he felt safe there.

To maintain the balance between prisoners and staff, as I always wished, I was pleased to find that the staff facilities were also excellent which greatly reduced the number of complaints found in some older prisons. In all this, I provided security but I also demanded no nonsense in exchange. Discipline had to be consistent so they could understand where they were with regard to that red line, and it had to be visible. I had always been very strong on discipline but my heart did soften as I saw my charges often achieve standards they had never even considered at home.

Finding accommodation for the boys on their release was an essential task for us. If housing could be found for them and a job put in place they were far less likely to re-offend.

Today, Thorn Cross, although a closed prison, maintains its very low rate of re-offending which has to be put down, not only to first-class governorship but to the training and facilities provided. It was all about jobs and these could be quite diverse in their nature. One boy loved horses and mucking out stables and a local farmer, I found, recognised the lad's wish to continue when he came out. The farmer sought and obtained permission to take him to the races and from there he was taken on by the farmer on his release. It was one of those many happy ending stories.

The pride and self-esteem of the boys came from the smart uniforms they wore; good quality green cotton shirts and track suits and trainers were provided free. The pride overflowed into their cells which they kept clean, keeping up to the demands of good bed-making; it was run on the lines very close to an army barracks in some ways. Individuality reigned. Each youth was tailored into specialist work of his choosing with many boys learning to cook. The greatest pleasure in the job was to watch them, over the period of four years I was there, to see young boys grow into educated men. So many of these young offenders had never had a pat on the back but, by receiving certificates of passing they were able to show these to their girlfriends, fathers and mothers on visiting days. It made both parents and prisoners immensely proud, sons who were able to take up jobs when they left.

It was nice to get away from work early at last. A quiet evening, feet up, I thought, as I headed towards Wilmslow at the ridiculously early time of six. It was strange, silly almost to see a man walking along the side of the motorway, the M56, something he should not have done but, maybe, he had broken down back towards the turn-off although I had seen no car with winking lights. I got home, and began to think what I was going to have for supper when the phone went. It was work...what else?

'Five of them Miss. Five of them got out.'

'Five!' I had only been gone an hour. 'I'm on my way.'

While I drove, I considered all the options open to me. Five was serious and would not go down well at Headquarters. It was, therefore, a relief to find on arrival back at the prison, without my supper, that four of the five had been recaptured.

'Keep looking,' I said, having put all the necessary actions into place for a missing prisoner. One was certainly a lot better than five, I had to admit but it would still be a mark on my file I would rather not have.

It was eleven that night when I got back into the car, driving up the M56 when I had a thought. The man walking on the side of the road at six. It had to be the same one. I drove on and there he was, still walking. Ahead, I saw a policeman who had stopped a lorry for some rashness or other.

Officer, I'm a prison Governor. One of my prisoners has escaped and I have just seen him. I think he saw me for he's jumped down the bank.'

The policeman turned to the lorry driver. 'F--- off now and don't do it again. Right Miss, which way did he go?' Off he stumbled through the thick grass to find the prisoner too exhausted to go on. It was an easy arrest I was told, although there was a sequel to this episode. When I got in the next morning I learned the police had held the man at arm's length if you understand what I mean. The prisoner had contracted chicken pox and was now covered in spots!

I would imagine his fellow cell-mates found it all very funny.

The problem with such a prison as I was in charge of, is that the prisoners were permitted to go to the gym after their evening meal. If they want to disappear no-one knows until the last roll call of the day, giving them, a head-start on us.

Such an event, if that is the right word, made me think of how we could support the prisoners more, so that the idea of walking out could be reduced. A decision was made to entertain the whole prison with a visit from a celebrity. There was a real purpose behind such a plan. Someone the prisoners could recognise and who they looked up to could be cajoled into giving a talk, understanding why they had gone off the path and giving them hope they could climb back on. Importantly, they could impress upon them how senseless some of their actions had been, what damage, physical and psychological they might have done to householders of a certain age but, they also needed hope for the future.

One visit was, in my opinion, as good as weeks of education. Our choice was Frank Bruno who had grown up in Hammersmith with a Jamaican mother and a Dominican father. It could not have been a better choice, for Frank was at the height of his career and fame, having had a bruising fight the year before with Mike Tyson. Although Frank had lost the bout he was still a mega-star for taking the other heavy-weight boxer on in the first place. He was also a man of great character and charm with his cheerful face often filling the television screens of the time. His value lay in his appeal for even those who were not interested in watching a boxing match.

We had arranged the day through the Prince's Trust, agreeing for Frank to fly in by helicopter. I was detailed to look after him, which raised the first laugh of the day when he climbed out of his transport. He was six feet three inches tall to my five feet five inches; little and large came to mind as I gazed up at our man attempting to shake hands with the giant paw. He was dressed in a rather snappy suit but he wasn't happy.

'Veronica. I've got to get out of this kit. It's killing me. He ran his fingers under the tight collar. I need to be relaxed when I meet the boys. Know what I mean?'

'What, your suit?'

'Suit, shoes, shirt, the lot. Shoes size 14 that is.'

'Hmm. I'll see what I can do.' But where do you find clothes for a giant and just happen to know where a size 14 pair of shoes might be lying about ready to be picked up at a moment's notice? I pulled out a reliable prison officer who was only too pleased to help the famous man.

'There's Geoffrey. He's big. He has big fisherman's boots. Might be a bit muddy though.' The man ran off, leaving Frank and I to discuss the day's arrangements. The news which had been circulated around the prison was electric to the boys. Here was an ultra-famous man in their eyes, a real-life hero.

The officer returned, having dug out an enormous track suit and a large pair of trainers from one of our larger prison officers. A shirt was found which strained the buttons but Frank was ecstatic with the change and wore the clothes for the rest of the day.

The day succeeded brilliantly. It was best described by a fifteen-year-old prisoner who told me '… it's been the happiest day of my life, Miss Bird.'

Frank turned to the boys and, as he delivered his words I could see every lad leaning forward to catch every word. It was as if they were spreading heather honey on fresh bread and they did not want to waste a single drop.

'You don't have to do these things,' lectured Frank in that quiet rumble which started inside his huge torso. 'There are other things to do which are not illegal.' Heads nodded in full agreement. If only we could have such visits like this every week, think of what we might have been able to achieve for these boys?

As he was leaving, now back in his suit, Frank turned to me. 'A word of advice Veronica. Always feed your celebrity first, before he meets his audience. I haven't eaten a thing as my hand was shaken so many times I thought it was going to drop off by itself. Everyone wanted to touch me as if I was Jesus.'

'Next time Frank, I will make sure you have a banquet before you meet my charges, but at least, we made you comfortable for the day. Perhaps you should come in a track suit?'

Frank's rumble was louder. 'Know what I mean Harry.' He touched his nose and sighed, genuinely concerned for the boys who were laughing and joking as they leaned forward to wave him off.

It had been a very different scene on the day I had arrived at Thorn Cross. As I entered the site two boys were slugging it out with bare knuckles until they were finally separated by officers. Two hundred plus alpha males, their testosterone brimming over with unreleased tensions means continual trouble unless they are constantly occupied, which is why we spent so much time in education and training. For the first time, many of these boys were obliged to listen and learn (as opposed to playing truant from school as they had done) and often surprised themselves in the interest they gained from beginning to believe they could excel in a trade.

There is a point here. I know I have repeated myself over the issue of training but these offenders were still very young. If we could get to them even earlier, there was a chance we might never see them in Reception collecting their bundles. With Frank Bruno's bee in a bottle droning in their ears, 'know what I mean Harry' they could relate his freedom to their own in the future.

Step forward yet another Home Secretary, Douglas Hurd, to make a visit. He came, I am sure, because our re-offending rates were dropping to very low figures and he needed to carry the good news to other prisons. It might also be quite useful to find out how we did it. No doubt, he would also be able to advise Cabinet, the Government was doing something right. He clearly approved of the humane conditions and showed his pleasure at the facilities and the prison regime. Especially so, he learned that a group of young trainees were working with a group of handicapped patients every week in the gymnasium. This sort of news does not get into the newspapers nearly enough and he recognised the fact. He called our prison a 'show-piece' as he later described his visit.

Like his predecessors, his intellect often pushed one into silence, yet he hid it behind a façade of school at Eton and Trinity College, Cambridge with an accent from the past which was always reassuring. He would, I think, have placed a firm hand on any tiller he was asked to hold.

Thorn Cross never ceased to amaze me. Prisoners here designed and patented a braille bingo board which has now been sold around the world. In some ways, it was like a school.

I would watch these young lads growing up, their whole lives before them, realising that maybe, there was something in life out there other than pinching cars, fighting or stealing from shops. Some of them could have been my children, naughty children I know, but I wished them well when they left and they would often thank me with awkward words but genuinely delivered.

Thorn Cross was my first job with males. It was an open prison so no hardened criminals. For that, I would have to go to Armley and that was a different ball-game altogether.

CHAPTER 11
ARMLEY – THE HARD ONE

'I've done it!'

'Oh well done. Well done,' Joan said, delighted into the phone. There was genuine happiness in her voice. 'Who is it? What's his name? Where is he from? What-'

'Hang on, hang on.' I cut her off. Crossed wires. 'No Joan, I haven't got married. I've made Governor Three. At Armley.' I let that sink in for a moment. Joan, like the family, had always believed I would go off and marry secretly, and tell them all after the event. She did not understand I had become wedded to the Service years before.

'Oh!' Again, though this was said without quite as much enthusiasm, until realisation of what I had achieved sank in. 'Armley! For God's sake! That's a dangerous place, isn't it?'

Armley was, at the time, one of the biggest prisons in Europe with over a thousand male prisoners confined there, holding many lifers, many fanatics and the like of The Ripper had passed through the enormous and forbidding main gates. There were IRA men there as well, not the most dangerous of those who had been captured, but these ones had tried to blow up Marks and Spencer's with explosives. They were eventually moved on to Durham to give them a fair trial.

I had been told Armley was in a mess, not made any better by the fact I had never visited the prison and had not been able to make my usual brief call before taking up the post. My job as Governor 3 meant I would run the prison under a delightful Governor 1 who was fully engaged in the long-term planning of the Service while ensuring Armley moved forward at the same time. Robin Halward was one of the brightest and youngest Governor 1's in the Service. He was constantly called upon to sit on Committees and consultation meetings despite the fact he was a sick man, but he never let his ill health slow him down. Even when in hospital he would have his papers brought to him so he could continue with whatever he was working upon.

Robin had been asked to set up a team culled from the Prison Service to bid against Private Sector companies for the running of Manchester Prison. This was the first time the public sector had been permitted to bid. (today, there are 14 out of 118 prisons which are private or contracted out).

My job was to ensure the prison ran like clockwork. I was also charged in seeing if the number of suicides could be reduced. To show how serious a problem it was we had several Samaritans who were highly skilled, training up prisoners as *listeners* in shared cells. They would watch and report back any concerns if they suspected a deep depression setting in on a fellow inmate.

One of the first things I did for these special cases, was to install curtains in the windows, place a duvet on the bed while we also provided a kettle to make a cup of tea. Anything to soften the grimness and get these particular people through the worst time of their lives.

Then came the sex offenders wing where all the paedophiles were dropped in together, as much for their protection as anyone else. On an early, first visit, I met a young offender in this wing, the down still on his cheek. He was on remand awaiting trial.

'What on earth are you doing here?' I asked. I had to admit to total astonishment as I could not reconcile this young face with the serious charges levelled against him.

As I spoke, the young man collapsed in tears pleading his innocence. It was a ploy I had heard a thousand times before.

'I didn't do it,' rang in my ears as I walked back down the corridor. That night he did not return, so the judge had obviously seen sufficient evidence to clear his name and sent him home. But, that trauma of those awful weeks would remain with that lad for the rest of his life.

Apart from the sex offenders wing, Armley was divided up into other distinct offence sections. Each of these wings had an Assistant Governor in charge of them all reporting up to me. I found this out on my arrival, having mounted the steps which brought me into a main corridor where I could see the Governors' offices nearby. Ahead, lay a week of induction where I was to meet all my senior officers, so I could sort them out into my strengths and those weaker than the others. There were issues, problems, conflicts and misunderstandings which would all need to be dealt with before I could think of moving forward with my ideas.

My attention was drawn to the hospital wing, an area of great importance. I made it one of my first inspections at which time I recognised a prison officer, a woman from an earlier prison. She also had noticed me and, in so-doing turned to a number of her colleagues grouped in a semi-circle waiting to hear me talk.

'She'll sort you lot out. Just you wait and see.' It was a strange comment from a junior officer and it remained with me until I was debriefing with the Governor, Robin.

'Why do you think she said that?' I asked a trifle crossly. His reply was to suggest I should not take things too personally. 'Just a comment to lighten the mood,' he advised.

But, it was the same member of staff who then came forward a few days later, laying some very serious charges against several prison officers. It became apparent there was some evidence the woman, the whistle-blower, was correct. Only in to the job a few days it still left me with no option, but to suspend four officers and refer the whole matter to the police. As these accusations were serious, the trial was moved to another city to ensure the officers received a fair hearing, unbiased by the location. The case was proved and I lost a good officer in the woman who had to be moved to a prison of her choice to continue her career with all of her moving costs paid. It would have been impossible to keep her on my staff. I also, of course, lost four officers. At the time, I believed I had lost a first-class woman officer though, later, it turned out to be quite the opposite as she was found to be having a corrupt affair with a dangerous prisoner.

This small crisis came with my arrival, a calling card almost and the pressure was never to ease off from then on. But the resolution satisfied Robin I was in control, and he went off on holiday leaving me all alone at the top.

It was a week later. I was commuting to work every week from Wilmslow and I was home at the time, awoken at three in the morning, when the news reached me saying four of my prisoners had escaped.

'Buggar,' was the technical term escaping my lips, still groggy from sleep. It was a label used by all governors when they are up a gum tree. Normally three in the morning was when the Gestapo came to call – normally. At the beginning of the week I had got into the routine of packing a small case for I was living out of hotels until I found a house to live in. Packing was one of the least things I had to worry about; I had to get back to Armley as quickly as possible. It had happened on my watch and my watch had only just begun. I was totally responsible. Responsibility travelled up the ladder until it reaches the top rung. As there was no top rung it stopped one down, that was me, Bird. I opened the back door of my car and bunged in knickers and blouses and roared off still half-dressed making my pink slippers press down hard on the accelerator pedal.

When I arrived, the first thing which held me up was a young policeman.

'You can't park here madam. We have four-'

I cut him off. 'I know officer. I'm the Governor.'

The young officer looked down at my pink slippers which

were just beginning to emerge from inside the car. 'Oh, yes madam.'

I threw my bunch of keys at him – quite hard – 'I'm going in. you park the bloody car where ever you wish.' Now was not the time for niceties.

Inside was chaos. The Duty Officer could not even give me the correct number of missing prisoners. 'Well, is it four, or is it five?' I demanded, appalled that this vital piece of information was not present for me. A mumble followed. He knew an angry Governor when he saw one from four feet away, still in night attire. 'I want a full roll check, NOW!' I slipped into my office and brushed my hair. My bag arrived with some shoes. My Assistant Governors began to report in one by one and gradually I brought Armley back under my control.

'Right, how many are out?'

'Four Miss Bird.' Heads bobbed up and down in unison so it *was* probably four escapees I had to deal with.

'And how the bloody hell did they get out?'

'It's not our fault Ma'am, he said brushing his hair down with a hand, after his disturbed night's sleep. 'They got out through the dormitory ceiling into the roof-space.'

The new wing, still being finished off, was a hospital extension and an education block. 'But, that doesn't explain how they got out. Christ-!' I had to report back to Headquarters on this one. I began to tap my fingers on the top of my desk which was unquestionably not a tune I could recognise. 'Who is out?'

A young Assistant Governor leaped forward with four names, one of whom was extremely dangerous, the other three were run of the mill prisoners not in the same league as the first. Deployments made by the police already were laid out in front of me enabling me to take stock. I was on my own with at least one very bad guy on the run. It was a scary moment for by now the Home Secretary would have been notified. The Press would be next, yelping in full cry.

My assistants left, all now composed and serious, thankful, I think, they could pass the buck to me. I switched on the early morning news to learn I was at that moment in a helicopter hovering high above the prison taking a 'bird's eye view.' That was nice to know. I'm not sure if the reporter had his or her tongue in cheek on this one but I was not in the air, not even outside the prison. Don't believe everything you read in the papers.

As the picture began to come into focus it became more worrying. All four prisoners had been accommodated on the top floor in a dormitory so it had been easy for them to plan their escape. Three of the men, for whatever reason, had not left but climbed up onto a roof, refusing to come down. It might have been a diversion to allow the fourth man to get away. It was certain that the bad man was well away on the run and there were no sightings. He it was who was likely to harm or even kill anyone who stepped unwisely in front of him, with intent to capture. It was time to order in the riot squad and to send trained negotiators to deal with the three still on the slates.

Then a report came onto my desk which I found hard to believe as the news had been widely spread for several hours. Our escapee had been seen walking alongside the M1 and had been given a bottle of milk by a milkman…for God's sake! The excuse, I presume, if I had questioned him was he had got up before the news of the break-out. (but didn't it appear strange that a man was walking up the M1 at that time of the day and had no money to pay for the milk? And why had the milkman stopped anyway?).

The three prisoners were finally talked down at eleven that morning, news which I transmitted on through the Command post I had set up on my arrival which felt like a century earlier. The fourth man, sentenced to fifteen years for armed robbery was not caught for a further two years when, in a smooth targeted response to information received, he was returned to prison having lost his remission.

It meant an enquiry, but first I had to get Robin up to speed. I left a note at his house telling him to contact me before anyone else on his return to the country after his holiday. Meanwhile, we got on with running the prison with one less inmate.

Robin had had no idea of the 'incident 'on his return from France but, good as gold, he rang me as soon as he got in through the door. He was concerned. He had to be, for the escape had sent tremors all the way up to Kenneth Baker, the Home Secretary who, in turn, would be obliged to provide answers in Parliament.

The enquiry threw up many questions mostly directed towards me. My job was on the line but, Robin, bless him, backed me to the hilt. The results of the enquiry showed that the most dangerous of the prisoners had climbed out through the ceiling of a room onto the roof and from there out of a window using knotted sheets, lowering himself until he dropped down to the builders' compound where he was able to make his escape. The others dug the mortar out of some new brickwork and crawled through a hole into a roof space It was all put down to an inadequate budget, *plus ça change*. Importantly though, major changes were made – everything was rethought through from then on. If a knife or a screwdriver went missing, the prison would go into lockdown while everything was turned upside down. If nothing came to light the whole process was repeated.

When such incidents arise, it becomes essential to clear the area around the presumed escape area but in all other aspects, the prison has to continue to function as normal. Other prisoners need to be kept calm to prevent the infection from spreading. With this being my first major incident, I had been able to depend upon a loyal staff which was reflected in the enquiry's final report.

Another small, but satisfying snippet came my way. I learned that when the escape was announced together with the fact it was being controlled by a woman, the Press had stood by for fireworks believing I would not be able to handle the fast-on-going action. This was twenty-five years ago when sexism in all its sad forms still showed its face plastered over the wall on many occasions. I was content to learn that the results had finally filtered back to the editors' desks where they quietly filed the report for a later day. Score one to Veronica.

*

Eighty percent of my time, I was to find, was taken up running the prison myself. Robin was kept extraordinarily engaged by his masters on strategic long-term planning. So it was, I was approached one day by the family of a young man who had committed suicide in my prison. Prior to his arrest, he had tried to kill himself by jumping off a bridge in Leeds, but had failed in his attempt. His parents had insisted on seeing me to assure neither myself nor my staff were to feel any kind of blame. 'He was always going to do it. It was in him all the while.' It was a nice gesture.

Suicide was always deeply upsetting for I felt I had failed in getting inside one of my prisoner's minds. Often, I could feel the trauma, the desperation and, eventually the resolution that death by whatever means available, was the least evil.

Suicide was something I wanted to focus on, to try and understand what it was that drove prisoners to call it a day; to give up once and for all from the sheer hell of each day. Such despair could often find a way round our fifteen-minute monitoring cycle set up for deeply disturbed inmates. The mind of such a person becomes sharpened in its cunning as a calculation was made on what had to be done in the fifteen-minute window before the next inspection through the door glass. Just as babies must never be born in prison, no man or woman should ever die by their own hand during their sentence. We have somehow failed them and society.

As Governor, I was obliged to visit the punishment cells each day to check on prisoners' welfare. From there, I would move on to one particular arrival whose reputation went before him. Charles Bronson had been sent to us to give Wakefield, where he normally resided, a four-week break. Other prisons would help out as well. As he had proved so difficult to contain, he was circulated many times through those prisons which had the facilities and staffing to hold him securely. We had lodged him in the segregation unit.

If the name is familiar think of the American film actor. Charlie had adopted the name, changing it from Peterson. He had been a bare-knuckle boxer, an author and an artist, apart from building up a string of offences for armed robbery – he was already doing seven years for armed robbery by the time he was 22, wounding with intent, false imprisonment and blackmail. Being incarcerated for life, he was nonetheless a successful publicist. Charlie attracted a film producer who made a documentary on his mad, chaotic time in prison. Later, books would be written – in short, a celebrity was beginning to emerge from the character. He became famous as only the cheap magazines can deal with, and in full colour front page stuff, but he was still an extraordinarily dangerous and fearsome celebrity at that. He changed his name again to Charles Salvador in 2014 after the artist he most admired.

Charlie had known the inside of Rampton, Broadmoor and Ashworth, all high-security psychiatric hospitals. He has spent more time in prison than Myra Hindley. And now, here he was with me.

Charlie was quite a character though very unsafe to be close to, despite his demeanour towards me. Each time I sent for him he was accompanied by a considerable number of my burliest officers for he was reputed to carry out two thousand press-ups each day in his cell (he has written a book about exercising in small spaces). I never counted but his sheer bulk was daunting (he was like a bigger version of Jonah Lomo) and the impression he gave me was he was as broad as he was tall. He wasn't especially tall, five feet nine inches in his socks but the sheer menace of the man, some radiant force made him appear much taller than he was.

As I had to visit him daily, I got to know him quite well. He could never be allowed out of his cell with anyone else for fear of him taking another hostage (he already had three charges of kidnapping against him). To speak to him in his cell I was obliged to wait outside and I never got close to him physically. I was flanked by two officers standing on the balls of their feet. Yet, Charlie was ever the gentleman with me. He was calm and collected and never showed his other side, when he could go berserk as '...demons took hold of me.' And he never swore. He was a man of extraordinary contrasts; on the one hand, he had spent forty years in prison. On the other side of the coin he has raised cash for a disabled mugging victim and sells his artwork to help sick children.

We had decided to hold him on the ground floor as we would never have got him down the staircase from one landing above. Instead, he kept his cell spotless, not that there was any furniture inside save his bed. Anything else could have been broken up and used as a weapon. It was thus time-consuming to have him at Armley with the constant fear of hostage-taking but we had to give Wakefield a break from time to time.

One day when his cell was opened as usual to check how he was, he was found covered from head to toe in black shoe polish. They called me down.

'What on earth are you doing Charlie?' the officer asked, mystified.

'These blacks, they get everything they want, when they want, so I thought I would join them. They get more than I do.'

Very funny Charlie.

The idea of covering himself in boot-polish led to smearing himself in Lurpak butter when he attacked twelve guards after hearing Arsenal, who he hates, had won the FA Cup. The butter prevented the officers from grabbing hold of him.

The Press always wanted to write stories about his latest antics, painting him in the blackest light (sorry). But with me, he was a gentleman in both meanings of the word. Charlie represented all that was wrong with the prison system. As he said himself: 'I'm a nice guy but sometimes I lose all my senses and become nasty. That doesn't make me evil, just confused.'

There was no doubt he was extremely dangerous in particular environments or with certain officers. But, I was convinced he could be reached if only there was the time, the money and, above all, the patience to help him. I learned recently he is now contained in a Close Supervision Centre where he could be seen all the time. That is very sad.

Charlie Salvador has set up The Charles Salvador Art Foundation to help promote his art and '...help those in positions *even* less fortunate than his own.' The emphasis is on the word 'even'. I recall a time at my first interview saying almost the identical words.

*

Sometimes, coincidences can be useful. I had determined to reappraise our contingency plans for hostage-taking in the light of our time with Charlie. I had attended a 'Hostage Course' recently and was full of the new ideas safely stored in my head. The current plans were out-of-date and would not work in Armley so I put quite some time into getting a workable document together for my staff to read up and practice. Hostage-taking was always serious, always dangerous and here, it was complicated, due to the layout of our prison and the nature of our prisoners. What helped moving prisoners from one section to another also helped the hostage-taker. It was a Catch-22 situation.

One sunny day, approaching lunch-time, the busiest time of the day with prisoners returning from their places of work, I was told by an officer, 'Miss Bird, we have a hostage incident. Three prisoners have taken another prisoner hostage.' Shock and horror. One of the prisoners had killed previously and was serving life, while the other two were also extremely violent. They were now, enraged, frustrated and dangerous. Threats were being issued.

No testing of the new contingency plans had been carried out which now left me in a serious dilemma. I set up a command suite as soon as I could, while thinking about prisoners being fed, let alone my own staff. My team were the best there were, as they swung into action using both negotiators and an intervention squad while prisoners in the area were transferred out of the scene. Headquarters was updated. One prisoner said he would cut the frightened hostage to pieces if his demands were not met. The aggression in the man was palpable and he had nothing to lose as he was in prison for murder…and to hell with remission if you are that angry so you cannot think straight. There was, and is, an incredibly fine line between getting this right (that is, saving a man's life) and screwing it up completely. We also, as I have described, had to keep the prison calm and operating as if normal.

Robin arrived in the Command Suite and we worked back to back. The incident ran down to a stale-mate, so at five that evening I went home for some sleep and returned at nine to relieve Robin. It became a long, nervous night until Robin entered with the Chief of Police who had been in attendance observing the situation as a last resort provider. We sat down to consider what to do. I pulled out my plans which, after some discussion, were adopted with little change. We moved immediately from the academic to the reality, the latter which was developing worryingly as information was fed back from our team. Time was running out.

A crisis arose eventually as the hostage-taker declared he was not prepared to wait any longer and began to move his knife about as he prepared to move to the next stage of his plan. Without further reflection, Robin sent in the intervention team who were there on stand-by, and in the nick of time rescued the terrified man who had been cut, though not badly. The police had been in attendance as a last resort but my staff were, by now, so well-trained and equipped they did not need the extra support.

This incident (curious term which originally meant 'occasion') ended my first eventful year.

*

We had the inevitable but nonetheless important visit from another Home Secretary, this time Kenneth Clarke. I could measure the Parliaments and the passing years by the Home Secretaries I met and entertained. Without exception, it was not difficult to understand how and why they had been appointed to one of the three highest government's positions of power. Kenneth Clarke was just such a man, reaffirming even with his easy, laid-back persona, his razor-sharp intellect which continued to throw out a non-stop stream of questions. These were not queries listed by his PPS as an aide memoire for his boss but on the spot interrogations based on what he was seeing. He padded along in his ponderous, very unfit (seemingly), fashion, shod in his famous suede shoes and a ready smile. Surprisingly, his reputation had gone before him, so the prisoners he met were well behaved, some even polite. It was easy to understand why he was so popular with the public, well underlined when it came to the buffet lunch we had arranged. He moved along the dishes on the table with his plate piled high. It was a successful visit setting us up for Princess Anne.

You will, hopefully, recall the earlier escape from the half-finished hospital and Education wing. This had now been completed and Anne had agreed in her well-established position as patron of the Butler Trust (forty years) and long-serving Royal member to many prisons, to open the building.

By now, Robin had been promoted to Northern Ireland where he was to serve with distinction as Director-General of the Northern Ireland Prison Service. A new Governor 1 arrived in his place to take overall charge of us. He was, though, quite green when it came to his knowledge of the layouts of the prison complex so I arranged to have a whole series of discreet arrows placed along the route. Royals prefer a loop and do not like to go back on themselves, so it needed careful planning. This Princess was well-informed when it came to prisons and the prison way of life and she was quite willing to throw out awkward questions at awkward times.

An incident occurred that day which endeared me to her, a belief which has not changed in the many times I have had the considerable pleasure of my work coming into contact with her own.

I had learnt that one of my cleaners, not a prisoner, had terminal cancer. She was in the last stages of her life but was determined to attend the event, if only to catch a glimpse of Royalty. Her pale, shaky face hovered in the background press of people, anxious also to be seen. I was unaware her case had been passed on to Princess Anne. Making her way directly to the cleaner, she stopped to chat, taking her time to ease at least, some of the pain from the poor woman. The delight and sheer joy that this unscheduled stop brought was worth every penny. She died a week later but as a happy person leaving me having a large lump in my throat. That such a small effort could bring such pleasure. I was to see it again and again as I began to move into a very different world to Doncaster Road.

It wasn't all a bed of roses that day. Princess Anne and her entourage had been delayed in their arrival for reasons I have forgotten. So late, we had to lock up the prisoners as a result to maintain the absolute routine of the day. When she did arrive, the prisoners had been inside for some time and began to shout out *'comments.'* They started to call out through their doors, which rose to a clamour at one time. One of the more reasonable commentaries which I picked up while standing to one side of the main party 'heavies' was, 'you're a fookin' whore Anne.'

I died, naturally there and then, seeking a black hole deep enough to make Professor Brian Cox happy. But Princess Anne sailed on, deep in conversation, oblivious to the comments as if they had been a murmuration of starlings passing overhead. Later on, one prisoner began to become a real pain, shouting and screaming at the top of his head. Tony made an eye at me.

'Sort him out Veronica.'

How do you sort a prisoner out – big and male – when all of your staff are lining the route or are otherwise engaged on security detail?

I went over to the cell door. 'What do you want, Alan? Can't you see we are busy?'

'No, I can't Miss Bird. I can't see through a fookin' locked door. We need to get out.'

'Tell you what. If you shut up now, I'll give you an extra five minutes on your next visitors. How about that?'

The prisoner subsided into a reasonable state of placidity. He had won and he knew Miss Bird would keep her word. It was how things worked.

The rest of the tour went smoothly. It turned out to be a memorable day. One would have thought it would have been the female staff who would have shown the most enthusiasm but it was to be the men who twittered like those overhead starlings. Morale throughout Armley was lifted for weeks to follow, whether it was staff who rose to the occasion with their professionalism, or the prisoners having the crushing boredom shoved into the background for a few hours. By such incidental and seemingly insignificant events can we change people's lives. By such acts of kindness can the charge by the anti-Royalist brigade be dismissed. There is undoubtedly, gloom and despair in Armley but on that day a light shone brightly in the corridors.

*

As part of the promotion process I was told I would need to go on secondment. It was a wise move by Headquarters to farm out those Governors climbing the ladder, for we all needed to get outside our stone walls and experience how alternative management systems worked, and could work for us. We did live in ivory towers, in an environment which could live with the term, *hot house*. Few influences forced their way into our lives from the parallel universe of the 'free' world. It was not a healthy way to expand our own ideas and Headquarters at Victoria had long recognised this weakness.

'In six months' time, Veronica you will be at the stage in your career whereby you can take the fullest responsibility. So, we are sending you to Yorkshire Health Authority where you will be based. From there, you can choose companies which you believe are looking at the same issues as you. Smoking, drinking, drugs and stress management. Think you are up to it?'

'Yes Sir,' I was able to reply confidently. Six months away from the clamour and stench of prison life had to be good. 'Oh,' continued my advisor, 'and at the end of it all you will be required to write and present a report on your findings.'

Good-oh! 'Comfort zone' and 'right out of' crossed my mind, balancing, to some degree the fresh air and sunlight.

Yorkshire Health Authority opened my eyes wide, though not as you might imagine because of the information I gained which was, nonetheless, of value. What I did find, was that my own particular world of Armley was way ahead of this colossal organisation. I had long ago made up my mind on how to save time and money, remembering the time of removing a tomato from the bag to save a penny.

I worked with senior managers and statisticians and had a deep discussion on those subjects we had listed. It became clear, there were many links between hospitals outside the Service and prisons with these four big problems in all our lives. Smokers, drug takers and alcoholics might steal to exist and end up in Armley. The converse was equally true, for when prisoners came to the end of their sentences, they became a charge again upon the NHS with built-in drugs issues which demanded continuing care.

At the end of what I considered was a satisfactory meeting with top professionals in the Health Service, one of the statisticians thanked me.

'When is the next meeting Veronica? 'Pad and pens were poised, expectantly.

'Er, another?' I had not planned on any more meetings. There was no need. 'I hadn't planned another meeting John.'

'But, we always have meetings. We can't work without meetings.' He was confused, no doubt about it. I smiled, somewhat ruefully with the professional meeting-maker. 'It would be a waste of my, our time, and of office space. Think of the coffee saved. And paper. We would just be repeating ourselves.'

John nodded his head acknowledging the sense in what I had said, but was now in a vacuum, completely out of his depth. No more meetings? Wow!

I returned to my desk to plan out the remaining time. I had been given a list of about two hundred companies which had agreed to work with me on the survey. There was a need to send these out and ask them to return them as quickly as possible, so I could analyse the information and put it down in some sort of coherent order. To be truthful to myself I would have to admit that the size of the form I had designed was somewhat daunting – well, perhaps twenty pages in all. Probably for that reason alone, I did not receive back nearly the number required to make sense of the statistics. The form had been sent out with the title 'Look after your health' for I wanted to find out what the private sector companies were doing about it with their employees. Some bubbled to the surface almost straight away. Fox's Biscuits of Batley and an amazing construction company, Shepherd Construction. They really taught me how it should be done. Fox's had a policy of employing young mothers. Their children were looked after professionally including the school holidays for the older ones and provided a mini-supermarket at discounted prices. Who on earth would want to leave such a job?

But, many companies had not responded at all. So, there was no option but to ring them one by one and go on ringing them until all the questionnaires had been returned. They proved only too happy to answer the questions with my help on the phone…if only to get rid of me and allow me to fill in their form.

At the end of my secondment, came the bit where I had to step outside my comfort zone and present my findings to a panel. One member stared at my returns with slight disbelief.

'How, Miss Bird, did you get so many responses? This is far higher than anyone else has achieved.' I definitely got the feeling he believed I had just made the answers up.

'When I didn't hear back, Sir, from companies which had agreed to be involved, I rang them and, if they still were not there, I rang them again. In the end, they were only too pleased to get me off their back by answering the questions there and then so they could get rid of me, so to speak.'

The Board member's cheek twitched behind his papers. It was the end of my six months in the other world in which I so rarely trod. I learned a great deal; I believe others also learned how we operated and what we were all about. It was good, two-way traffic and the Service was able to hold its head up high at the end of it.

An envelope dropped through my letter box whose back bore the familiar emboss of the portcullis surmounted by a coronet. The letter was jointly signed by Dame Angela Rumbold and Elizabeth Peacock. It invited me to become a member of the Westminster Dining Club. This meant joining a group of four hundred and fifty women all of whom were in influential positions in all walks of life. They met two or three times a year to promote a better understanding of opinions on current issues.

The idea was very nice. The cost was very high, even for one lunch a year but there was a further carrot as it was likely, members would be invited to No.10 Downing Street to meet with the Prime Minister, John Major at the time, and others of influence, who just might be able to help me in the Prison Service. I wrote back, accepting and, realising I was being viewed as a person who had the ability to put a different slant on prisons to other women who almost certainly would not have the slightest idea of what my working life was all about. The promises came good.

Five months later I received an invitation to attend a Reception at 10. Downing Street to meet The Right Honourable John Major.

Walking through that much-photographed door where so many famous people had been before me, I continued up those stairs with its portraits of past Prime Ministers, onto the landing, where I waited until my name was called. To a small, Yorkshire lass from a two-up and two-down in a threadbare dress it was, simply thrilling. I shook hands with my Prime Minister and received his ready smile. Later, I was able to share my love of cricket with him when I was invited to Headingley as a guest of honour at a lunch with Dickie Bird and Michael Parkinson. I remembered Michael from the days when he would call at Fred's shop at lunch-time to buy a piece of fruit and would always stop for a chat, always interested in what I was doing. I found we shared many other interests in sport which had been born in Ackworth school an aeon earlier.

I still wonder where I might have landed up if Fred had not taken me away during that fatal and awful year of 1959. Leaving Downing Street that day, I shook my head wondering if it had all been a dream. Little did I realise I hadn't even scratched the surface of my new life.

*

Soon after I completed my secondment I was sent to London as an evaluator for the Contracts and Competitions Group. There were massive changes afoot in the Service as the Government began to contract out the running of prisons to private companies which led to the reason for my secondment. Familiar names such as Securicor, Sodexo, Group4, Premier and Serco were making their bids to manage Buckley, and my job was to check the required staffing levels these companies were suggesting would be sufficiently safe, and value for money. Their figures along with a great deal of padding, were contained in large, very weighty boxes which were carried in, one by one. (never mind the quality, feel the width). There were ten boxes and an awful lot of paper. To make it worse, each bid described the everyday actions in differing terminology so it became almost impossible to compare handcuffs with handcuffs. For example, one company might call a working area, The Main Gate. Another might describe it as Reception. Both titles, to me, had separate and well-defined tasks; prison officer grades too, did not match present day descriptions. Call *confused.com* perhaps?

G4S decided they did not want to contaminate their staff by bringing in well-trained and experienced Prison Service personnel. By contaminate, I mean they did not wish to take on the militancy of the Prison Officers Association with its bad practices such as sick leave which, at the time was higher in the Service than in any other profession. This, as you might well appreciate, was a recipe for a cock-up. In a prison, it is experience which is an essential ingredient of the jig-saw which makes up a well-run prison – there is no ready alternative to it.

When Buckley opened, on time, staffed by G4S, one prison officer, who had been instructed to carry out a job on the security mesh fence, leant his ladder against it while he went off to get some tools. Four prisoners found it very convenient to use the ladder to escape. 'Red' and 'face' are two words with which this officer, I am sure, would agree were applicable. Compounding the whole farce, the newly trained staff exited the prison en masse to try and catch the prisoners as if the tower of Babel had collapsed around them. This left the prison dangerously unattended. Controllers, therefore, appointed at the time of the awarding of the contract provided great value and sense in bridging the chasm between take-over and being able to run the prison with as much competence as the Prison Service itself. Guess who was appointed to do just that at Buckley?

CHAPTER TWELVE
BUCKLEY HALL – IN CONTROL

Those in charge, those who were experienced in running prisons, knew from the start it would never work. To allow unskilled private companies to run our establishments, built up over many years of learning at Her Majesty's pleasure, was not a sensible idea however much the Government of the day believed they could save from their budget. Thus, it was wisely determined, that control must never be lost entirely, and each prison would have a Controller installed who would monitor the progress of the contract, provide advice and carry out statutory duties which a private prison director did not have the powers to execute.

As a Controller, newly appointed, I was to be the eyes and ears for the Prison Service reporting through to London Headquarters. A spy in the camp you might well think, but it was impossible to allow handovers to private control without some form of supervision or, at the very least, experienced advice being close at hand. It had been agreed that a Director of a prison would not have the full powers as could be found with a Prison Governor.

Buckley Hall was the third private prison in Britain. Normally, it took twenty years to plan build and open a prison – I have no idea why – but here, they knocked down an old prison and built a new one on the same site, pre-fab in style, in ten months. It was a near thing for Michael Howard, the Home Secretary in 1994 as he had informed Parliament that he was going to have Buckley opened for Christmas. He forgot, or was quite unaware of the clause, 'Inclement weather' in the contract and slippage on the end date loomed as the weather never ceased to stop raining. Nervous, the powers that were, sent me down to the site to see why everything was getting bogged down…. only for me to find that everything *was* becoming bogged down. I was acutely aware of Mr Howard's eyes boring into my back. Provided with a hard hat, Hi-Viz jacket and gumboots several sizes too large, they enabled me to stride off across the site to find out for myself what the real problems were, which, I hoped, would allow me to send a positive report back to those waiting for an optimistic reply.

The problem lay in the unarguable fact the site was waterlogged – unarguably. I could and did report back this detail but did not add the rider I had become stuck in the mud. I mean, stuck. Immovable. Bonded to the earth. It was embarrassing or perhaps excruciating, for eventually I had to be hauled out vertically from the mire, mud dripping from my heels, by two large navvies who, gleefully, returned me to terra firma amply aided by their sniggers. There had been a suggestion, unkindly, that a crane should be used but, in the end, that was not found to be necessary. I did not go back to fetch my gumboots which remained forlornly in the mud like two of Titanic's funnels sinking into a brown Atlantic.

We brought in nine trustees to help with the final kitting out and who were then able to move in as the holiday arrived. It permitted the Home Secretary to report back to Parliament, he had kept his word. A small irony there for it had been the co-operation of the prisoners which had made it all possible.

It was very soon after I moved in as Controller to Buckley that I was approached by a prisoner who I had never seen before.

'Good morning Miss Bird. Do you remember me?'

'No, I don't think so.' I didn't think, I was sure.

'Well, I remember you, very well.'

I wracked my brains, trying to recall his face. Most of my memories were of women's' faces. 'Sorry.' I shook my head.

'My Ma told me all about you. You used to push me about in my pram around the yard. You fed me. I was born at Styal, in the hospital. Ma is Elsie.'

Dawning arose. This fully-grown prisoner who I had bathed and fed as a tiny baby had completed a full circle. Now *he* was in prison, an adult, reminding me of all the years in between. He was one of the prisoners at Buckley who looked after the carpark and gardens and attempted to use this relationship later when he was a few days away from completing his sentence. He wanted to be with his mates on the last days, not trimming grass and cutting edges.

'All my tools, Miss Bird. Some buggar.…. begging your pardon ma'am, has stolen them all. I will have to stay inside won't I?'

I eyed him balefully, but, having no tools in sight, I let him go and began an investigation into the loss. It wasn't until after he had left, that I was told he had got rid of them himself. It did not surprise me. Many prisoners could be very devious and cunning to suit themselves just to make their lives a trifle more bearable. And how sad was it, the man had continued the life of crime which his mother before him had led him into?

Although I was not running Buckley as a Governor, I could feel the mood in the prison was beginning to change, and it was not for the better despite it being a new facility. Yes, G4S was, slowly finding its feet, as the staff came to terms with the routines of the day which were essential, but there was no doubt about the tense atmosphere which was one notch away from a riot. From my experience, I could feel the mood rising. The rumour mill reached out to London.

One night when I was clearing my desk for the night, the Area Manager for the North-West walked in unannounced. It was nine in the evening.

'I want to carry out a full inspection Veronica. Now if you please.'

As we proceeded down corridors at a pace to begin with, my Area boss would suddenly stop as he met any staff he saw. He would ask them the same question.

'What is the name of the Director, when did you last see him and what is the name of the Deputy Director?' He was met with blank stares and mumbles.

'But, you know who this is?' He jabbed a finger me.

'Oh, yes Sir. It's Miss Bird.' While I liked the answer, our man apparently, did not. He pursed his lips which, by the end of the tour ended in a thin line. Deeply concerned we left the prison.

'I'll be here tomorrow Veronica. Set up a meeting for 7.30 with these particular members staff.' He handed me a list of senior staff he needed to see in the morning. That includes the Director and his deputy... whatever their names are,' he added. And with that, he left.

The next day, the assembled staff were as tense as the prisoners had been. He moved quickly into gear.

'This place is filthy. You,' he turned to the senior staff, 'are contracted to ensure it is kept clean. You are failing in your duty. You are contracted to provide work. You are not. Have you any idea how dangerous it is, not to provide our inmates with work. Idle hands and all that. Do you really think you can keep the lid on this volcano by not providing work?'

One of the staff attempted to interrupt but the Area boss was in full flow. 'You are contracted to keep prisoners unlocked for specific periods of the day. You are not doing so. Provide work for prisoners.... you are not doing so. I suggest we start with the basics and move up from there. Then our felons inside can complete their terms as humanely as possible. Listen...and learn.' He turned to me. 'You are going to have to get into this one Veronica. We cannot leave it like this. Find some work for them and apply some of your Yorkshire cleaning and get the place clean.'

Saying that to a Yorkshire lass is like giving ice cream to a child. 'Yes Sir.'

The news got out to the prisoners. G4S (now reverted to HM Prison Service) found them work and the prison began to shine again. You might believe my Area Manager had been too hard on what was a brand-new prison, still finding its way. But Buckley was not a low category site. It held a criminal who I found more dangerous, more scary than any others I have met before or since I entered the Service. While the private companies began to understand, and comply with their contracts, and grew professional in their conduct, it took longer for them to understand the mind of the very dangerous criminal. And such a man was being looked after by them.

This man had kidnapped several women, hiding them in the boot of his car. Arrested, tried and sentenced, he never admitted his crimes nor showed any remorse. As Controller, it was one of my jobs to approve any home leave. With this challenge to my authority, I could find no circumstances in which I could grant him his leave.

As he came to the end of his full sentence, having had no reduction whatsoever, I took an enormous, but justified risk (in my opinion). I sent him out with a Prison Officer to have a cup of coffee in town to begin his readjustment into the real world. It was not a success, but not for the reason I had thought. He simply could not stand the noise and bustle around him in the café. Even the clamour of cups and the constant twitter of coffee talk irritated him and they left, the Prison Officer getting him back safely to his cell. It was curious, for prison life is full of noise; it must be his ear was attuned to one set of noises only. Anything else was alien and thus disruptive to him.

I had to try again and found a hostel willing to take him on and, with his release he finally found a real life. The end of this story is more upsetting. One day, acting as a good citizen, he went to the aid of a man being attacked in the street and was killed for his efforts. Before this tragic event, I had received a card from him, thanking me for trusting him. It is a bizarre world we live in. Sometimes things just don't seem to add up.

*

I have described the regular visits of government Ministers, all of them meeting the benchmark of high intelligence and an interest of getting under the skin of their appointed job.

At Buckley, we had another, a Prisons' Minister and a woman to boot, my first as a visitor.

Buckley had had a series of issues as it settled down; fires, fighting and escapes all were logged into the record. The idea of contracting out the management and day to day running of Her Majesty's prisons was beginning to attract a great deal of publicity and Ann Widdecombe needed to find out why these problems kept coming across her desk.

She arrived with Liz Lynn the MP for Rochdale which fell within her constituency. As a member of Parliament, she was one who did not agree with the contracting out of prisons. I gave the two of them the statutory coffee and biscuits before the tour and briefed them on what I saw were the main issues.

Ann Widdecombe appeared nervous – this was only the third or fourth prison she had visited, and I had been advised by the Director-General, this was new territory to her. He advised me it would be my responsibility to get her moving on the tour as she would not move until she was led.

As we progressed she wanted to know just how prisoners had escaped over a fence, climbed up onto the hospital wing from where it was a simple matter to raid the drugs cupboards. The Director of the private company was hard put to answer the barrage of questions (I don't think he had got up to speed with one his most important properties he was charged with managing) so I had to fill in the gaps.

It was later, during our rounds when I had been freed from attending, needing to sort out some important papers, a prisoner rushed into my office. 'Miss Bird! That Minister of yours, and the MP, Liz something or other. They're having a punch-up!'

'A punch-up? What do you mean, a punch-up?' Prisoners were prone to hyperbole and this sounded like one of those moments. I still felt I should go and investigate, which I did, but it turned out, the two women had been having, what is called in government circles, *a robust argument* on principle which, I was assured on my return, was resolved.

Ann Widdecombe quickly expanded into her role, no more nerves, visiting every prison in the country and not all by prior arrangement, especially when she believed something was far from the actualité. It was a sign of the strength of character of the lady. At one establishment, she arrived demanding to see the governor, only to be asked by the gate-keeper, 'Who are you?' To which Ann Widdecombe did not provide a sufficiently strong enough reason. Calmly yet probably forcefully, the Minister for Prisons told the man to pass on her message to his Governor, 'if he was there,' to be told she should wait in her car until the message had been relayed. Not unexpectantly for the Minister, the Governor emerged from his place of work, at the double, hastily patting his hair in place and straightening his tie.

Ann Widdecombe was always supportive of the prison staff she met. She was well aware, as a government Minister, of the tightness on funding – and we never had enough – but always showed her concerns and understanding of the difficulties we all underwent on a daily basis. She remembered me when I received my award, sending me a congratulatory letter which I appreciated very much.

We finished that year with a big surprise for the staff. They had been arranging a charity event which was to be held in the Visitors' Hall. Some sort of main attraction was needed to pull it all together and, as luck would have it, it was one of our prisoners who succeeded beyond anything the staff could arrange. This prisoner had contact with Manchester United Football team; what the connection was I was never able to find out and I felt it was better that I did not enquire.

David Beckham and Paul Scholes, I remember well, but the whole team came, giving of their time along with a signed ball and shirts to auction. It was odd in its way, seeing these super-star footballers mixing cheerfully with tough prison officers in the middle of a hall designed for prisoners to meet their families. I imagine the anonymous prisoner who had arranged the entire event had a few relaxations and additional benefits provided for some time.

It does show there are kindnesses shown on both sides of the fence. It never ceases to amaze me that although prisons are collecting centres for those of us who ignore the laws of the land, or are just incapable of keeping their feelings in check, there is an inner goodness inside many of these wretched prison dwellers, which needs us to re-examine the whole principle of locking up.

CHAPTER THIRTEEN
BROCKHILL – A BASKET CASE

I had now been in the Prison Service for thirty years. I have no idea where the time went as I spent days, years, dealing with hardened criminals and those, who patently should never have been sent inside in the first place. My reputation for never having to raise my voice, 'always speak quietly to them,' was advice I constantly doled out to my staff.

'If you treat them with respect, you will get respect in return,' I would propose, and it usually worked. My philosophy of never wanting to know why a particular prisoner was incarcerated in my prison, continued.

Maybe it was that reputation for keeping calm, to ensure that peace reigned, had worked its way up to Headquarters?

I was asked to go and visit a prison in Hull with a view to taking it over. I made a trip down to Wolds prison, made an inspection and arrived home ready for the weekend to learn, '…. there's something far more pressing Veronica. Brockhill. Do you know it?'

'Brockhill?' for God's sake, everyone in the Service knew of Brockhill! It had previously been a male only prison though now for females. Brockhill was in Worcestershire, a pretty county with nice countryside, but a dreadful prison. What I did know about it was the layout was similar to Pucklechurch, but there, the comparisons ended. I cleared my throat and managed to reply. 'Er, yes. I've heard of it. I'm going on holiday tomorrow Sir. Let me think about it while I am away.' I assumed, correctly as it turned out, he wanted me to go to Brockhill. He would not have raised it otherwise.... but Brockhill!

There was no doubting the frustration in my Superior's voice but there was little he could do about it. He knew I had to feel comfortable if I was to accept the post, taking on the worst prison for women in the country.

So, I went on holiday but was unable to get away from the long arms of the Service, for I received three more calls asking if I had made up my mind.... yet!

'Have you been able to visit?' They knew I hadn't, as I was still on leave.

'It's a mess, Veronica, a right mess,' was the nearest expletive I could put down here on paper.

Brockhill was a failed prison. There had been no money to improve its infrastructure, no maintenance on the buildings. The place looked abandoned and I was to learn quickly, staff morale was at rock-bottom. It consisted of a mixture of buildings, all poor in design, materials and construction. Newer cells had lavatories and hand basins in the cells. Quite a mixture of the old and the very new. When I got back from leave, something struck me straight away. Brockhill had nowhere to go but up. I would be working with a women's population again which had always proved worthwhile, and I had bags of experience in dealing with female issues.

I was in. I made up my own mind on the matter. I rang up and confirmed a start date. Sir David, later Lord Ramsbotham (Chief Inspector of Prisons) made comment to me, '.... it's well past its sell-by date. Just hold on to it tight Veronica for a year, then we will find something better for you.'

'But Sir, I'd like to have a proper go at it. Give me a year and I'll turn it around.'

Sir David studied me as if I needed to lie down quietly with a cold compress on my forehead. He almost said but didn't, 'there, there,' but instead he replied with a shake of his head. 'There's no more money for this one Veronica. It's just a holding situation.'

This got my back up. Was such a facility all I was worth? Now, I'm a quiet sort of person up to a limit. I learnt my place in life a long time ago but I also knew what I could do, what I was capable of and I was certain I could do the job, with or without funding. All at once, ideas began to burst into my head and I wanted to get on and show him what I was made of.

'Give me chance Sir. I'll turn it around in the year, I promise.'

A long, pregnant pause ensued. 'Well, I'm impressed with your belief. Alright, you've got your year but I have to tell you no-one has ever turned around a prison in such a state before. Certainly not in a year. And Brockhill!'

'Quite so, Sir.' I clamped my lips together and smiled to reassure him.

It turned out it was a lot worse than I imagined it was. My heart sank when I saw three hundred women prisoners who were all wearing men's' pyjamas at night and track suits, too large for them, in the day. Brockhill had previously been a male prison and all that had been done for its conversion to women only, was to remove the men and replace them with female versions. Everything else had remained.

The walls had been painted in dark-green, Hollybush I believe it is termed, tiles were missing and floors were clogged with heavy dirty wax from years of application. Underneath the grime was a modern prison subsumed under a lack of care and an absence of communication between the previous Governor and his staff, for he had had no experience of working with women. As I viewed the depressing scene, it was indeed a low mark in my life but I had made my bed and I had to lie on it.

But, I had experience of working with women, I countered, lifting my head and recognising my experience. I brightened for the first time since arriving. I had to start somewhere, so I began with the Young Offenders, those aged fifteen to twenty-one years old. Eighty-two percent of our inmates were under twenty-seven years old, a difficult age group to control.

We had some spare cash in the books with which we bought duvets and curtains and we bought in enough paint so we could lose the green mire which dominated everything. I begged the use of a powerful steam cleaner from the male prison next door which, eventually and after much effort cut through the blackened surface to expose the original wood floor in all its glory. The dining room simply sparkled as light began to pour into the gloomy corridors transforming the prison into a much more acceptable place to last out one's sentence. Lastly, importantly for the women, I put them all in clean clothes magnificently provided by the W.I. Now, they looked like women, rather than pantomime clowns in trousers too big for them. To paraphrase those immortal words, 'one small step for man, one giant leap for Brockhill.'

Another issue was to find work. Prisoners had been spending their time on the landings with nothing to do all day. With a clean dining room, they were able to move back in to eat rather than, as before, take their meals in their equally dirty cells. The women found jobs laying up the tables, washing up in the kitchen and getting involved in all the activities which the spanking new room demanded. They could mix and chat, occupied, forgetting the deadly boredom of the previous regime. Morale rose.

What was equally fundamental, was to ensure my staff could see there was effort being put into their lives as well. I created what I called a rest room, stuck a television in so they had something to watch while they ate their lunch. Before this, staff had hunched up on a landing with a cup of coffee. This really had been a ridiculous state of affairs and I could well understand why morale had been so low. Nor was it necessary: brains were not needed to see what was wrong and then to right it…. quickly.

Next, I looked at improving the education facilities, upgrading health care and very soon the Category B prisoners began to take a pride in themselves. This was heightened when the W.I. again, brought along nighties and more clothing. We had not only removed the strait jacket of the uniform but brought a personal care into their lives which, converted, turned into a large number of smiles. The women began to look like women again, and they knew it.

The Chief Inspector was due for an interim visit having heard how we were doing. I decided it would be nice if we filled up all the dead planters in the front, colour to brighten his arrival which we did with bought in flowering plants. The next morning, we found that the bloody rabbits had eaten every one of them and we hadn't even had a chance of taking a pot-shot at them for jugged hare.

It was a warming note to see morale rise, particularly as I knew that the staff were more male in numbers than female. This had come about as it had been a male prison earlier in its life and staff had stayed on. Without my staff, I might have stumbled in front of the man to whom I had made a rather rash promise. Instead, I could report we had no need for more funds and the threat of a major disturbance disappeared below the horizon.

One year in, I attended a Prison Service Conference at which the Director-General addressed us all from the platform.

'Why is it,' he asked, his eyes boring into our heads, that Veronica here, can turn around one of the worst, if not the worst prison in the country in just one year and you need three to four years, plus,' he looked at me for a moment and smiled, 'plus, you always ask for a wodge of cash at the same time? She didn't claim a penny.'

He continued. 'I have rarely visited an establishment where the relationships between staff and prisoners are so self-evidently healthy.' He grunted to himself in agreement with his own words.

Now it was my turn to feel the eyes boring into the back of my head. There was bound to be some resentment at the big boss having singled me out for praise. It would make their own tasks that much more difficult, and I am sure some of their issues were intractable. But, as the saying goes,' it isn't rocket science,' it is simply using whatever resources you can grab hold of, and then leading your troops together into the fray.

We started up a 'listener' service to watch for potential suicides and my own interest in the subject enabled me to attend a Conference on *'Suicide in prisons'*. I managed to take with me two redbands, trustee prisoners. At the bar, the night before the Conference began, I bought them both a couple of drinks which went down very well and they reciprocated with money they had been given. This was their first taste of freedom and it *did* taste good, I could see it on their faces. Their first comment, however, on entering the hotel was to enthuse about feeling carpet beneath their feet again....and proper cutlery. Two things in life we take for granted without a thought. It is much harder working your sentence than some may think, when you are outside the walls drinking a gin and tonic in the evening sun with your bare feet pushed into a grassy lawn.

Helping my staff to enjoy better facilities and conditions paid off in a most unexpected way. I had been involved some years earlier to help and advise on nominations for the Butler Trust. The issues had boiled down to one big problem. One of my Prison Officers' key tasks in Brockhill had always been to take prisoners to Court each day. They had not considered instead, of checking first to see how many staff were needed to man the prison and go on from there. This was changed quickly allowing my officers to have a much more ordered life around which they could build their family life.

Happy again, they turned their attention to, of all people, me.

RA Butler the reforming Home Secretary from the late fifties and early Sixties had given his name to a new Trust, which, every year recognised the outstanding work of Prison Officers. It had, over the years become the most prestigious set of awards in the country and was held annually, headed, naturally, by Princess Anne the patron. It later become my job to help arrange the Award ceremony and to lead winners to their seats and tell them to be ready to go forward when asked.

There is always huge anticipation in the audience, for prisoners as well as staff can nominate the winners. Usually, about three hundred and fifty staff are put up for the awards with ten of these winning one or other of these honours and a further twenty would be commended. The ceremony was normally held at Buckingham Palace or St. James' Palace depending on the availability of the room. There's excitement and evident pride. This was the best day of the year for the Prison Service.

Imagine, therefore, my own surprise when in Millennium year, undoubtedly as a present from my loyal staff at Brockhill, I received notification I had been awarded the Butler's Trust, the first Governor to do so. I learnt my own secretary had organised the application with another member of staff.

This was a day of happiness. The award was presented to me by the Princess Royal in Buckingham Palace surrounded by more gold cherubs and red carpet than the Oscars could dream of. A splendid lunch with the feel of crisp damask, cut glass and silver came with a printed menu in French, of some elegance. So much so, I was clutching the menu tightly as I left the Palace and walked across the forecourt to the main entrance. Seeing me leaving, dressed to the nines, (the hat gives it away I think), I was approached by an American who must have realised I had been at the Award ceremony. I showed him my menu.

'Say, Ma'am, I'll give you two hundred dollars for that little 'ole menu.' I shook my head.

'Guess I could go to two hundred of your English pounds' sterling.'

I shook my head again.' Not for a thousand pounds.' But I did allow him to take photographs which drew a gaggle of Japanese tourists anxious to know why there was such a commotion around 'liddle 'ole me'.

What would George Bird think of his daughter now, I wondered?

My staff were equally delighted. Together we had turned Brockhill from a basket case into a model prison.

My work in the Butler Trust did not end with me winning one of the awards. I became, as the airlines would declare, a frequent flyer to the Palace, allowing me to get to know my way round inside the furlongs of corridors until I could confidently tell arrivals where the royal loo was. This was more important than you might think, for nerves were often stretched to breaking point and a lavatory became paramount in the lives of some award winners.

The Committee was like a well-oiled machine, for we had enormous support from two stalwarts in the shapes of Terry Waite and Trevor Brooking. Terry was another giant who towered over me. His always, calm voice, belied the terrible time when he had known what it was to have been locked up in a black hole in Beirut. But the Lebanon was a far, far different prison to one we could offer. I simply could not imagine, even with my experience, how he had sustained himself in the long darkness and kept his mind from falling off a cliff. He and Trevor between them, with their abilities, ensured the Butler Trust Awards built, year on year to the ceremony it is today.

On my return, it was to find an 83-year-old woman had arrived, sentenced for non-payment of the now, disastrous and ill-thought out Poll Tax which finally caused Margaret Thatcher to lose office.

It had become fashionable, with some scattier people, to prefer jail to paying the tax and in this case the judge had decided it should be prison no matter what age she was. The lady in question only stayed with us one night as a good citizen paid for her fine and she emerged from the prison gates to a waiting Press. Asked what the food had been like inside she smiled. 'Well, I've never had pizza before and I must say I found it rather nice.'

Somehow there has to be room for flexibility whereby a judge can stand back from the idiocy of such sentencing and say, 'Don't do it again Mabel,' rather than waste Her Majesty's time and money on such a case.

*

When I left Brockhill in 2000, my staff gathered around me to say goodbye. They told me in no uncertain terms, '…don't give all of your life to New Hall as you did here. Get out and enjoy life.'

The truth of it is, that life flashes by at such a rate, one only has to blink one's eyes and there is a new job to come to terms with, a new promotion to celebrate (Governor 2), being dangled, new ideas needing more changes. Fast it was and faster it became. I was happy and content with my life albeit one that challenged the accepted norm of a family, children, weekends together and building sandcastles on some beach in August. In the end, every one of us must do what we want to get the most out of life.

Almost repeating word for word, a previous request, my Area Manager commanded me one day to, 'Get up to New Hall, Veronica. Sort that bloody lot out. It's a bloody mess'… and a lot more like that. Happy he wasn't. Now where had I heard that before?

The idea of going back to Yorkshire was a nice one. Retirement was only a couple of years away and I had every intention of remaining in the county after I departed the Service. As I liked to do before I took a job, I travelled up to Wakefield to suss the prison out, a long journey but I knew it would be worth it so my mind could be settled as to how I could tackle the job. There was a need to list the problems before my arrival.

On that day, I found some of the staff outside the prison boundary (ah, 'bloody mess', I see), shoulders hunched, hands in pockets whereupon they proceeded to tell me that Prison Officers were taking industrial action across the country. I had no option but to turn around and drive all the way back. I could not get into the prison. Back in Brockhill I heard from a colleague the prisoners at Newhall had gone without their breakfast (a very dangerous situation to allow). Luckily, experienced prison officers recognised the danger signs and went back in to provide breakfast, rather later than normal, but putting the lid back on the pressure cooker. By lunch the action was over and, for the second time my car took me back, the now familiar route. I was starting a job without having made that first inspection; I had no brief to guide me.

It was one thing to be promoted to Governor 2, a level at which I was fully in charge of the prison so, no-one sat above me who I could talk to and seek experienced advice. Being unmarried and with not even a partner to toss out issues at night, it was a bigger leap than normal. As I steered my way north, news had been passed on to me that, this time, the young Offenders at New Hall had begun to riot in their wing, smashing their furniture and destroying anything which could be removed. 'Déjà vu', 'seen it all before' and 'so what's new?' might have passed through my mind if I had had time to think. Instead, I rushed to Command Control which, the Deputy Governor, with foresight had seen fit to set up in my absence, and grabbed the reins. By lunchtime, (again) all was back to normal though the young female Turks in their cells were now bereft of their desks and chairs. My new staff went, thankfully, off to lunch leaving me at my desk to munch a sandwich. I had hardly had time to pull a biro from my bag when a member of staff popped her head round the door.

'Baptism of fire today Miss Bird.'

'Well it's all over now,' I replied with a small grin.

'I don't think so ma'am.'

'What do you mean?'

'Sorry, a prisoner is giving birth in her-'

'Woah. Do you mean *in* her cell?'

'Yes ma'am.'

I grabbed my keys and called for a nurse who had no midwifery experience, but was at least, a pair of hands, then I called for an ambulance.

'The head has begun to appear ma'am. Thought you should know.' I was told by a breathless officer at the scene. It was pure luck the ambulance arrived quickly. Mother and child were whisked off to hospital, thus removing the stigma of a child being born in my prison which would have been on my first day!

Day One ended and we were in the first year of a new Millennium.

New Hall lies in the village of Flockton near Wakefield and holds 446 women. Originally, in 1933 it had been built as the first open prison for men as an experiment to see how the Service could deal with prisoners coming to the end of their sentences in nearby Wakefield. In 1987, it was converted to hold women as a closed category facility and had dormitories installed inside Nissan huts. The washrooms, showers only, were communal and provided no privacy. When the new cell blocks came along they were luxurious in comparison with in-cell toilet and wash basin. Quite a step in the right direction.

By the time I arrived on the scene, parts of the prison had had its services contracted out to private companies. This included the all-important canteen which supplied tobacco, sweets, stamps and biscuits. It had to be kept fully stocked as it was only three days before Christmas. As you can imagine, these were essential for many mothers – there was a mother and baby unit – wanting to give their visiting children presents in the form of some chocolate. Mischief came to call; chocolate had run out, tension rising fast.

On top of mischief was Mr. Sod; remember him? Because I had worked every Christmas Day since I joined the Service, I felt I was entitled to take this Christmas Day off and to spend it with a very old lady friend of mine, aged almost 100, together with a male friend who was entering the stage of dementia. A singularly unique trio perhaps but they were both good friends from the past and I wanted to enjoy the day with them. When I heard the news of the unstacked shelves and understanding there could be trouble at any time from now on, I jumped in my car bringing with me my confused friend as company, and for his own safety. It was pouring with rain and, dangerously, the streets and pavements had begun to freeze over, turning Harrogate, where I lived, into a giant skating rink. The two of us dashed into town and began to load up the boot with boxes of chocolate and other sweets pre-ordered with Woolworths. I spun around attempting to keep dry at the same time as loading. My feet went to the right, the rest of me departed to the left. I spun for the second time, now directed towards the pavement at speed. This meant my wrist connected painfully with the concrete and before I knew it, I was also on the ice with an interesting combination of a multi-fractured wrist, a man with dementia not knowing what to do, a 100-year-old lady wanting to know what had happened to us as we had not returned, and a potential riot on my hands in my own prison (remember, no-one else to turn to) if I did not get back with the goodies. Now, that *is* Sod's Law with a capital 'S'.

All this I had to relate at speed to the Harrogate police as I was lifted into an ambulance, assuring me they would deal with my car – which they did – and ordering a taxi to cart the chocolate to Wakefield ladies. They were outstanding in the service they brought to me as they resolved the issues one by one. I felt a bit better when I learnt that it was not only my feeble ice-skating ability even as I slowed up with age, for thirty other shoppers had slipped, fallen and broken a limb or two during a night to remember at Harrogate Hospital.

The out-sourcing contractor had a great deal to learn. The seemingly innocuous empty shelves in their shop could have led to a nasty riot at Christmas. Leave would have had to be cancelled for prison officers who otherwise might have hoped to be with their families.

As it was, the inmates of Wakefield had a peaceful Christmas, their children stuffed full of chocolate. I had to return to hospital straight after the holiday as the doctors had not been able to set the wrist properly before the hospital geared down. Unable to do anything in the prison, as I could not even turn a key in a lock, I took myself off to Italy where, amongst the Chianti and the Spaghetti Carbonara, an

English lady told me my wrist would be locked as it had been set wrongly. She proved to be right. The third operation took a long time to heal but was alleviated to some extent by the flowers and a food hamper from my staff.

So, ended my first Christmas at home.

Amidst being driven to work, finding my feet again, literally, I had to plan another visit from Princess Anne. This amazing woman never held back on her duties to the Prison Service and it was agreed with her secretary, she would visit on St. Valentine's Day. Our planning even went as far as setting aside a loo for her which was spruced up by the maintenance team. She was, once again, delayed in her arrival, this time by two hours, fog, I seem to remember. It did give time for her security guard who had come ahead separately, to advise me the loo was too far away from where we were to eat, which was the chapel on any other day. Attached to this room, disused perhaps, but a still functioning lavatory. It contained buckets and brooms, old dusters and half-used tins of cleaning fluids. (This may seem depressingly familiar to some). We had two hours to sort it out so I instructed some trustee prisoners to clear the room out, clean it up and make it presentable for a Princess. I was under pressure at the time. 'Don't paint anything,' I ordered. 'We don't want the smell of wet paint.' Apart, I realised, from a royal bottom sticking to a shiny varnished seat causing a nightmare image of a cry for help issuing from under the said door, 'Help. I'm stuck.'

Two hours later, Anne's helicopter flew in, we shook hands and began our tour, before ending up in the chapel for lunch. It was so easy to talk to someone who knew the prison service as well as she did. The time passed quickly until we were due to say goodbye. Helicopters do not have loos. 'The Princess Royal would like to go to the loo before she leaves.' I was asked to show the way. I pointed out the chapel lavatory at the same moment in time recalling I had not checked their work. Images of a Princess sitting among brooms and mops made me pale. Varnish/bottom/stuck/fast. I did pray.

A short while later, Anne emerged, chortling and giggling as she came over to say goodbye.

'Can I have the card?'

'The card, ma'am?'

'Yes, the one in the loo. It reads, 'If you feel stressed, bang your head here. (the cistern). 'I would like to take it back to Gatcombe for the staff.'

I began to breathe, agreeing rather too effusively with her request.

'How do you manage with 150 kids? I have trouble with just two.' It was her parting comment.

It was another good day with a very good Royal maximising her time with us. After the helicopter had taken off I went back to the loo and peered inside. The prisoners, detailed with the rushed workload had indeed cleared the whole room before attaching a black band of cloth around the walls. The cloth was over-printed with what appeared to be dead flies but on closer inspection were in fact, dark-green flowers. I imagine the card adorns the dresser in the kitchen at Gatcombe.

It was to be a royal year. Just two years earlier I had been to Buckingham Palace, not in my role as a Butler Trust member but to receive such an award myself. It was, sincerely, a great honour, a recognition by my peers of the work I had put in at Brockhill. Now, I was to go again.

I had received a letter at home from No.10 Downing Street. Another survey required by Tony Blair who needed, in those days, constant updates on street crime statistics. I felt that opening the letter could wait while I went out shopping with my 100-year-old lady who I was caring for. The letter remained in the hall for two days until I was reminded of its presence. I sighed. There was no getting away from my duties I was sure the contents would reveal.

It was indeed, from Tony Blair's office but not asking for statistics. Instead it merely required me to confirm, or otherwise, my acceptance of the Order of the British Empire from the Queen. I laughed out loud. My staff were playing another prank on me – I was quite susceptible to their jokes. *Taking the Mickey.* I put it down again and it was not until nightfall when my charge's nephew called. He noticed the letter and I explained it was a spoof.

'I don't think so, Veronica. That is an official letter. You should not have shown it to anyone, not even me, as they can take the award away before you even get it.'

Mortified, I took back the letter as if it was the Holy Grail. 'I won't tell anyone, honest,' he said with a smile. 'Congratulations by the way.'

I had to confirm I would receive the award and keep extremely quiet telling no-one. It is difficult, to say the least, to do so, the second part, that is. I posted the letter off and went on holiday to Italy again to find, on my return, my telephone answering machine stuffed full of calls from the Press, having got wind of something while I was away. I said nothing and did not return their calls. I did not want to be interviewed. That evening I watched teletext where the award was confirmed for my still disbelieving eyes. I had been told the full list would be published after midnight. And there it was. Miss Irene Veronica Bird OBE for services to the Prison Service. It was a shock seeing my name float up alongside so many worthies. Veronica Bird OBE, late of Doncaster Road, Barnsley.

In the night, after I had gone to bed, friends who had also picked up the news arrived with flowers and champagne. Finding no reply at the door, they had thrown pebbles up at the window, then, believing they might be reported for attempted breaking and entering, they withdrew hastily leaving the said flowers and bottle on the front door step. Within a couple of hours of me getting up, flowers and presents began to arrive, warm wishes from so many friends and colleagues. I had to ring the family one-by-one unsure of their reaction, but time is a great healer and they were all delighted with the news.

One small piece of trivia. I found out that from now on, I could get married in St. Paul's cathedral, if I so wished. Well, that's all right then.

A follow-up letter told me where to be and when. The best news was to learn I would be presented with my award by Her Majesty herself and it would be at Buckingham Palace where I had walked down those red-carpeted corridors only two years previously.

On that special day, we the Award winners were directed one way and our guests on an opposite path. There were no drinks for us as we waited – this was probably born out of experience, for there were many already almost incapable with nerves, but at least, sober. It was the Queen no less, who they were going to meet on a one to one basis, up front and personal, not at a distance waving a union jack in the air. One man was so frazzled I told him to stay close behind me, 'then you will be alright. There is really nothing to it.' He stuck close, though I do not believe he took in a word I had said and he was probably the first who might have sunk a snifter or two if it had been on tap. He remained behind me, prompting memories of something similar at the end of *A Tale of Two Cities*.

We were briefed, lined up in order (I lost my companion at this moment) and had a pin placed on my lapel so the queen could hang the medal with ease. I walked forward as my name was called, a single question from her Majesty, a handshake with the slight but firm push away to signify it was all over, to say thank you and goodbye; the whole process took twenty-five seconds.

Such memories do not go away. Though I was to return to Buckingham Palace several times in my role as a member of the Butler Trust, being presented with the award had to trump everything else in my life.

There were garden parties in the summer. One hot event caused thirty-four guests to faint in the heat and women could be seen leaving the gates carrying their shiny new shoes in their hands, red, swollen feet making the point on many occasions to signify their state. In contrast, my trip to Ireland for another party was flooded out with a downpour. I was able to understand why Ireland is so green as one looks down on that lovely country from the air.

It felt right to me to enjoy this pampering at the end of my career. Perhaps you may feel such awards and parties are an anachronism these days in this egalitarian world, but how else do people, and yes, governments, show their thanks and appreciation for the work you have done for the country if not with a flurry of hats, red carpets, nervous giggles in the Ladies loos and a glass of champagne?

I will leave it to others to decide what drove me into the Service and then compelled me in an upward direction. There is no doubt I missed out on many of the comforts and events which occurred during my thirty-five years. What it did do, I am convinced, was to give me the feeling of security I had always craved as a child, having lived in fear for most of my formative years. As I grew into the job, that secure feeling enabled me to see ways of running a prison which went against (and, no doubt, still does) the accepted methods of making our prisons safe places to be for staff and prisoners alike. Many speak out, few changes are made and these, usually, are against a background of Human Rights legislation and the EU trying to create an anodyne service where one size fits all, especially with twenty-eight nations (27?) having who knows what, differing ideas on how to control their prison populations.

Thorn Cross was undoubtedly a success. It could, in its way, show a new direction to manage prisoners' lives. We must always seek to develop alternative ideas if only to reduce the re-offending rate. Is there a better way I asked myself, as I prepped up to go and see the land of Pushkin and Putin?

CHAPTER FOURTEEN
IVANOVO

The second week of April had nudged its way into in my diary. The year was 2002. I was beginning to close down my work and plan for my retirement when I received a telephone call one day in my office in Wakefield which proved to be of considerable interest.

'This is Rannoch Daley, Veronica. I'm involved with the Council of Europe and we've set up a project to see if we can establish greater protection of Human Rights with Russian pre-trial prisoners. It's part of a three-year study.'

'Oh right. Why just pre-trial?'

'They don't have any,' came the brief reply.

'Ah,' was my shorter response. 'Possibly a good idea then.'

I was aware of a venture to spread European values further eastward. There was a plan to twin British and Russian prisons. (A bit different to attempting to twin Bourton-on-the-water and Colombey-les-deux-Églises) but Ranuch's voice had a touch of anxiety in. He was continuing.

'I would like to know if you will represent New Hall prison, that's Wakefield, isn't it? Would you like to go to Russia representing the women's' viewpoint in prisons in the United Kingdom? You can take two officers with you and the Council of Europe will pay all expenses, which, I might add, are very generous. But,' he paused to ensure I would understand the catch. He could hear I was getting ready to say yes. 'But, you will be expected to receive a similar delegation from over there and to entertain them later in the year.'

'When would you expect an answer?'

'Oh, in the next three minutes, say. We have to leave in six weeks.'

'Has someone backed out then?'

'Yes.' He didn't mention the name of the prison. 'It is one of your colleagues in a female prison and it is for this reason we need you, for we will be visiting a female prison which is in quite a mess. We need someone experienced to go with us. And, TB is out of control. They need a lot of help.'

I didn't think twice. It was in with both feet. When I put the phone down having been promised to receive all the details by post along with the air tickets, I had no idea where I was going (Russia *is* quite a large country). It appeared on my map as quite large, in fact it covered most of the top of the world. Did I have to submit a group report or an individual report and what was in the itinerary so I could do some research? How long was I going, might be helpful and who else was going would also be useful?

There was also the small issue of implied favouritism to overcome. I was a planner, a maker of lists, a time-keeper. If I was to take two officers with me, how was I to choose? This last point I resolved by holding a very public raffle with an independent drawing two winning tickets out of a hat. The result was a jubilant Jan, a female prison officer and a very happy Tony, an Assistant Governor, so both male and female sides would be represented. I felt I could not have been more fair.

Information did arrive. It was to be June but no report was required of me which made me doubt the seriousness of the project. *Junket* was a possible noun which drifted across my mind. There were, though, visas to obtain, passports to be checked. What to wear in a hot Russia?

The Group had drawn up a training manual for prison staff entitled *Human Rights in prisons* and this had been translated into Russian and sent on ahead of our party. Was this, I pondered, just to be another discussion forum? Reports I knew. Reports I wrote all the time so, no report was, to say the least, curious. Was this to be just an excursion?

Between the three of us, no-one had any idea of conditions in Ivanovo, the town, or was it to be big enough to describe it as a city? Ivanovo certainly did not fall under the list of recognised cities such as Moscow or St. Petersburg or even, I remember from school days, Vladivostok at the far end of some fabled rail journey. (Vlad was the shortened name for Vladimir, the first name given to Putin). My Collins World Atlas, size eight inches by four inches only covered those three cities.

I learned we would be met in Moscow and provided with an interpreter, a driver and a guide. The hotel rooms had been reserved. Nothing was left to chance with the EU planners behind us; nothing could go wrong. Nice feeling.

Two mistakes were made early on in my planning. Normally, when I travel, I take tea, coffee and biscuits, just in case I am caught out somewhere, something to soften entry into a strange country (rather like the heat shield on a re-entry cone). For some unfathomable reason, I did not. I was to regret it. Secondly, I had always worn a skirt or a dress in the Service. It was part of my recognition, my handle, '.... that must be Veronica coming. She's the one in the skirt.' Besides, I found a skirt more flexible. This time, I did not, take a skirt that is, I took trousers. Why, you might ask, did you, Veronica, do that?

I had some notion I might be walking up many open-treaded staircases (I had probably seen one picture of such a Russian stair) and, not wanting most of Russia looking up my skirt, I plumped for slacks.

We flew from Leeds Bradford Airport down to Heathrow and, not being much of a traveller, was delighted just to gaze down on London and identifying the famous landmarks as they grew out of the clouds.

We landed without a smidgen of a bump and disembarked

to a minor annoyance. As I have said, I have not travelled a great deal so we did not 'patch' our cases through from Leeds to Moscow. Thus, I was obliged to tow my case around as if it was an obedient dog until we arrived at our new check-in desk. One lives and learns.

We took off on a brilliant Sunday sunny afternoon in what one can only describe as a rather basic aircraft, an Aeroflot Ilyushin which was so forgettable I cannot recall eating anything on board. This must have been the case for by the time I arrived in Moscow I was very hungry. (my biscuits were still in the tin in my kitchen).

The day we flew was during the first week of a no-smoking policy had been declared on international flights. This naturally, divided the law-abiding races from those others, more used to doing what they considered was right. Ghenkis Khan syndrome I believe it is called. Quite unperturbed, our Russian friends on the flight migrated, after negotiation, to the port side so they could continue to smoke while the British, as would be expected, flowed to the starboard side and quite firmly decided not to smoke. Thus, are all great concordats agreed. It made no difference to the result, as the smoke, for some curious and partisan motive, curled and coiled its way over to us as if the tide was coming in on St. Ives beach.

Emerging into the fresh air of Moscow removed me from the misery of the equivalent of a London smog but into the bedlam which comprised *Sheremetyevo* airport on a holiday Sunday evening. Over the glass wall arrivals entrance, I gained my first sight of Cyrillic lettering. Добро пожаловать, or 'Welcome' to you and me.

Most of Russia, or so it seemed to me, was on the move, as if this part of the world was caught up in some great moose drive from the Mongolian steppes, as they arrived back from wherever they had been, just as we spilled out of our transit bus.

No-one likes to queue in Russia – something to remember if you are thinking of going there for a holiday. However, the Immigration queues snaked back and forth (it took an hour) so every five minutes we saw the same travellers reappearing alongside, giving slightly embarrassed smiles. (Hullo, haven't I seen you somewhere before?). Eventually, tired out with shuffling, and wearing out my shoe leather, I handed over my passport to an Immigration official and firmly asserted that I was here for business *and* pleasure. I received the all-important stamp and the woman handed it back to me with a curt nod of her head.

As we emerged into a new throng I heard a shout. 'Ver-on-ikah!'

The voice came from an elegant gentleman, a psychiatrist from the prison hospital who spoke excellent English. Now this is better, I surmised.

I gathered my thoughts together. Civilised, educated and very welcoming. We all shook hands. 'Ver-on-ikah, we must get your currency changed here. So, you can pay the hotel when we arrive.'

I knew this as it had been explained to me back in Britain. Besides, Tony had already pointed out the *bureau de change*. We had a problem for we had no idea what additional roubles we would need as we did not have the faintest idea of where we were going. Adding in the hotel costs, we guessed; it proved to be passably accurate. Armed with a sheaf of dirty notes, the six of us walked out to climb into a black limousine (was this a Zil?) and off we sped into a very late night, hungry, confused and tired, but we were there, St. Petersburg, Pushkin and Putin in our minds.

About one and a half hours later somewhere on the E115, our interpreter leaned over the seat back. 'Ver-on-ikah, we stop now. We eat.' Good-oh, I thought. At last. It was a roadside restaurant and we were met by a very welcoming restaurant owner. I did not though, receive three kisses on the cheek.

Six glasses of vodka arrived on the table although I had seen no-one place an order. It was clear, like gin, although I had been told I might expect it to be brown, like whisky, if it was local. Straight vodka, by federal law, has to be clear, for what reason I know not, but vodka is also aged in oak barrels and there is considerable dispute in Russia as to whether it is lawful to call brown vodka, vodka! What did become clear as gin was the sheer volume of the spirit which was consumed, drunk is another word and drunk is the more apt word I feel. Russia leads the world in alcohol related deaths by far, with two-thirds of murders in the country caused by intoxication. As has been reported recently '...Russia is quite literally, drinking itself to death.'

The psychiatrist spoke again as he got into his stride. 'I order for everyone. Okay?'

'Anything, anything,' we responded in unison.

'Okay, I order meat with variations.'

Sounded good to us. I assumed it might mean a mixed grill and the variations would almost certainly be vegetables. The Russians then proceeded to swallow their vodka by a swift jerk of the hand and a well-practised, almost dislocating move of the neck, backwards. My colleagues followed suit.... except me of course. I needed food, not neat vodka on an empty stomach.

Six more vodkas arrived.

While we waited, we all introduced ourselves, during which I witnessed the swift action with the glass, still, excusably, as a salutation to us. By now, I had two glasses, so I passed them across to the interpreter to deal with. He passed one to our driver, so not such a good idea really. Thus, two of our team now had three vodkas inside them.

Aha! The food was on its way. I was very hungry and the idea of a mixed grill with sausage, bacon, liver, chop, steak, a fried egg (or two), mushrooms and crispy frites would go down well with minted peas picked early in the morning on a local farm, felt good.

A plate was placed in front of me.

Well. We did have peas. The meat was tongue, circular in shape and cut neatly to fit the bottom depression of a saucer. Under the meat, and well over it, sat the peas, processed, more

241

grey in tone than garden green, although in retrospect, I did see a pale, greenish slime beginning to emerge from the pile starting to spread, highlighting the whiteness of the plate. Our Russian friends tackled their own food without further delay as if they had not eaten for a week. I had to admit I felt the same, so I bit into the edges of the tongue as if I was a *garra rufa* fish giving a fish pedicure to someone's feet.

A third vodka arrived – well, why not? Mine was passed over again and I knew I had made a friend for life. Yes, who else but the driver?

Off we went again, our driver now four up on me with drinks, driving in the darkness though by now there was a pallor in the east from the arriving northern sun, suggesting to me it wasn't so much very late as very early morning. Jan, I could not help notice, was very quiet; so were the two men in my party but all three had been topped up with three vodkas, 'shots' I believe you call them. I can think of quite a few prisoners back home who would have enjoyed the party.

You may think I am portraying the image of a naive young girl rather than an experienced, ageing prison Governor more used to dealing with hard-bitten lags. I had spent most of my life in one prison or another, isolated from the impact of external influences`, aligned to prison food, prison generally, prisoners, prison rules, prison staff, all these I could deal with but, heavy drinking at three o'clock of a morning in Russia was not something I did, nor was I going to start it now.

Finally, with sighs of relief all round and two hundred and fifty kilometres from Moscow, now only a distant memory, we arrived at our hotel in the city of Ivanovo with its population of just over four hundred thousand which is a bit bigger than Leicester. In style, though, it was a mirror of Manchester as it had once been a centre for textile mills which had once dominated the skyline. Money had moved in, up went the large pre-revolution houses until, finally they were split up into many apartments after Lenin came to power. As Confucius once said: *Everything goes round in a circle.*

*

We gratefully spilled out into the foyer with considerable sighs and much stretching of backs and arms. I rubbed red-rimmed eyes trying to take in the first Russian building. The floor was covered in dark brown linoleum, well, more dark than brown. The furniture too had been chosen by the same enlightened Architect, for this was also dark brown. The whole vast space was lit by one sixty-watt bulb which sat inside a glass dish of circa nineteen-fifty, possibly pink glass, though quite a long time ago. It was so dim no shadows were cast in the centre of the room, let alone into the corners. Oh, I almost forgot, and the walls were brown wall-paper too, unless they had been cream once.... but were not now.... cream that is. I was allocated a key by a sleepy looking night porter and welcomed to the hotel. I nodded, too tired to speak. Our lift though, stopped at the first floor so we could be shown where we were to have breakfast. We had been beaten by the Architect who had made the decision to cover the floor in dark brown linoleum, more dark than brown. I could go on but you must have the idea by now. Getting back in the lift I said to myself. 'What on God's earth am I doing here?'

But, as I emerged onto the bedroom floor the scene transformed itself. Clean paint, pictures on the walls, good lighting. My bedroom was the same. Basic but bright and clean with my own shower room. It was as though the Russian authorities did not want their own locals to see how the Europeans lived; that the foreign tourists (in Ivanovo?) got a better deal than themselves. It was though, almost impossible to imagine a single reason to visit the town.

I struggled awake at seven for we had to leave for the prison at eight. Before though, I had promised Mary, my ancient but very good friend of mine, that I would ring her to say I had arrived having previously told her that she should not say anything on the phone for 'it might be bugged.' (Honestly, you couldn't turn this into a West End play). Many friends had given me advice before I left and I had absorbed it all like a sponge. I told Mary, once I was put through, that I had arrived safely and the hotel was fine. Mary, being made of sterner stuff took no notice of my treacly comment.

'How is the food?' She demanded to know.

That was another matter. I was just about to reply saying it was 'appalling' and 'interesting' when whoever was listening in decided, to maintain good relations with Russia, and cut us off. I was left with just the sad burr of the handset and I could only imagine what Mary was thinking. Whether anyone was listening in I have no idea, but all the stories I had been given, courtesy of Ian Fleming and John le Carré began to look as if they might be accurate. I put the heavy handset down and made my way down to the first floor where businessmen were eating their breakfast, mostly in silence. I was offered a sausage along with processed peas or, if not that, a hard-boiled egg and I mean, hard-boiled. The coffee was too strong to drink – *ersatz* as the Germans would have put it – and there was not a lot else. I ate the egg. I never went back to the restaurant.

A trifle wearily we walked to the waiting car, noticing Jan was still not with us. She had missed breakfast. A note followed us out. She would not be able to make today as she was too ill. (This lasted for two days). I was now quite pleased I hadn't tackled the vodka, and we drove off to the prison, one less but, after all, I reminded myself hastily, that is why we were here; to see what Russian prisons were like and to see where we, as representatives of the European Union, could help.

As we drove to the woman's prison I witnessed a type of poverty I had not expected in such a major world power in the Noughties. Men were hunched over pails half filled with potatoes hoping to earn a meagre meal themselves. Everywhere was unkempt, a lack of pride, a lack of ownership and a lack of care and money. Ivanovo had been, once, the equivalent of how Manchester had been one hundred and fifty years earlier, when it was at the centre of the cotton industry. But, Manchester had moved on, long ago. Ivanovo had not. Each dormitory of the town or should I call it a city, seemed to specialise in one sector of industry or agriculture, such as light fittings or melons. Melons! I could eat a melon on my half-starved stomach. 'Stop the car', I commanded. 'I want a melon.'

My driver looked round. 'Mees Ver-on-ikah, you cannot eat these melons. They come from Chernobyl and these farmers do not understand they are radio-active and dangerous.'

'Buggar!'

Whether this was true I have no idea but I got the feeling it was an excuse, as they were late for the meeting. If it was true, then I had been saved from a fate worse than the one Jan was going through. Studying a map later I could see that Chernobyl was some six hundred miles from Moscow and we were further north again, so the likelihood of radio-active melons being sold in Ivanovo was a long way from the actualité. Possibly, I could hire a taxi to take me back at night to see if they glowed in the dark?

The four-lane highway was busy with old buses trundling along, belting out noxious black fumes. They had obviously not been serviced for a long while, perhaps never. But the road eventually wended its way to the prison where we disembarked. The penitentiary sat in a countryside I would describe as real Russia, surrounded by dense silver birch forests stretching away into the hills. In front, there were pleasant green fields but I saw no animals. Possibly they were kept locked up safely somewhere for I wouldn't disbelieve it if I was told men would drive up from Moscow each night to pinch a few cows.

The prison could contain three to four hundred women in one dormitory alone and up to 1,000 women were held here in 2002. It was enclosed by a surprisingly low wall with a corrugated iron gate which anyone could have slipped over or under. Security at first view appeared very basic. We were welcomed by the Governor and senior officers both male and female who, touchingly, had clearly had a whip-round for us to buy a packet of what must have been very expensive biscuits. It was a first indication of how kind the local Russians could be. This was a world far removed from Putin's domain with its politics and need to prove itself as a major power to the world. It is like most places; remove the politicians and there is peace.

We sat around a table with our interpreter being called upon constantly as we discussed prison rules, the same ones we had been translated back in England. The idea for us all was to see if we could introduce European methods of running prisons into Ivanovo. We discussed visiting arrangements, washing and cleanliness generally, the no-smoking rules (utter amazement), security and staff benefits (more amazement). I asked what the women were in for and was told Russia had no bail system as we know it, so anyone arrested for whatever matter, could be held in a prison for a year or more. They might well be innocent. I was told the authorities had no idea how long a prisoner would have to wait before they received a trial. (Amazement from our side followed by much clearing of throats as we felt we had displayed too much overt criticism in the form of amazement). But such a thing would certainly start a riot in England.

I have already related the fact, when I am in England I always wear a skirt, it is more flexible than trousers but some reason, like the omission of biscuits perhaps, I decided to wear trousers on this trip. My decision caused a problem on this first day's visit when one of the male officers kindly suggested I might like to go to the loo before we moved off on the tour. So, I went to the loo, more of a hole in the ground. This now disgorged a rat (large and dark brown like the linoleum) interested to see who had invaded its kingdom. It popped its head out first then, emboldened, walked out onto the floor heading for my trousers now in the 'down' position. It and I filled the tiny cubicle between us.

Now, as I have said before, I do not like mice, rats, cockroaches or alcohol and certainly not rats the size of a tom cat. I leaped for my trousers to pull them up but they were new and unfamiliar, the buttons stiff, so I managed to get all tied up trying to make as much space as possible between myself and the original occupant. Eventually, shaking, I sprang from the ladies' loo like a jack-in-the-box to find the kind prison officer waiting for me. He was holding out a piece of soap the size of my thumb nail. It was plainly his own property and had been brought from his home, thinking of me. I smiled encouragingly concerned as to what he might have heard, and said I did not need it. He had, thoughtfully, not only realised I might want to go to the loo after my drink of Russian coffee but brought his very precious piece of soap with him. The other side of the Russian bear, I think? It was the smallest of gestures, the largest offer of peace I had seen.

The Governor then walked us into the grounds of the prison and I pointed with a finger at the low wall.

'Governor, what about escapes-?

'We do not have escapes in Russia, Mees Ver-on-ikah,' he replied firmly. He indicated a thin wire which ran around the perimeter inside of the wall. He leaned down upon it. Within seconds, his entire staff erupted from their buildings as a siren went off. They were in full uniform with Kalashnikovs' slung around their necks. The effect was somewhat spoiled by the fact the female staff were not entitled to free boots, so shoes had been purchased individually. As they paraded for us we were met with a long line of pink, green and blue shoes of sling-back, high heel and slip-on varieties. Their faces were also plastered with make-up, a strange mixture of feminism and butch reality. I asked the Governor, by now I was able to call him Sergei, the reason.

'Sergei, why such an interest in make-up?'

'They have nothing else to spend their money on Ver-on-ikah'

I noticed the women constantly checking the state of their make-up in tiny hand mirrors. There was a chasm between the rulebook and the reality of everyday commitment to the job. Our countries were so far apart it was hard to conjure up a single point where we could agree on even one action.

Back inside, we found the inmates living in huge dormitories, about one hundred and thirty per room in two-tier bunks each with a locker, nothing else. It was spotlessly clean and very military in its way. Very cramped but neat. There was no-one in the room but that was conceivably because they were all in the workshops. Women could attend church if they wished and there was a facility offered to very stressed inmates called a relaxation course which, I was told, helped a great deal, but I was never able to pin down if this was just propaganda or if such ideas had ever been put into practice. I say this now with wisdom for it wasn't long after this the interpreter said to me, 'Do you believe everything you are told Ver-on-ikah?' He did not embellish his comment but he didn't have to. He knew only too well an act was being put on for his British guests.

The dining room was awful. A large tureen was placed at the head of each table. Prisoners could help themselves with as much as they wanted which, today was potato soup with a helping of grease on the top. A piece of bread, the size of the palm of your hand was also available. When finished, anything left in the bowls was poured back into the tureen. No waste! This was the main meal of the day.

The women were not wearing uniforms. My first agreeable sight for they were allowed to wear their own clothes. Curiously, countering this avant garde idea, they had to wear a headscarf at all times. Failure to do so might mean a punishment of some form. As to other meals, I never did find out what they had for breakfast but assumed there might have been some processed peas available.

We moved on to the workshops, which were enormous, a factory no less, making uniforms for prison staff, the armed forces and the police for national distribution. They were beautifully made. All the various stages of making a suit were here from the cloth cutting machines, sewing, checkers and packers. This work must save the State a lot of money. I learned that other women were deployed in the kitchen and some had been detailed to grow fresh vegetables outside to supplement their diet and I could see flowers brightening the rows of cabbages. I never understood why the growing of vegetables in Britain for the Service was stopped for it seemed such a good idea. I would have thought prisoners would have welcomed any chance of being outside in the fresh air and sun. Gardening could reduce boredom, the ever-present fuse to the powder kegs of the more anxious and restless inmates.

One disadvantage of being a female prisoner here was that there were relatively few female prisons in Russia compared with their male counterparts. This meant families had to travel vast distances to see a daughter or mother and, with poverty prevalent in so many villages, it could mean they were separated for the entire period of their sentence.

I was quite used to having a punishment block in my prison but I now saw how women were treated in the Russian equivalent. The door opened on a 15-year old. The cell contained just a wooden board which was let down at ten at night. There was no radio or television, no chair to sit on, nothing to read. While there was a library for the other women, this young girl had nothing to read and nothing to do. I saw a set of scales which made me believe her bread and water diet was rationed – and this was the twenty-first century! It was very hard seeing her there but we were not told why she had been sent to this most dismal of places.

That night the men in my small party suggested we go to the hotel bar for a drink but I was too tired after the lack of sleep the night before and excused myself. The next morning, refreshed from sleeping well, I asked them how they had got on.

'Er,' said one looking at the other. 'Er, we were approached by a beautiful woman who said she had six equally beautiful women to choose from. Tony said:" What a shame I'm too tired." The other man said, 'Hang on a moment, let's think about it. Only joking of course.' He went on. 'Did you see the woman on the landing as you went up last night?'

'No,' I answered truthfully. Maybe I had my head down in weariness.

'Well, she was there, at the end of the corridor with her ladies in waiting.'

I repeated my mantra to myself, 'What on God's earth am I doing here?'

As you will have totalled up in previous pages, I do not like rodents, members of the sub-class Apterygota and Order Orthoptera, nor distilled potato juice, which were all here in abundance. Now it was prostitutes on my bedroom floor. Well, not *my* bedroom floor, per se, but the corridor floor on which my bedroom was sited! It was not until a couple of days later that I managed to fall into a dead sleep and was down several levels of consciousness when the telephone rang. It was three-thirty in the morning. Slightly alarmed, for it could only be someone ringing from England who was making the call (and how did they get my number?) I picked up the old, heavy handset.

'Гулло, с кем я разговариваю?'

'Hullo.'

There came a blast of Russian, spoken by a male, very quickly. I tried to answer by speaking more loudly, as if one is in France, but to no avail. With rather lurid magazines being all that had educated me in the past on such matters, I was certain the KGB were attempting to find out if I was in, so I climbed out of bed and looked out of the window. It was two floors down to safety. Although I was athletic in many ways, I grabbed, instead, the only chair in the room and jammed it under the door handle, just like in the *Thirty-Nine Steps*, and waited with bated breath. (I should make it clear that in 2000 it was not the KGB of course but the Federal Security Service, the FSS, same jobs, different titles but KGB spins up quite nicely when dining out, and well away from their wire taps).

No-one came, no-one burst in through the door and eventually, I went back to a chilly bed. What that had been all about I have no idea and I had to add this event to the growing list of things for which I had no answers.

It was time to see how the Russian men fared for there was

also a men's' prison in Ivanovo. This visit was as upsetting as we had been warned. I had worked in Armley in Leeds, reckoned to be a tough prison but here, no Human Rights existed.

I could see, as our car rolled up, the security fence was much higher and as we ground to a halt, commands were barked out causing the scattering of prisoners to scurry towards the far fence where they turned towards it faces averted from us. They were kept that way until we passed them by.

The men were corralled (this is the right word – to use the term, lived, would be a misuse of the word) in dormitories, not cells, packed in twenty-three hours a day. They smoked, ate, defecated together in the one room measuring thirty feet by thirty feet. The stench was, of course, appalling aggravated by the fact the officers had boarded all the windows up tight '… to prevent escapes' even though there were bars on the windows. There was no fresh air or light entering the room, and the whole thing was a nonsense. No wonder TB was spreading like wildfire throughout the Russian prisons. It did not need a medic to tell me that.

We were shown the exercise yard where the prisoners were packed into a courtyard, just a long narrow pen, for one hour, so tightly they were unable to move. They could smoke if they could get their hands to their pockets. To see them, we climbed up an open-tread ladder, my first, (see what I mean about wearing trousers) onto a metal platform. It was as though we were at a zoo looking down into a pen of animals, none of us could recognise. As we were taking in the miserable scene a man shouted up to us in English.

'When are the conditions going to improve?' I hate to think what punishment was meted out to him. I had always considered battery hens to have a rough time but this was too much for anyone to stomach. There was no physical exercise although we were told there was a gymnasium on the site but that was very difficult to believe. These men were here to be punished, harshly, not to rehabilitate them for the future.

Tony, our hardened Assistant Governor with many years'

service and experience could not stand it. 'This cannot go on,' he said in a low voice, not wishing to broadcast his thoughts. He was shocked, horrified and in tears.

The TB was spreading through the combination of lack of light and fresh air and there were no washing facilities. It had become out of control which, for very little money could be reduced considerably.

We needed a drink. While we attempted the strong coffee, the Governor told me that the ratio of prisoner to officer was one to six hundred. 'And what ratio do you have in England Ver-on-ikah?'

'One to six,' I replied waiting for the astonishment to rise up on his face. Instead, he just shook his head. My own prisoners would complain officially if the ratio increased by one or two. And I thought I was here to learn about security. There was little chance of an escape when the prisoners had no leg muscles to run, nowhere to run to and the rest were dying in hospital.

Tuned in to my thoughts, we moved on to the prison hospital where doctors and nurses were all dressed in white coats. The beds were full of very sick men suffering from HIV/Aids, TB and alcoholism. The interpreter told me many of the men had Tuberculosis. How do you recover from such a disease when the food was so poor?

Another day, another week, we were taken to Vladimir prison, closer to Moscow on the same road we came in on, in fact it was one hundred and eighty kilometres from the capital. When we arrived, the officers' faces lit up when they knew we were being told this was the prison Gary Powers, the U2 pilot, had been held. He had been shot down on a spy-plane mission and brought here in much triumph. Now, the prison capitalises on the museum they have developed by showing off Power's uniform and framed documents of the day. You might remember the film *Bridge of Spies* which showed the capture of Powers and the negotiations which went on to release him. This was also the prison where Greville Wynne had been imprisoned for eight years following the Oleg Penkovsky spying affair.

The prison had been built for high-security prisoners, terrorists, murderers and lifers. Eighty men, slept head to toe in turns, with a leader appointed to each dormitory to report any sickness or depression to ward off suicides. How anyone could commit suicide in such a crammed dormitory where every one of your actions would be seen by several men was difficult to imagine.

'We have no suicides in Russia,' came the comment, reflecting, neatly, my own thoughts.. 'Not like in your country I believe?'

'Hmm.'

The real issue quickly became apparent. The men could not get out into a workshop to alleviate the boredom, to exercise their muscles and to get fresh air. They needed fresh air, not nicotine in their lungs. And with the stench and the long-term confinement, it was astonishing that re-offending rates were still high. It was, as usual, a lack of funds which drove an uninterested populace to keep their prisons as they had been since the revolution. Or, was it just a lack of information seeping out into the cities and towns which might have brought change? During one period of government with budgets at an all-time low, the staff could not be paid. In desperation, the Ministry supplied free vodka in its place with the inevitable result that large numbers of staff became hooked on alcohol. The corner is now turned, thank goodness. The solution – to wean the younger ones off with beer. Oh, so that's alright then!

We had been told there were no escapes in Russia. I am certain the prison governors had been told to pass this fact on to us for we were advised that no-one, but no-one, escaped from Russian prisons. This had to be the staff anthem for, we were advised, if anyone escaped from a prison, the Governor and senior staff were immediately sacked from their jobs and, I assume, there would be no recompense in the form of a pension. Hence, no escapes, real or imagined. I was reminded of this after I had returned to England when I received a begging letter from one of our interpreters saying he had been sacked following a prison escape. I can neither confirm nor deny whether this was true or false.

But, on the brighter side of our visit, the Russian countryside was beautiful. It was as if nature had taken hold of the land once it had left the grip of humans. There was no doubt the people had desecrated the landscape for miles around yet, here was sap green pushing through the rusty piles of junk. The grasses, wispy tops, bent in the slightest wind. They swayed towards our group as we approached as if to berate us for not stopping to admire them. Beyond, in the near distance, hung gold onion domes sparkling in the sun. This was the real Russia; the one I had seen in the advertisements for Aeroflot, and the one I imagined. It was cathartic after the horrors of the prisons as I tried to clean my mind of the reek of the men.

Later that week we were taken to see the Volga in what was euphemistically described as our 'free time' when on a tour. Each day we were bounced between one meeting and the next, but someone supervising the whole operation, perhaps, decided we needed a break. It took us about an hour driving north-east until we parked by an enormous river with calm waters. There was, this time, a church with green onion domes, white painted walls and red stone gables looking down on the serene river as if it had never witnessed the terrors of the revolution. It was a romantic day and sunny and we all forgot our work for a while and tried to learn a few words of Russian. Our hosts were so kind in clubbing together to buy me a linen tablecloth and serviettes care of the Ivanovo mills. I went out and bought some glassware to fill up my cabinet at home.

We had peeped, and pried, gaped and gasped while nodding our heads in commiseration, pitied, protested and professed our dismay. It was time to go home where we could, as individuals, pass on our concerns to those more capable of bringing them to the notice of President Putin.

Harrogate was green beneath our wings; my sanity had

remained intact but had been broadened, usefully, I think, by my experiences in Russia. It meant I could speak from strength in the future. Back to a way of life I understood, I was also pleased I had been and seen the disturbing scenes in Russian prisons which I had previously witnessed only in columns in a magazine. I hadn't believed them, putting them down as fictional claptrap forged through some hack's foetid imagination.

Coming in to land I could see fields, this time filled with sheep and cows though without the dense forests of birch. I was home but I knew there was a lot of work to do before the Russian prisoners could get anywhere near our own Prison Service and that was for the staff as much as the prisoners.

*

I need to insert here a note or two on my visit to Australia. I was there ostensibly on holiday, staying with friends but someone heard I was in town and informed the Governor of the local prison. This was in Perth. I then received a call inviting me to visit and, why not? I had heard of the comfort, the prisoners in Australia, enjoyed. It would form a good contrast to Ivanovo.

The first thing which I realised were the similar travel distances prisoners had to travel. Travelling in Australia meant immense distances. It could take three days to get one inmate from Perth to Sydney for example. But there, all idea of similarity ended. Here was paradise. Here was extreme comfort. Here was brightness and light with prisoners walking in couples from building to building as if they were strolling down a path in a campus. This in its way was as big an eye opener, as Ivanovo, if at extreme ends of a spectrum. Somewhere in the middle was the right path and it was my feeling, now reinforced by experience, that Britain had it about right.... for the time being.

*

Three months after my return – it was already September – we prepared to receive the Russian delegation in response to ours. It was made up of one female, an Assistant Governor, one other male officer and the necessary interpreter. They arrived in Leeds where we picked them up and drove them back to New Hall prison in Wakefield. As we drove along the Yorkshire roads filled with traffic, I explained that the county was one of the industrial giants of our country and always had been, its wealth anchored in wool many years before. This was their first surprise because, as they asked, if it was such an industrial giant, where was the dirt, where was the depressing grime? And these disbeliefs continued for the entire length of their stay. It was as though they wanted to look behind the hoardings to find the real Britain.

We had to take them into Leeds to collect cash from a specific bank so they could pay for their hotels, and then continue to New Hall. During their entire stay, I did not see one of our visiting party spend so much as a penny. They wanted to keep the meagre subsistence allowance and take it home with them. I could understand why, having seen how they lived. Our Russians saw how we treated our prisoners, and staff, our ideas on Bail and Remand, the food we provided and the washing facilities. Even our punishment facilities could be described as comfortable when compared with that little girl in Ivanovo sleeping on a bare board with nothing to do all day.

This focus on money, or the lack of it, boiled down to three constantly asked questions. 'Where do you get the money to pay from to pay the staff?' 'Where do you get the money to feed the prisoners?' And 'Where do you get the money from to heat the prisons in winter?' Nothing about the welfare of the prisoners themselves.

Probably a mistake with retrospect, but, as they asked, I took them to see my own house. This caused much shaking of heads, when they realised there were three toilets in my house and the kitchen was fully fitted. Not a lot of vodka though in my cupboards, I must admit.

To cement our relationship, I felt it would be a good experience with a visit to an Italian restaurant, a traditional trattoria in Harrogate. The Italian owner had found out who our guests were, and asked me if I spoke any Russian myself.

'No,' I said. 'Except thank you.'

His face beamed. 'What is that please?'

'*Spasibo.*' I was quite proud of my pronunciation. As we left after a delightful meal where everyone could relax away from the tasks set us for the prison visits, Luigi came up to us and shook hands, one by one, saying 'Spasibo' as if he was fluent in their home tongue. They became wistful for their own country as they realised how far away their home town was from Harrogate perhaps metaphorically even further, as much as physical.

Dr Edward Tierney was one of the good men of this world. He gave me enough money to take the group to London for the last day of their stay. It was extraordinarily kind and a very generous gesture, typical of the man and I made sure the party was aware of the private gift. They had heard so much about London and the Queen, causing them to lean forward urgently at the slightest comment I made, in case they missed anything of value. We drove down the M1 in two cars and went to see all the sights. Big Ben, of course, the Houses of Parliament, Trafalgar Square and when we arrived on Westminster Bridge to gaze down the Thames their eyes glittered with tears in their happiness. My *piece de resistance* was a visit to Fortnum and Mason. I had explained that this was where the Queen would do some of her shopping after the proletariat had left for the day. They stood in the entrance at attention, expecting a glimpse, perhaps, of a diamond tiara, taking in the rows and rows of quality goods and the well-heeled customers. They simply could not absorb into their Russian minds, the variety of foods, the way the chocolates were packed, the soft lighting and the luxury floorings. They did not spend a penny, of course, keeping to their wish to take as much money home as possible, but one of our party went up to the Cashier desk and through the interpreter, asked for '.... two F. and M. carrier bags, the ones with your name printed on their side.' These were duly handed over and they became the most precious souvenirs of the trip. We ended the day going to a London pub where the party chose steak and ale pies, mash and a pint of beer, allowing themselves to be driven back to Wakefield in the late night.

I had one more surprise in store. I had packed up large carrier bags for each of them. They had been filled with all the sort of goodies they could not get, such as soap, toiletries, and biscuits. There was much hugging, tears and three sets of kisses for each of us.

Their plane took off on time and we went back to our work. We had achieved two things, amongst others. The first was, they, and we, had come to a better understanding of how to improve the lives of prisoners, especially those waiting on their non-existent remand. We had given them fresh air and light, a tiny step perhaps, but to a prisoner shut up all day it was a giant leap forward. The other was we had come to understand that people are the same all over the world. They have fears as well as aspirations, they all want a better life for their families and they could see no reason to need politicians arguing in the U.N. about this transgression or that contravention.

We all want to live in peace. It was, if nothing else, a good re-affirmation of a basic tenet in life.

PART THREE

WHY DO WE LOCK PEOPLE UP?

CHAPTER FIFTEEN
IT'S AN IRONY

It is an irony, is it not, that Veronica's family is called Bird. It is almost as if she latched on to the secondary sense of her name in its penal implication, that is, 'doing bird' (to endure a prison sentence) at an early age in her life, which caused her, unconsciously perhaps, to steer a course towards the Prison Service. She certainly did her bird, thirty-five years of it, some of it in the harshest prisons in the country.

On the very day Veronica finally broke free of the family bonds which had held her tightly, Myra Hindley entered the Prison Service on the wrong side of the door. She died, almost as Veronica hung up her keys once and for all. Her future life would be predicated on the need for two simple, and free fundamentals which in anybody else's circumstances might never have been considered as essentials in any retirement plan. They were, fresh air and sunlight.

After I met Veronica and agreed for me to write her story, I logged seventy-three years of her life onto my dictaphone, over two hundred thousand words in total, which needed distilling down to about half that figure. Having no knowledge of, nor any preconceived ideas about the Prison Service (I was still describing staff a few months ago, as 'Warders' and prisoners as 'convicts' which goes well against the grain of today's position of labelling prisoners as 'men'). To understand what they did and how they carried out their daily jobs, I could only sit back and listen to the recordings…and learn. It was a steep mountain path to walk, and I made numerous mistakes in my interpretations but, gradually, a story of ultimate triumph began to emerge from my fog of ignorance. Through excellent arrangements with Bob Duncan who wrote the Foreword to this book, he managed to take me into Pentonville prison, a 175-year-old Victorian institution where I received a full-on experience. I was able to touch, feel and smell – tangible senses which brought wisdom and a better understanding to my thought processes and underwrote my belief that prison could never be for me and, I believe, it is not for you either.

Using a much over-used but appropriate word in this case, I feel privileged to be able to say I know Veronica Bird, who, in the end, through her utter determination, built a happy story around her.

*

About one hundred years ago, give or take thirty-five, I was living with my mother and sister in a small house almost, if not quite on the roof of Dartmoor. The prime position was already occupied, a wild swathe of bracken and gorse with the occasional pony displaying a long fringe covering its eyes, to bring scale to the desolate scene. Bent and coiled, like one of Dartmoor's adders and forming part of the A386 leading to Princetown and thus, the prison, is the aptly named Devil's Elbow which was always impassable in winter after an icy night.

We were closer to this forlorn spot than to Plymouth, which drew us daily to its Dockyard, and close enough to hear the Dartmoor Prison siren's fearful moan, intruding its way onto the moor, often when the mist hung just above the gorse. It was, of course, the best time to escape. We knew only too well another prison break was on the way and we lay somewhere in an escapee's path.

In the swirling fog, a prisoner, lost, soaked through to the skin and demoralised, terrified of the stories of quaking bogs, might well imagine Baskerville's hound howling at his heels, as he sought shelter in the first available house which hove into view.

We had a reasonably sized dog of our own, not a Baskerville breed perhaps, but a red setter, which slept alongside our coke-fuelled Rayburn every night. (That is the old type of coke, not the modern expression). There seemed no point in locking doors up there. No-one would call after dark where we lived. So, we never worried about a convict calling for cocoa at midnight. Us?

It was the night after the siren had sounded its warning. We were asleep and did not hear the back door being tried cautiously, before being opened wide enough to allow a shivering body to enter. The convict, hungry after a day on the run, made for the pantry, almost tripping over the dog which, woken, was now keen to share the biscuits which had been purloined by his new mate. This they did together with considerable pleasure. Bread, more biscuits and bananas disappeared into a bag and, I am sure, with a pat on the head for the dog, 'Copper,' (good name for a guard dog) he was off. He had not disturbed us by demanding money with menaces and left the kitchen in such a tidy state, other than some muddy footprints (which gave the game away) it took us quite a while to realise we had been visited in the night by the escapee.

I relate this incident in my life to make a point. Dartmoor held at that time (1951) the hardest criminals in the country. Like Colditz Castle, one prison was designed to hold the whole rotten bag of potential escapees and most of the men had nothing to lose. Forget Human Rights, it hadn't been invented. In those days, you were on your own, struggling just to survive.

'You will never escape from here,' was the oft-repeated phrase in the Second World War Stalag, but, also in the middle of Dartmoor. That must have been the thought of every woman detainee as the heavy steel door sealed behind her on her first day in Holloway.

But that cold, wet convict could have benefitted from

demanding whatever cash we had, 'money and car keys,' let alone 'warm, dry clothes and maps of Devon.' Why didn't he do so? Was it just his utter resolve to get away unchallenged that prevented him from disturbing our slumbers on that night or was it the thought of being caught and returned to an extended sentence in hell, which made him have his supper with our dog, before merging into the blackness and the fog at the very earliest opportunity? Or, was there a thread of decency retained within his hardened heart?

Things have changed radically since those days. The brutalised men had held their captors in some respect. The hierarchy of class remained, affecting to some degree one's thinking processes. If you conformed, you might have your sentence reduced. If you killed someone, the State would kill the murderer – an eye for an eye, if you like, straight out of the bible. (Exodus 21:24).

Today, we have lost the class system effect, and the scaffold, replaced by a professional army of Prison Officers, well-trained, though sometimes struggling to find those extra funds to allow them to go the extra mile. They now have to deal with better educated prisoners, many of them aware of their 'rights' and willing to use them where ever they can. There is the rise in the use of drugs, and ingenuity shown from those outside the fence smuggling in all sorts of contraband. As technology advances, the Prison Service has to continue to be ahead of the game and have, I learn, achieved considerable success in reducing, if not stamping out the flow of illegal goods.

On this basis, the Government has to plan to continue to improve standards generally in our prisons, to prevent the system falling back to those dark and now, forgotten, Dartmoor days. The plan is continually under pressure, for the peoples' aspirations rise pro rata, so what was judged acceptable yesterday will not be so in the near future.

Let's use Brockhill as a real example. It had previously been described by others as a 'basket case,' – in other words, to our sophisticated standards in twenty-first century Britain, this was as bad as Dartmoor was fifty years ago. On such a foundation, it will always prove difficult to outrun our desire to improve conditions in our own prisons as we judge them, for they are constantly being pushed ahead of the reality.

So, should we be locking men and women up in prison at all?

What if we don't want to follow this tried and tested method of crime prevention? What if we were to take away the system altogether? What then? One only has to reel back to nineteen sixty-nine in North America to remember the Murray-Hill riots (Montreal's night of Terror) ending in the murder of a policeman, with one hundred and eight normally law-abiding Canadians, arrested (and they are not the most volatile nation on earth) when the Montreal police withheld their right to protect the public – and that strike was only for sixteen hours. Imagine what a week could do?

We lock up because we still adopt in our hearts, the biblical proverb, *'an eye for an eye, a tooth for a tooth'*. We have all used the phrase, but it is a strange, awkward set of words when examined more closely. The principle is that someone who is injured by another person should be penalised to a similar degree. Hence murder begets hanging. When you take away hanging, this must beget long-term imprisonment as there is nothing else we can replace it with, at the moment. If we have nothing else, how can a victim receive an estimated *value* in compensation? This is not a simple swop; there is an insistence here you *will* swop, to the same value, otherwise someone is going to get very upset.

Mohandas Gandhi once said: *'An eye for an eye only ends up making the whole world blind.'* *'We should not seek retribution',* says someone else, *'for personal slight. Enforcing an eye for an eye is the magistrate's job; forgiving our enemies, is ours'*. But, on the other foot, Mohammad Ali was quoted as saying: *'I'm a fighter. I believe in the eye for an eye business. I'm no cheek turner. I got no respect for a man who won't hit back. You kill my dog; you better hide your cat.'* There are, as we all know, always two points of view, both earnestly given, both believed in – you take your pick, but, remember, both could be wrong.

When I worked in the Middle East, forty years ago, the principle of retribution was still very much part of life, an accepted norm. The amount of money could be calculated down to the last riyal and everyone was happy or, if not happy, was able to save face, which could be as important as the cash. But in England, how often does an angry victim's family, cry out, when a convicted criminal receives a lesser sentence than the public deems fit, (in other words, lesser than an eye, in their perceived wisdom) despite a judiciary responding to laws set by the same public?

A second reason is, we lock people up because we have lost most of our mental institutions. These far-away people have nowhere else to go. It's good isn't it, that these awful, often Victorian, monoliths have been closed, the screaming which had run bouncing along the tiled walls, stilled now, as stinging nettles grow in the once tended gardens? It's good that we know the Government have dealt with the issue once and for all, so the politically incorrect term 'madhouse' can no longer be applied in our effete society. Isn't it?

If we were to stop for a moment, gazing with unfocussed eyes, might we not ponder on where these sad, desperate people have gone? Surely there are just as many cases as there were fifty years ago, maybe more, with the pressures of life heavier on their shoulders, stresses greater, the probability of a breakdown more likely?

Released back into an uncaring world they seek only the sanctuary they knew and, not finding it, take it out on the 'heartless' public and end up in prison where they cannot understand the callous attitudes of the new neighbours around them.

So, where else do they go? Unless they are known to be dangerous to the public there is nowhere else. That is where we lock people up so we can be safe. But to be mentally unbalanced does not mean you have committed a crime; some do of course, but others are as innocent as you or me. Those in prison, confused and restless, mix with rogues and ruffians, many who have no moral compass at all; the virus takes hold in new stock. But that is what we do. We lock people up yet we don't stop the killing. On average eighty-seven people are killed every year in Britain by unstable minds. Are you certain we are still safe?

We lock people up through our belief, dangerous men and women should be prevented from continuing their careers in crime. A wall, a fence or both, high enough, (and ladder proof), between them and us has been the way to deal with criminals since before we became a nation. The first people we locked up in Dartmoor Prison were French prisoners-of-war. The initial group of captured soldiers arrived in eighteen hundred and nine. These were, on the whole, good, loyal men, fighting for their country; it had been their misfortune to get caught up on the losing side of an argument. They weren't criminals. Quickly the cells filled up, in fact Dartmoor became packed to the bulwarks, leaving the Frenchies twiddling their fingers during the day. They turned their attention to making the most exquisite models of men-o'-war fabricated by carving their bacon bones into miniature ribs, gun ports and deck planks. This is not the picture we usually imagine of Dartmoor's past, a place of Dickensian grimness.

The government, naturally, did not want to allow fighting men to return to the war as soon as they reached France. A sensible idea. But, the war over, our Government realised they had a solidly built and available prison, and moved quickly in deciding they could lock up their own people here instead. Out on the moor, in the mist and fog where they had no hope of escaping….and, hopefully, out of sight, out of mind, the flotsam of Britain could be conveniently forgotten.

There is yet another, a fourth group of convicted offenders to consider. (Felon is too harsh a word to use for this selection of sinners). What about those sent down for manslaughter where, perhaps, a teenage son borrows his father's car, drives it into a mother pushing a pram across a road and kills both the woman and her child. He or she pleads 'not guilty' naturally. 'I didn't mean to do it,' and 'the sun was in my eyes,' are probably the tearful truth, but it doesn't give the bereaved husband release from his fearful tragedy. So, lock the lad up. The widower demands an eye for an eye. He wants, as the press love to term it, closure.

Is therefore, the real idea of prison to bring solace to the grieving, haunted by death or serious injury? Is it to allow the sufferer a feeling of justice having been served which has, in the end, been decided often by the votes of just twelve men and women? Are we not simply pushing the problems further down the river, hoping they will eventually float out to sea?

Veronica described how the removal of prisoners' uniforms could improve the self-esteem of her charges. In nineteen fifty-one it was unthinkable such an idea would one day come into being. Dartmoor convicts (they were always convicts in those days, a mid-fourteenth century word, stemming from the Latin, and a much loved and well understood term) wore jacket and trousers with black arrows stamped over the material just as we see in cartoons today. Did you know their boots also had an arrow made of studs on the sole? It allowed warders to see if their escapee had passed by in a particular direction even when amongst other footprints. Insisting on keeping this Victorian status quo, would not go down well with the Prison Reform Trust or the Howard League of Prison Reform in today's politically correct society. But, as so often in life, the cry is raised: '…he hasn't apologised.' So, a prison sentence carries with it – to the victim – a catharsis of a kind. 'I knew I was right,' he says, as he folds his arms in satisfaction.

It does highlight, does it not, the changes which have undergone the Service, especially since the end of the Second World War? Time and again, we hear, of prison governors speaking out saying, '…. There needs to be much more intervention into that rung of society who have never had a chance in life. We need to reach out to them much earlier to prevent a boy or a girl entering upon a life of crime.'

The first urgency, therefore, surely is to divide those who must be contained at all costs. The second group, those being men and women who follow a life of crime for no other reason than they had few other options in their short lives, could be looked at differently.

In the first category, we have people such as Frank Mitchell, the Mad Axeman, who escaped from Dartmoor never to be found. (much later he *was* found. He had been murdered by the Kray Twins). He had always been a thorn in the side of authority and had been birched and given the cat- 'o -nine tails, as if this country was still living in the eighteenth century. It made no difference, and he continued to terrorise the staff until, one day he disappeared into the mist.

There were committed IRA prisoners who were never going to change their political beliefs; the Ripper comes to mind though in this case he would need to be protected from the public, an ironic twist of fate. And there was Charles Bronson who Veronica was to meet, a man so dangerous he must be contained in a special cell with open grilles so he can be monitored at all times of the day and night. Such people, unfortunately, need to be kept away from the public, as there is no knowing how they will react to any set of arising circumstances.

This leaves quite a high percentage of the remaining prison population. Some psychiatrists venture to suggest eighty percent of prisoners should be in a mental institution; you can argue that statistic for as long as you like, but, there are many, surely, who could be re-trained as plumbers and electricians or plasterers; or what about software designers, engineers or working on a farm in the fresh air and sunshine? God knows, we need plenty of all these and there is a nice living to be made, independent of officialdom and free of a cell measuring twelve feet by six feet, providing you pay your taxes, of course, and there we go again!

Yes, you say, impatiently, this is being done already and has been for years.' We train, we help with housing, but they still re-offend.

I need to return to the Dartmoor theme. Harold Webb known to his fellow inmates as 'Rubber Bones' for the speed he could slip a pair of handcuffs and to the delight of the newspapers, escaped down a heating duct just a few inches' square such was the urgency of getting away to join his true love, Joan Kinsley. He declared he would give up his life of crime if he could be sure she would be waiting for him. 'I'll go straight if...' is a familiar story.

Is there any truth in these pleas? Can we trust a felon to go straight if only we were to give him or her a new way of life? Should we, could we not spend the £65,000 it costs to arrest, charge and imprison one criminal for a year on changing the way he or she thinks, possibly at home, if they still have one, of course. It costs a further £32-45,000 a year thereafter, which for a sentence of five years averages a staggering £225,000 to hold that person safely out of reach.

It is a very small percentage of our island population who have ever set foot inside a prison, nor have they any desire to do so. The message coming out of prison is a deterrent itself for most of us; being shut up, locked up for long hours of each day is enough to keep us on the straight and narrow. If we do end up on the wrong side of the wall, it is likely to be through stupidity, not ignorance of the law. I spent a few hours in Pentonville prison in close contact with prisoners and their environment; I have no desire to repeat the experience.

At the very top of my wished-for list is the word: *rehabilitation*. Surely, the whole aim of prison is, in the end, to reclaim the prisoner's ability to live in society without the urge to steal, maim, kill or strike out blindly at his neighbours? If we fail, and we do, often, to achieve this aim, Prisoner 4242 will be back one day casting a surly nod of recognition to the Prison Officer as he arrives at the Reception desk.

Is there some good in everybody which we might tap and build upon during the last months of his or her term? After all, they have almost served their sentence; they will soon be free. They can look ahead in a few months to being a free man again, 'I've served my sentence, I've paid my debt to society. How about a clean slate?' It is surely time to see if we can prevent a man, or a woman from re-offending. It is a question I first asked myself at the beginning of this part of the book.

Veronica is very aware of the effects of prison on prisoners. She is experienced in handling those who were also mothers with babies. The influence on the child, who is not a thief, but is there because the mother has her own rights, begins as soon as her kid is old enough to understand. The child grows up surrounded by foul language and other mothers of similar attitudes. When they are eventually released, they can often end up in a less comfortable, more problematic life in the *free* world. To a young child knowing no other, it can be a harsh reality where the best and safest accommodation is right back there in Styal. There is also the danger of a mother rejecting her offspring in the struggle to find a new partner or, failing this, move into prostitution to make ends meet. The growing youth might well feel it is safer, warmer and better feeding, back inside. The cycle begins all over again.

One more element should be mentioned. A large proportion of prisons are run on humane grounds, well managed and sensitive to the very reasons I have set out above? There are a few, as in all life, that are rogues, which the media love to publicise, and it makes good copy for the *Mail* and the *Mirror,* but they *are* in the minority. Let us remember there is a chance that a prisoner, released, will not re-offend if strong support is provided, particularly towards the end of the sentence. What then, of prisons which do not have this softer approach? Often in the past it has been a boot camp attitude, what was called a short, sharp shock. But, like a cricket ball struck hard, it can go off at all angles, often into the hands of evil men, waiting for the opportunity of taking on a recruit to do their dirty work for them. It creates bitterness towards a cruel system, a need to kick back at society which has let them down totally. There is a greater chance of driving a fragile mind deeper into the system rather than be able to pull back from the chasm.

The contrast between the two approaches becomes such a gulf it makes little sense.

This really requires the arrangements to be fair to all. If all offenders knew without a shadow of a doubt, they were going to be treated humanely, when they get out, might some not consider giving the real world a second chance, and go straight? Perhaps not, you will say. It is difficult to unscramble an egg and the evidence is there for anyone to look at.

The heroine of this story, Veronica, was able, against all the odds, to turn one of the country's prisons, within a single year, described as a 'basket case,' into a calm, well ordered place in which her prisoners could work out their sentences in something approaching amity. Riots became a thing of the past, attacks on staff were minimised. She could be alikened to a Headmaster or Headmistress of a large school. Replacement of that single person in a poor or non-performing school can turn the establishment around in months. You can see the same thing with an incoming hotel manager or the newly appointed Commander of a ship. It is the individual who connects with the people which counts. And it is that individual who builds a team around them who believe in the same principles. This works. It is applicable to the Prison Service who, no doubt has a just cause for claiming their job is extraordinarily complex today, which it is, but, my own discussions with Governors show they are rising to the challenge.

All of this may still turn you off. 'What on God's earth can I do about it...and do I care anyway? The government's dealing with it...and I've paid my taxes. Get a life, can't you? I can't help you.'

But, Veronica wanted to help. She said at her first interview she '.... wanted to help the less fortunate than myself,' This was at her first interview when she was one of the least fortunate people in the north of England, indeed it would be difficult to find someone less fortunate. She made this her mantra at a time when she had her whole world packed into a small overnight bag. It was not only her physical possessions, but her lack of mental width which she had to overcome, notwith-standing the fact she is an intelligent individual able to think on her feet in conditions of extreme stress. It was a fact, when she began her career, she couldn't recognise a condom lying on the Sergeant's desk in front of her, yet she could understand, immediately when a sobbing youth claimed he was innocent of the crime of paedophilia.

Veronica's world has been a closed one, almost as if she needed the comfort of prison herself. An umbilical cord for the foetus? Her father and brother-in-law had kept her chained to their persuasions in life – both self-centred and greedy for themselves – leaving her little time to become streetwise.

It came through sheer hard work and determination and a desire to better herself. There was an awareness she would have to come into contact with the most hardened and dangerous crimi-nals being held within the system and, from all reports, she found a way to communicate with them, a method not understood per-haps by other officers who viewed the job solely as a job.

But, at such a cost. Veronica, locked away, saw little of life outside the stone walls and security fences. Theatre, cinema, reading, building for the future were not for her to enjoy.

How is it that such a diminutive lady with such a slight-ness of figure could talk sense to Charles Bronson, a man who needed up to six burly officers to escort him back to his cell? Did this man recognise another tortured soul albeit in a com-pletely different form?

This cry of 'it's not fair,' will be levelled at me I'm sure. 'It is not showing bias surely, to imprison criminals?' you will say 'Think of the victims'.

Of course, it's not fair; life is not fair and never will be, no matter how hard we work at getting a balance into our day to day lives. Remember, many of these offenders never had a chance in life either; it wasn't, and it is not fair to them. As another Prison Governor said. 'Change,' he declared with some vigour, 'change will not come until we change the system and tackle the real source of the problem.'

This is Veronica's mantra. We cannot go on locking people up without realising what we are doing to them. To all these lost people, we have to give them a new chance in life.

I am not making a case for removing prison as a means of dealing with crime. What I am trying to clarify is contained within the last few words above. We must realise what is happening in the minds of this inactive population, almost one third the size of Barnsley. We carpet the cells, we give prisoners their own cell key; a flat screen television; we can give them a choice for lunch and we can give them their human rights, but for all this, there is no apparent contraction in the re-offending totals. Nevertheless, the nettle has been grasped, there is a greater understanding of the issues and there seems to be a determination to remain in control and on top. Meanwhile I do not pretend to know how to offer a solution; I just listen and try to understand and hope to communicate these issues to someone perhaps, who might read this book, who can come up with a better idea than the one we live with daily.

*

At the end of Veronica's story, her '*bird*', I hope you have been as impressed with the end of her story as myself; certainly, Veronica's life has become smoothed out as she cast her old existence into a cardboard box along with her other memories. There were always going to be poor odds that Veronica was going to make it in life. She could have so easily succumbed to continuing to work in the market at a pittance. Instead, came that day when she met a friend who told her '…. you are nothing but a little slave'. At that moment in time, Veronica grabbed the nettle; it was now or never, she seemed to say to herself, and she took it. It was Veronica's tipping point in life.

This is one of those feel-good stories you want to come right on the last page if not before. This was true for me also. It is a story of a real-life Cinderella, whose glass slipper brought her out of the misery she had lived in for so many years, into a world of respect and responsibility even if she did not collect a Prince on the way past GO.

I interviewed Veronica over many months. She is a good communicator, apt to making mental notes which she files away in her head until later, she returns and proffers the result of her research with a smile of reassurance on her face.

This story has not covered her siblings' involvement, save Joan, her eldest sister, and her husband, Veronica's loathed brother-in-law. Her brothers and sisters are only distant foot-notes to be called upon from time to time to clarify a point. They had no connection with the prison service. Because there was so little contact between them during their working lives, none of their activities would divert Veronica's own telling of the story. They are all surviving, other than Jack who died far too young, air-brushed out of history as cleanly as a high tide on a sandy beach.

Fred Ward was a man of his time. He was skilled at his trade, understood thoroughly what his customers wanted, and built up a small empire before the Supermarkets moved in to undercut his prices. His name repeats itself all too often in the early part of Veronica's life as he ferreted around, unable to leave anyone he knew, let alone her, to get on with their life without continual interference.

Fred is dead now. Joan lives on at the grand age of eighty-seven. She is in much closer contact with Veronica these days and indeed, they have liaised with each other, over the detail of this book. That, in itself, has to be a happy ending

It is ironic, is it not, that Fred and Veronica's father, George Bird were the instruments which drove Veronica like a trem-bling doe into the Prison Service. That doe, that Bambi, would grow as a result, into a nine-point buck of a Governor, holding safely, some of the most wicked people in the country.

It wasn't long before the questions began to flutter around my keyboard. The fine points of detail were answered quickly, and accurately but, as if they were flour lumps in the bottom of a sieve, some refused to pass through the grid. One remained obstinately. It was a question to myself, arising from Veronica's story, a question which would tickle at my conscience for a long time. It continues to do so.

Why do we lock up those who, palpably, should never be in jail?

POSTSCRIPT

It was several years after she had retired when Veronica learned the news Fred Ward, now in his eighties was very ill. She had been told he was dying in Barnsley Hospital, so she rang up his nurse and explained it was difficult for her to get away and drive up at a moment's notice, for an evening visit. They agreed she could come and visit during the morning.

Veronica did this deliberately as she had no intention of upsetting any of Fred's family by being by his bedside if they were to call, so she seized the opportunity offered, arriving early the next day filled with the need to see if he was remorseful in any way for the years of abuse he had given.

She found him lying in bed and could see he had recognised her.

'Hullo Fred. It's Veronica.' It was pointless asking him how he felt. He knew he was dying and so did she. Fred did at least nod his head though neither pleased nor angry with her presence by his bedside.

'I want to ask you Fred, are you sorry for all those things you did? Do you regret removing me from Ackworth at the time I was due to take the most important exams in my life? Especially as there was no need.'

He turned his head slightly but the word 'sorry' was not in his lexicon.

'You almost destroyed me, Fred Ward-' she stopped. What was the point?

'It doesn't matter now Fred.' Veronica patted one of his limp hands but he turned away to stare out of the window. Maybe a thousand apologies were boiling under the surface, but he just couldn't bring himself to acknowledge the facts.

Veronica must have left the ward with very mixed feelings. She knew she would never see him again. He was flawed, but he was also a human being. Just someone else who had turned off the track as so many of her prison inmates had done. She was so familiar with the pattern it was part of her life.

Perhaps Fred could not help himself; there is a possibility, I suppose, he became sucked into his obsession of her that he was quite unable to find the exit to climb out, even when it was clearly marked by a green running man? He must have seen Veronica's father's brutal way of life on numerous occasions, and felt he could get away with it, especially and most conveniently, when she came to live under his roof.

There is no way to say it other than by removing Veronica from Ackworth was an act of pure evil, for he did not have to use her in the market. He would have been able to find a replacement but that would have been more expensive. Her fees were paid each term by the school, and she was quite prepared to give up all luxuries so she could continue to work for her exams.

Whatever the rights and wrongs of this case are, it would be fascinating to speculate on seeing where Veronica's career would have taken her if she had been allowed to remain at school. If her father and brother-in-law had not had those streaks of cruelty within them, she might have plotted a course in life with a husband and children, spending time on taking them to the 'flicks' or a picnic on a Sunday afternoon.

Who knows?

Maybe it was the very fact she made a conscious decision to withdraw into herself and behind bars which allowed her to understand the Prison Service as well as she did. In the end, there are many ex-prisoners who will be forever grateful to the woman who brought a light into their lives during some of their darkest moments.

There is an epilogue to this postscript It arrived on my desk as I was reviewing the first draft of the manuscript.

I needed to pass the document on to Joan, Veronica's eldest sister, to receive her approval, or otherwise. At the same time, Veronica went to see her in Barnsley where they '…talked for hours and hours.' Then, Joan said, most surprisingly, 'I am happy for anything to be written even if it is upsetting…. I will not stand in your way.'

She hugged Veronica – for the first time ever – and said, 'Tell Richard, I do not mind even if he had written a load of bullshit about me, I am happy to go along with it. It will not cause a split between us.'

Veronica went on, 'There is no doubt, she is proud of me now and so much so she encourages her grand-daughters to follow in my example. Not just Joan, but the whole family are proud.

'Next weekend is to be another big first. Joan, Pat, Ghislaine and her two grand-daughters are spending a week together in London. They are going to a show, lunch in Harrods, and they have invited me to join them!

I have accepted the invitation.'